*(continued from front flap)*

initiating, persuading, and sustaining loyal partisan audiences. In Britain and America, millions of men participated in a democratic political culture that spoke their language, played to their prejudices, and courted their approval. Today's readers concerned with broadening political discourse to reach a more diverse audience will find rich and intriguing parallels in Robertson's account.

Andrew W. Robertson teaches history at the California Institute of Technology. He has been a Fellow at the Shorenstein Barone Center on the Press, Politics, and Public Policy at Harvard University and writes about contemporary political rhetoric and press-political relations.

Jacket illustration: Richard Caton Woodville, *War News from Mexico*. 1848. Courtesy National Academy of Design.

D1300412

*The Language of Democracy*

# The Language of Democracy

POLITICAL RHETORIC IN
THE UNITED STATES AND
BRITAIN, 1790–1900

ANDREW W. ROBERTSON

*Cornell University Press*

ITHACA AND LONDON

First published 1995 by Cornell University Press.


Printed in the United States of America

⊗ The paper in this book meets the minimum requirements
of the American National Standard for Information Sciences—
Permanence of Paper for Printed Library Materials, ANSI Z39.48-1984.


**Library of Congress Cataloging-in-Publication Data**

Robertson, Andrew W. (Andrew Whitmore), 1951–
    The language of democracy : political rhetoric in the United States and Britain,
1790–1900 / Andrew W. Robertson.
        p.   cm.
    Includes bibliographical references (p.    ) and index.
    ISBN 0-8014-2899-8 (cloth : alk. paper)
    1. Rhetoric—Political aspects—United States.    2. Rhetoric—Political
aspects—Great Britain.    3. Press and politics—United States—History.
4. Press and politics—Great Britain—History.    5. Electioneering—United
States—History.    6. Electioneering—Great Britain—History.    7. United
States—Politics and government—19th century.    8. Great Britain—Politics
and government—19th century.    9. United States—Politics and
government—1789–1809.    10. Great Britain—Politics and government—
1789–1820.    I. Title.
PN239.P64R63   1995
808.5'1'08835—dc20
                                                                        94-44597

*To  E. C. R. and O. C. R.*

# Contents

[vii]

# Acknowledgments

I very much appreciate the time and attention of J. R. Pole, Rhodes Professor emeritus at St. Catherine's College, Oxford University, who has been a friend and a good critic. I also thank Michael Brock, formerly Warden of Nuffield College, Oxford, for his close and careful attention to my work. I could not have asked for better advice and direction than I received from these two scholars. David Hackett Fischer directed my early research at Brandeis University and later offered many helpful ideas while he was Harmsworth Professor at Oxford and on many occasions afterward.

Among the many scholars who offered their time, suggestions, and close attention along the way are Joyce Appleby, Robert Becker, Matt Gallman, Samuel Hays, Stephen Howe, Morton Keller, Morgan Kousser, James Kloppenberg, Susan Marchand, Colin Matthew, Marvin Meyers, Edward Muir, Richard Neustadt, John Rowett, Marshall Schott, Byron Shafer, and Carter Wilkie; I am especially indebted to the late Philip Williams.

I am grateful to the staffs of many libraries; I would like to express my appreciation to David McGrath and John Westmancoat of the British Library, Clark Evans of the Library of Congress, and Allan Lodge and Alan Bell of the Rhodes House Library at Oxford, all of whom were extremely helpful and pleasant. Jill Cogen and

Elsa Sink of the Huntington Library Reader Services went out of their way to provide assistance. I am also very grateful to the staffs of the Nuffield College Library, the Faculty of Modern History Library and the Bodleian Library at Oxford University, Houghton Library and Widener Library at Harvard University, Goldfarb Library at Brandeis University, the John Carter Brown Library at Brown University, the University of Delaware Library at Newark, the Pratt Free Library in Baltimore, University of North Carolina Library at Chapel Hill, Florida State University Library at Tallahassee, Hill Memorial Library at Louisiana State University, Baton Rouge, the Historical New Orleans Collection, the University of Texas Library at Austin, University Research Library at UCLA, Honnold Library at the Claremont Colleges, Clapp Library at Occidental College, CPU Library at Pomona, and the Huntington Library and Millikan Library at Caltech.

I am indebted as well to the staffs of the American Antiquarian Society, the Massachusetts Historical Society, the New Hampshire Historical Society, the New-York Historical Society, the Delaware Historical Society, the British Newspaper Library at Colindale, and the Library of Congress. I thank Barbara Quinn and John Sullivan of the Huntington Library for their assistance with the illustrations. Jeanne Netzley provided excellent and efficient assistance at Caltech.

I am very grateful to Cynthia McLoughlin for her editorial suggestions. I have been fortunate in having Peter Agree as my editor at Cornell University Press. I have appreciated his good instincts, his patience, and his courtesy. Risa Mednick and Philip Harms, formerly of Cornell University Press, were also attentive and considerate, as was Carol Betsch. Terence McKiernan-White was a scrupulous and erudite copy editor with a sensitive ear for rhetorical nuance. I am grateful for his careful attention.

I dedicate this book to my father, Eugene C. Robertson, and my mother, Olivia C. Robertson. They have provided many varieties of support over the years, and this is a small gesture from me to acknowledge many large gestures from each of them.

I could not complete this list of acknowledgments without expressing the incalculable debt I owe Pamela Deidre Kelly Robertson, who, among other things, is my wife. I never asked her to do the typing or the editing, but she volunteered for late night copying in Newark, Delaware, and early morning faxing of archive material from Tallahassee. She cross-checked references in the Book of Revelation aloud until our neighbors must have thought we were starting a religious cult. She provided moral support, much patience, and a sane appraisal of my scholarly endeavors. Our labrador retriever, Beauregard, made his own sane appraisal of the life of a scholar by devouring my copies of the *American Historical Review.*

A. W. R.

# A Note on Sources

In this study of electioneering rhetoric in the press, I felt I should convey a representative sample of the language from as many newspaper sources as possible. A century of sources in two countries forced me to be selective. I have attempted, however, to choose newspaper sources from areas in both the United States and Britain that experienced regular competitive elections. For the most part, the newspapers quoted are ones that survived at least twenty years and had consistent party allegiance for long periods of time. I also tried to select cities with two or more newspapers expressing different party affiliations. This criterion sometimes meant concentrating on the biggest cities in the two countries, particularly New York and London. Since this work is mainly concerned with the interaction of parties and editors on the one hand, and voters on the other, I have drawn most of my sources from the month immediately preceding presidential elections in the United States and general elections in Britain. To be faithful to particular forms of rhetorical speech, I have occasionally used extended quotations.

This book concentrates on the rhetoric of the partisan press. Independent newspapers and yellow journals have been included, but the majority of citations come from the party press. In determining which newspapers were partisan, I have relied on

standard reference works and monographs to aid my own judgment.[1] I have quoted extensively from the two best-known "newspapers of record": *The Times* of London and the *New York Times*
Despite their protestations of "independence" in the nineteenth
century, the partisanship of these two newspapers at election time
was often unmistakable.

Some of the best political rhetoric I have been forced to leave
out: I have largely omitted electioneering in Ireland and in the
Lower South before the Civil War. The political context in these
two regions was so exceptional that I concluded it would require
too much explanation to incorporate many examples. The language of the South *after* the Civil War increasingly resembled the
rest of the United States. I have thus included examples from
many southern newspapers in the Gilded Age chapter without the
necessity of additional explanations. Why the South, especially the
Lower South, persisted in employing laudatory rhetoric until the
eve of the Civil War is an engaging question. Oral performance
by the gentry and oral protest by the populace carried far more
weight in a political culture that had lower rates of literacy. Newspapers in the South did not achieve the same circulation or the same
influence enjoyed by newspapers in the North and West until after
the Civil War. Ireland also had a tradition of oral protest that
seemed to carry more weight in its political culture in the nineteenth century. Southern Irish oral culture included the Celtic
language tradition, despite the rapid disappearance of Irish as
a spoken language. To offer an adequate explanation for the
"otherwise-mindedness" of the American South and Ireland would
mean a four-way comparison and a different sort of book than .
the one I have written.

In a work that addresses the visual dimension of newspaper
appeals, I have strived as much as possible to reproduce the

[1] Arthur Aspinall, *Politics and the Press, c. 1780–1850* (London, 1949); Stephen
Koss, *The Rise and Fall of the Political Press in Britain* (London, 1981), vol. 1; Clarence
S. Brigham, *History and Bibliography of American Newspapers, 1690–1920*, 2 vols.
(Worcester, Mass., 1947); Culver H. Smith, *The Press, Politics, and Patronage: The
American Government's Use of Newspapers, 1789–1875* (Athens, Ga., 1977); Thomas
C. Leonard, *The Power of the Press: The Birth of American Political Reporting* (New
York, 1986); Michael E. McGerr, *Decline of Popular Politics: The American North,
1865–1928* (New York, 1986).

actual layout and typeface of the original source. The use of large type, small type, italics, and boldface has been recorded and reproduced on the page to convey the visual impact of the original. Another important form of visual communication was the political cartoon. Reproduced in this book are only a few of the large number of cartoons, caricatures, and broadsides from more than a century of political satire. These are only meant to suggest the larger body of sources.

*The Language of Democracy*

INTRODUCTION

# Causes, Conjunctures
# Occasions, and Relations

Politics in the United States and Britain gradually evolved from government by gentlemen at the end of the eighteenth century to government for, if not by, the people at the end of the nineteenth century. This change occurred more rapidly in the United States and more gradually in Britain. At the end of the eighteenth century, even after the American Revolution, electoral politics was carried on in similar style on both sides of the Atlantic. Early in the nineteenth century, however, political discourse in the United States and Britain began to diverge, partly as a result of the expansion of participation in American politics. For adult males of European descent, the extension of voting rights occurred rapidly in America. In Britain, on the other hand, the franchise was extended in very gradual steps. Even at the end of the nineteenth century, suffrage for adult British males was quite far from universal. In the United States there were also limitations on democracy: by law and custom, African Americans had been disfranchised and American women remained excluded from politics.

Despite the limits on American and British democratization, the changes are still remarkable. Perhaps the greatest challenge facing the two regimes in the nineteenth century was integrating a mass audience into meaningful political debate. These two political cultures peacefully, albeit grudgingly, absorbed new voters into a discourse once exclusively composed of, by, and for "gentlemen." The new voters became enthusiastic participants in a politics that courted their attention.

How did this successful absorption come about? One important aspect of this process which has not been thoroughly examined is the role of political language as an instrument of integration. A new means had to be discovered in the United States and in Britain by which politicians could communicate with the large number of new participants in the political system. Political language as a consequence underwent a profound transformation between the end of the eighteenth and the beginning of the twentieth century. The change in political language was more than stylistic. As the style changed, so did the subject matter and so did the role assumed by the mass audience in political communication.[1]

Comparative history seeks to explain a course of events beyond the context of national boundaries. Studying the relationship between language and politics limits historical understanding when confined within a national context. Language and politics react to changed contexts in different ways and define identity in disparate ways. Recent comparative studies have made historians aware that the United States and Britain shared many features of political culture.[2] One important common feature in the eighteenth century was the important role deference played in political deliberation. As Gordon S. Wood has said of the American Founders, "They believed that their speeches and writings did not have

---

[1] As Gordon S. Wood has observed, "The republicanizing tendencies of eighteenth-century thinking actually challenged the age-old distinction between the aristocratic few and the common many. . . . By assuming their inferiors had realities equal to their own, they . . . gave birth to what perhaps is best described as humanitarian sensibility—a powerful force that we of the twentieth century have inherited and further expanded." *The Radicalism of the American Revolution* (New York, 1992), p. 235.

[2] J. C. D. Clark, *The Language of Liberty, 1660–1832: Political Discourse and Social Dynamics in the Anglo-American World* (Cambridge, 1994); Robert Kelley, *The Transatlantic Persuasion: The Liberal Democratic Mind in the Age of Gladstone* (New York, 1969); John M. Murrin, "The Great Inversion, or Court versus Country: A Comparison of the Revolution Settlements in England (1688–1721) and America (1776–1816)," in *Three British Revolutions, 1641, 1688, 1776*, ed. J. G. A. Pocock (Princeton, 1980), pp. 368–453; David Hackett Fischer, *Albion's Seed: Four British Folkways in America* (New York, 1989); Jack P. Greene, *Pursuits of Happiness: The Social Development of Early Modern British Colonies and the Formation of American Culture* (Chapel Hill, N.C., 1988).

to influence directly and simultaneously all of the people but only the rational and enlightened part, who in turn would bring the rest of the populace with them through the force of deferential respect."[3]

From Aristotle through James Harrington, political theorists had conceived of a distinction between the function of the few and that of the many in a hierarchical political order. In the *Oceana*, Harrington referred to this as the difference between "debate" and "result": the few assumed a deliberative role in policy, while the many rendered a positive or negative verdict by means of their votes on the result. This distinction persisted in the classification of modes of rhetoric, categorized according to the speaker, subject, and audience. Rhetoric addressed to the assembly adopted the future tense, in what Aristotle called the "deliberative" mode of discourse, which concerned itself with the question "What is to be done?" Rhetoric addressed to a mass audience Aristotle called the "demonstrative" or "epideictic" mode of discourse, concerned with the question "Who is worthy of praise and blame?" By the end of the eighteenth century, these distinctions had begun to break down; a century later they had largely disappeared.[4]

This change occurred because distinctions between the functions of the few and the many, between "debate" and "result," were less clear. One need only compare the way orators referred to "the people" in political speeches of the late eighteenth century to the way they described them in the late nineteenth century to discover the profound change wrought in political communication. In one of Britain's most famous political speeches, addressed

[3] Gordon S. Wood, "The Democratization of Mind in the American Revolution," in *Leadership in the American Revolution* (Washington, 1974), p. 67.

[4] James Harrington, *The "Oceana" of James Harrington, and His Other Works; . . . with An Exact Account of His Life, by John Toland*, ed. John Toland (London, 1700), pp. 48, 217–21; J. G. A. Pocock, "The Classical Theory of Deference," *American Historical Review* 81 (1976): 517.

See Aristotle, *De Rhetorica*, in *The Basic Works of Aristotle* ed. Richard McKeon (New York, 1941), I.iii and I.ix: ἐπί + δεικνύναι = intended for display. For a definition by two modern philosophers of rhetoric, see Ch[aim] Perelman and L. Olbrechts-Tyteca, *The New Rhetoric: A Treatise on Argumentation*, trans. John Wilkinson and Purcell Weaver (South Bend, Ind., 1969), pp. 47–48. See also Edward P. J. Corbett, *Classical Rhetoric for the Modern Student*, 2d ed. (New York, 1971), pp. 146–49, 152–55.

to his constituents in Bristol, Edmund Burke expressed an eighteenth-century view of the people's role, a view close to that held
by many American politicians of the time.

> No man carries further than I do the policy of making government
> pleasing to the people. But the widest range of this politic
> complaisance is confined within the limits of justice. I would not
> only consult the interests of the people, but I would cheerfully gratify
> their humours. We are all a sort of children that must be soothed
> and managed. I think I am not austere or formal in my nature. I
> would bear, I would even myself play my part in, any innocent
> buffooneries to divert them.[5]

Ninety-nine years later, when Gladstone addressed the Midlothian electors at the Music Hall in Edinburgh, he professed to have
a very different view of the role of the people in politics—again, not
unlike that of many contemporary American politicians.

> I really have but one great anxiety. This is a self-governing country.
> Let us bring home to the minds of the people the state of the facts
> they have to deal with, and in Heaven's name let them determine
> whether or not this is the way in which they like to be governed. . . .
> What we are disputing about is a whole system of Government and
> to make good that proposition that it is a whole system of
> Government will be my great object in any addresses that I may
> deliver in this country. If it is acceptable, if it is liked by the
> people—they are the masters—it is for them to have it.[6]

The most obvious difference between the two speeches is the
change in the role of "the people" in relation to representative
government. In a deferential political system, the people were

---

[5] Edmund Burke, *The Works of the Right Honourable Edmund Burke,* ed. Frank H.
Wills (Oxford, 1906), 3:45–46.
[6] William E. Gladstone, *Midlothian Speeches, 1879* (Leicester, 1971), p. 50.

called upon not for deliberation but for decision.[7] Burke does not believe that their decision will rest on sound collective judgment. For Burke, it was necessary only to "consult" the people's interest. He maintained that "political complaisance" must be bounded by externally imposed limits of justice. As a representative he aspired to create a favorable view of government in the popular imagination. This popular view has no necessary connection with the reality of government's acting to serve the general good.[8]

In Gladstone's speech, the people were no longer to be "soothed and managed" into a political decision. Those adult men who possessed the franchise had been assimilated into the deliberative process: they were consulted on the facts, and they had become the ultimate arbiters of policy. Thanks to the instantaneous communication provided by the national press, Gladstone did not simply address the audience in the Edinburgh Music Hall; he reached a national audience of newspaper readers. Whether the national electorate acted justly or behaved like children, he professed to believe that the electors were "the masters," and they must have their way.

Less obvious than the change in the people's role in politics was the change in the purpose of political speeches. In keeping with a typical demonstrative speech of the late eighteenth century, Burke sought to show that he was a praiseworthy representative

---

[7] Pocock explores the meaning of deference in "Classical Theory of Deference." See also J. R. Pole, "Historians and the Problem of Early American Democracy," in *Paths to the American Past* (New York, 1979), 223–49. One useful working definition of deferential political culture is provided by Ronald P. Formisano, "Deferential-Participant Politics: The Early Republic's Political Culture, 1789–1824," *American Political Science Review* 68 (1974): 473–87; another is found in Daniel Walker Howe, *The Political Culture of the American Whigs* (Chicago, 1979), p. 2. See also Wood, *Radicalism,* especially pp. 11–92, 145–68, 229–86. For a description of deferential politics in pre-reform Britain, see Richard W. Davis, "Deference and Aristocracy in the Time of the Great Reform Act," *American Historical Review* 81 (1976): 532–39; for a somewhat more eccentric view of post-reform "deference communities," see D. C. Moore, *The Politics of Deference: A Study of the Mid-Nineteenth Century Political System* (New York, 1976), pp. 12–13, 414–15. The clearest description of a deferential society, unclouded by jargon, is Walter Bagehot, *The English Constitution* (London, 1872).

[8] On Burke's references to the people, see James T. Boulton, *The Language of Politics in the Age of Wilkes and Burke* (London, 1963), pp. 71–72.

of Bristol in Parliament. For an eighteenth-century candidate, that meant calling attention to his character and his conduct. Gladstone's purpose in delivering his Midlothian speech, on the other hand, was to rouse the nation on a series of policy questions and persuade the electors to act upon their changed opinions at the next general election.[9]

Rhetoric changed dramatically in response to the challenge of democratization. In turn, rhetoric helped transform politics by framing political discourse to suit new themes and values. And the new rhetoric had a new purpose. While the older political rhetoric followed classical forms, the new rhetoric combined the style of a demonstrative speech with the deliberative purpose of debating policy.[10] The extension of participation and party competition also stimulated a more fervid style of rhetoric, and, in turn, the transformation of rhetorical style helped to sustain unprecedented levels of political participation. The new style of political language fostered the creation of a durable sense of party identification among the electorate.[11]

The new rhetoric, like the old, often referred to policy questions only incidentally: electioneering speeches and editorials frequently relied on emotional appeals to prejudice, fear, and envy in mobiliz-

---

[9] H. C. G. Matthew has provided an insightful analysis of Gladstone's rhetorical innovations. Matthew believes that Gladstone's style of discourse at Midlothian could be as effective as it was only because the franchise was still somewhat restricted in 1879. See Matthew's introduction, William Ewart Gladstone, *The Gladstone Diaries:* (Oxford, 1978), 9:xxxiii–lxxiii; see also Robert Kelley's observations on Gladstone's contribution to Anglo-American political culture in *Transatlantic Persuasion*, pp. 180–237, especially pp. 221–27, 233–37.

[10] Georges Louis Leclerc, Comte de Buffon, *Discourse sur le style* (Paris, 1753), p. vi; Clifford Geertz, "Ideology as a Cultural System," in *The Interpretation of Cultures: Selected Essays by Clifford Geertz* (New York, 1973), p. 219. Karl Mannheim has gone so far as to argue that democratization is a prerequisite for synthetic thinking. "The process of democratization first makes it possible for the ways of thinking of the lower strata, which formerly had no public validity, to acquire validity and prestige." *Ideology and Utopia: An Introduction to the Sociology of Knowledge*, trans. Louis Wirth and Edward Shils (New York, 1936), pp. 8–9.

[11] Richard P. McCormick, "New Perspectives on Jacksonian Politics," *American Historical Review* 65 (1960): 258–301; David Hackett Fischer, *The Revolution of American Conservatism: The Federalist Party in the Era of Jeffersonian Democracy* (New York, 1965), pp. xv, 191; J. R. Pole, *Political Representation in England and the Origins of the American Republic* (London, 1966), pp. 544–64.

ing voters. But political rhetoric, new or old, was not merely bombast, florid in style and vacuous in substance. Whatever its theme, whatever its style, electioneering rhetoric invariably concerned itself with choice.

This book examines the choices implicitly and explicitly presented to the readers of the political press.[12] Changes in rhetorical themes, the values they expressed, the style in which they were fashioned, and the frame of reference on which they relied, all have much to teach us about the interaction between party elites and voters' political behavior. Change and continuity of language reveal much about the role of language in what we might call the sociology of political knowledge.[13]

Rhetoric, acting as a mobilizing instrument, played an indispensable role in the development of a participatory political culture. Yet the purposes and interests of mobilizers and mobilized were rarely in unison and sometimes not even in harmony. To review electioneering rhetoric in the United States and Britain through the course of the nineteenth century is to recognize the importance of I. A. Richards's definition of rhetoric as "the study of misunderstanding and its remedies."[14]

[12] See Kenneth Burke, *A Rhetoric of Motives* (Berkeley, 1969), especially pp. 19–37. See also J. L. Austin's definitions of "illocution" and "perlocution" in *How to Do Things with Words* (Cambridge, Mass., 1962) especially pp. 91, 101–31; John R. Searle, *Speech Acts: An Essay in the Philosophy of Language* (London, 1977), especially pp. 44–48; Quentin Skinner, " 'Social Meaning' and the Explanation of Social Action," in *Meaning and Context: Quentin Skinner and His Critics,* ed. James Tully (Princeton, 1989), pp. 79–96; Hayden White, *Tropics of Discourse: Essays in Cultural Criticism* (Baltimore, 1978), p. 4.

[13] Gareth Stedman Jones, *Languages of Class: Studies in English Working Class History, 1832–1982* (Cambridge, 1983), pp. 21–22; Marvin Meyers, *The Jacksonian Persuasion: Politics and Belief* (Stanford, 1957), p. ix. For a very clear and insightful analysis of words conceived as "tools," see Daniel T. Rodgers, *Contested Truths: Keywords in American Politics since Independence* (New York, 1987), pp. 8–11.

[14] I. A. Richards, *The Philosophy of Rhetoric,* 2d ed. (New York, 1964), p. 3. Classical theorists defined rhetoric as "persuasion." According to Aristotle, the art of rhetoric is not to persuade but to discover the existing means of persuasion. Aristotle was reacting against Plato's *Gorgias,* in which Socrates draws a distinction between science and opinion and maintains that rhetoric can inform us only about the latter. For their differing definitions of rhetoric, see Aristotle, *De Rhetorica,* I.i.14, and Plato, *The Gorgias,* trans. Donald J. Zeyl (Indianapolis, Ind., 1986), secs. 20–36. Modern philosophers of rhetoric such as Richards and Kenneth Burke are more concerned with rhetoric's ends and less with its means. Burke

If it would avoid misunderstanding, rhetoric must dwell in the realm of the familiar. Rhetoric may be radical or reactionary in its motive but it is invariably conservative in its mode. "Every revolutionary," says Quentin Skinner, is "obliged to march backwards into battle."[15] Rhetoric's conservative nature inevitably limits the possibilities for effective political mobilization, since only a speaker with exceptional facility can convey a radically different political perspective framed within familiar themes. Change in language rarely coincides with political change. Political discourse changes gradually as collective perceptions alter. Such changes in collective understanding slowly produce a transformation of the political idiom, but this transformation is neither swift nor sure. The disjunction between rapid political change and more gradual changes in language means that even the most radical polemicist must rely upon familiar themes, common values, and proven rhetorical strategies if he or she is to persuade an audience.[16]

As David Green has observed, "The abstract nature of political labels not only gives them their evocative power, but causes politicians to fight over them. Because the labels have no fixed meanings, politicians are perpetually attempting to infuse them with politically useful connotations." In Britain and the United States, each succeeding generation sought to reformulate the meaning of political language to confer legitimacy on its endeavors. Even as the values of each generation shifted, they sought to connect them to familiar words and themes. The more radically divergent

---

distinguishes between the "old" definition of rhetoric as "persuasion," which seeks to "overcome resistance, to a course of action, an idea, a judgment," and a "new" (i.e., mid-twentieth-century) definition of rhetoric as "identification," which fosters "cooperation, mutuality and social harmony." See Kenneth Burke, "Rhetoric—Old and New," *Journal of General Education* 5 (1951): 203; Kenneth Burke, *Rhetoric of Motives*, pp. 19–20. See also Kathleen Hall Jamieson, *Eloquence in an Electronic Age: The Transformation of Political Speechmaking* (New York, 1988), p. 50.

[15] This is because, as Skinner has recognized, every political ideologist must rely upon "some of the *existing* range of evaluative-descriptive terms." Quentin Skinner, "Some Problems in the Analysis of Political Thought and Action," in Tully, ed., *Meaning and Context*, p. 112.

[16] See Paul Ricoeur, "Structure, Word, Event," trans. Robert Sweeney, in *The Conflict of Interpretations: Essays in Hermeneutics*, ed. Don Ihde (Evanston, Ind., 1974), pp. 92–93; Reinhart Koselleck, "Linguistic Change and the History of Events," *Journal of Modern History* 61 (1989): 649–56.

the values of an insurgent movement, the more imperative it became to frame its values in a familiar context.[17] The result of this need for idiomatic consistency is the phenomenon of thematic "recurrence": the same protagonists, words, and references arise in accustomed religious, literary, mythic, and historical contexts to suit shifting values, changing fashions, and often radically different rhetorical purposes. "Recurrence" thus exerts a profound but subtle influence on the development of political culture as old rhetorical themes are fashioned to suit new values.[18]

On both sides of the Atlantic, from the late eighteenth century onward, the press reached a large audience. Since most newspapers had a consistent political stance and a stable readership over time, we can learn a great deal about changes in political discourse by examining them. In the press, as opposed to broadsides and pamphlets, we have some assurance of knowing who wrote the editorials, and we have a more reliable and consistent idea of who read them.

One of the most important editors of the eighteenth century, Benjamin Franklin, observed that "Modern Political Oratory is chiefly performed by the Pen and the Press."[19] Until the late eighteenth century, the dominant form of political communication between officeholders and voters was the speech. Historians can only estimate the form and substance of oral delivery from printed reports of speeches. Beginning during the American Revolution and accelerating in the nineteenth century, however, printed forms of electioneering rhetoric came to dominate political communication to an enlarged and increasingly literate electorate.

[17] David Green, *Shaping Political Consciousness: The Language of Politics in America from McKinley to Reagan* (Ithaca, N.Y., 1987), p. 2. See also J. G. A. Pocock, "Languages and Their Implications: The Transformation of the Study of Political Thought," in *Politics, Language, and Time: Essays on Political Thought and History* (New York, 1973), p. 19; Rodgers, *Contested Truths*, p. 5; Joyce Appleby, "Ideology and the History of Political Thought," in *Liberalism and Republicanism in the Historical Imagination* (Cambridge, Mass., 1992), pp. 124–39; Ernst Cassirer, *Language and Myth*, trans. Susanne K. Langer (New York, 1946), pp. 83–95; Geertz, "Ideology as a Cultural System," in *Interpretation of Cultures*, p. 211.

[18] Nancy S. Struever, "The Study of Language and the Study of History," *Journal of Interdisciplinary History* 4 (1974): 414.

[19] *Benjamin Franklin: Representative Selections*, ed. Chester E. Jorgensen and Frank Luther Mott (New York, 1962), p. 203.

In fact, broadsides and newspapers adapted the cadences and emphatic stresses of oral speechmaking that had proved so effective in communicating to the masses in the eighteenth century. After the American Revolution, newspapers became more typographically innovative as broadsides became less so. By using emphatic punctuation, typographical devices, slogans, and woodcuts, newspapers conveyed the "presence" of speech. The printed page, ironically, did not relegate American oral electioneering to lesser importance.[20] On the contrary, speechmaking assumed a new importance for the mass audience in the United States, who read these speeches on the printed page. In Britain, on the other hand, as Thomas Gustafson notes, "print culture displaced the tongue as the medium of political communication in the nation state."[21]

Despite these differences, British and American political cultures had much in common. As Jonathan Clark has recently pointed out, the American Revolution was "a religious and civil war on both sides of the Atlantic."[22] British and Irish émigrés, in self-imposed exile to the United States, played a vital role in creating a language of insurgency in both countries. British prosecution for sedition obliged many émigrés to seek refuge in the United States. American prosecution of then-conservative William Cobbett for libel took him home to his native England where he eventually became the foremost polemicist for radical reform. Parliamentary statutes enacted to curb sedition in the 1790s were adopted almost word for word by Congress.

American rhetoric in the nineteenth century closely followed British texts, not only the standard texts on rhetoric by George Campbell and Hugh Blair, but newer works on rhetoric by Richard Whately and on parliamentary logic by William Gerard Hamilton. British workingmen in 1832 quoted the slogans of Jacksonian Democrats. Editors on both sides of the Atlantic often plagiarized

---

[20] Roger Chartier, "Texts, Printing, Readings," in *The New Cultural History: Essays,* ed. Lynn Hunt (Berkeley, 1989), p. 168; Georgia B. Baumgardner, introduction to *American Broadsides: Sixty Facsimiles Dated 1689 to 1800* (Barre, Mass., 1971).

[21] Thomas Gustafson, *Representative Words: Politics, Literature, and the American Language, 1776–1865* (New York, 1992), p. 373.

[22] Clark, *Language of Liberty,* p. 41.

caricatures, cartoons, and other visual devices from the other side of the ocean. American newspaper editors and publishers sought to appropriate the superior technology of the British press in the early nineteenth century. British newspaper proprietors and editors copied many features of American yellow journalism at the end of the nineteenth century.

In the 1790s, British and American electioneering betrayed many features of a common origin. One remarkable and largely unrecognized feature of electioneering discourse after the American Revolution is the extent to which it could still be described as Anglo-American. On both sides of the Atlantic in the 1790s, candidates framed their election appeals according to classical dictates, within the mode of demonstrative rhetoric. Demonstrative rhetoric in both spoken and written form used either panegyric or invective, that is, praise or blame, in appealing to the moral sensibility of a mass audience. Demonstrative rhetoric offered an audience the choice of accepting or rejecting a candidate according to its estimation of his moral qualities. Not surprisingly, therefore, electioneering appeals in both Britain and the United States often paid scant attention to politics narrowly defined. Since most electioneering language praised candidates, one might call this demonstrative rhetoric the *laudatory* mode of discourse.[23]

In the aftermath of the French Revolution, a different form of electioneering rhetoric began to appear in broadsides and in the press on both sides of the Atlantic. One might call this form *hortatory* rhetoric. Hortatory rhetoric was not new, but its impact on electioneering was dramatic. Accepting Rhys Isaac's suggestive dramaturgical analysis, we might imagine late eighteenth-century electioneering as an elaborate stage play, with actors (all male), stylized props (hard cider and bull roast), and carefully scripted lines.[24] Hortatory rhetoric was a cry of "Fire!" in the theater. It linked the audience in an immediate, emotional way to events, principles, or policies, mostly real, often exaggerated, sometimes illusory.

---

[23] Pole, *Political Representation,* p. 46; Jamieson, *Eloquence,* p. 146.

[24] Rhys Isaac, *The Transformation of Virginia, 1740–1790* (Chapel Hill, N.C., 1982), pp. 5, 350–56.

If laudatory discourse confined itself to praising and blaming the candidates, hortatory rhetoric looked to moral and political issues beyond the personalities of the contestants. Hortatory rhetoric urged its audience to choose policies as well as personalities, measures as well as men. Where laudatory rhetoric generated only passive participation, hortatory rhetoric inspired an active and enthusiastic political response. Laudatory electioneering was, in Isaac's terms, a form of "oral performance," like the rituals of the church and the courts, where constant recitation of literary texts assured their authority in the oral culture of the audience. "Within this tradition, 'learning' consisted of the skills to interpret the Scriptures and other authoritative writings," writes Isaac. Hortatory electioneering drew its inspiration from the oral tradition of mass protest, which involved spontaneous rather than ritualized expression. Mass protest took the form of the extemporaneous speech rather than the literary recitation; it was emotional, emphatic, and interactive with its listeners.[25] Hortatory rhetoric followed—to an extent we can only surmise—this tradition of oral protest: mass meetings, fiery speeches, and crowd action.[26]

Hortatory rhetoric drew upon sources not only in the oral culture but also in the printed polemics of earlier generations. Oliver Cromwell's speeches prefigure this rhetorical style. Protestant denominational idioms of resistance had critical influence in the formation of this style of address.[27] The polemical writings of John

[25] Ibid., pp. 121–31.

[26] Boulton, *Language of Politics;* pp. 11–72; for the sources of this language, see Bernard Bailyn, *The Ideological Origins of the American Revolution* (Cambridge, Mass., 1967) pp. 22–54; for a description of the style of persuasion in the early republic, see Richard Buel, *Securing the Revolution: Ideology in American Politics, 1789–1815* (Ithaca, N.Y., 1972), pp. 113–35; for a description of the British style of persuasion, see Olivia Smith, *The Politics of Language, 1791–1819* (Oxford, 1984), pp. 1–34; see also David A. Wilson, *Paine and Cobbett: The Transatlantic Connection* (Kingston, Ont., 1988), pp. 11–33, 99–111. For an example of Cromwell's rhetoric, see the "Dissolution of the Second Protectorate Parliament," February 4, 1658, in *Oliver Cromwell's Letters and Speeches*, ed. Thomas Carlyle (New York, 1855), pp. 390–93. On the influence of denominationalism on eighteenth-century transatlantic discourse, see Clark, *Language of Liberty*, pp. 29–45. On the significance of oral culture on the politics of the eighteenth century, see Isaac, *Transformation of Virginia*, pp. 121–31, 266–69.

[27] Clark, *Language of Liberty*, pp. 240–82.

Trenchard, Thomas Gordon, and Thomas Paine, and the speaking style of John Wilkes and Patrick Henry adhered to this form of rhetoric.[28] It was the style of British and Irish journalist émigrés, such as James Callender, Matthew Carey, and William Cobbett. In America, this became the style of the leading journalists, Republicans like Benjamin Franklin Bache and Federalists like John Fenno. Moreover, it had resonance with those who lacked social prestige but did not lack skill, resources for self-education, or a sense of self-esteem.

Harold Lasswell, in his classic study of political language, observed the many differences in language between despotic and democratic societies. In crises, however, the political language of democracies resembles the language of despotic regimes. In such times, "language is employed as missile and shield." Hortatory language acted as "missile and shield" in the crises of Anglo-America.[29]

The hortatory and laudatory styles were on a collision course in Anglo-America. The collision, however, took a very different course in the United States and in Britain. The hortatory style emerged as the dominant style of political rhetoric in the United States in the Jeffersonian period. In Britain, on the other hand, hortatory rhetoric was mostly confined to the periphery. Because of its marginal role in two-party politics, the British hortatory style retained a purity that had largely vanished in Jacksonian America.[30]

---

[28] Gustafson, *Representative Words*, pp. 169–74, 241–52; Isaac, *Transformation of Virginia*, pp. 267–69.

[29] Harold Lasswell, Nathan Leites, and Associates, *Language of Politics: Studies in Quantitative Semantics* (Cambridge, Mass., 1965), pp. 29, 36. See also Heinz Paechter et al., *Nazi-Deutsch: A Glossary of Contemporary German Usage* (New York, 1944), p. 6; Murray J. Edelman, *Symbolic Uses of Politics* (Urbana, Ill., 1964); Murray J. Edelman, *Political Language: Words That Succeed and Policies That Fail* (New York, 1977).

[30] Jeffrey A. Smith, *Printers and Press Freedom: The Ideology of Early American Journalism* (New York, 1988), pp. 57–73; Leonard W. Levy, *The Emergence of a Free Press* (New York, 1985), pp. 282–349. Daniel Rodgers cites J. A. Hobson's observation of 1897 that some British land reformers still spoke in the antiquated language of "natural rights." Hobson calls these reformers "typical English moralists." Hobson described them as "men of the lower-middle or upper-working class, men of grit and character largely self-educated, keen citizens, [and] mostly nonconformists in religion." Hobson, "The Influence of Henry George in England," *Fortnightly*

American newspapers came increasingly to rely on circulation and advertising revenue to maintain themselves. In the first thirty years of the nineteenth century, the number of American newspapers doubled and then tripled. Advertising revenue and the amount of space devoted to advertising in the American press increased even more dramatically as the press relied increasingly on commercial revenue.[31] The language and symbolism of commercial advertising became an important influence. The use of bold type, woodcuts, emphatic punctuation and, most important, the cadence and emphasis of spoken language proved an early and enduring contribution of advertising to American political rhetoric.[32]

In Britain, hortatory rhetoric reappeared in partisan politics during the Corn Law agitation of the early 1840s. Editors also used hortatory language in debating religious issues. Editorials reduced much political debate to a division between Protectionists and Free Traders on the former issue, and between Anglicans and non-Anglicans on the latter. Conservative election appeals proclaimed their support of "Protestantism and Protectionism," while the Liberals and Peelites extolled "Civil and Religious Liberty" and "Free Trade."[33] These usages made consistent party identification possible for electors at a time of great party instability in Parliament.

Across the sea, erudite references to ancient history and mythology gradually declined.[34] Editorials mobilized American public

---

*Review* 62 (December 1897): 841. This example is discussed in Rodgers, *Contested Truths,* p. 63.

[31] Alfred McClung Lee, *The Daily Newspaper in America: The Evolution of a Social Instrument* (New York, 1937), pp. 32, 60. Lee sees the trend beginning as early as 1760, when the first newspapers appeared with over fifty percent of their space devoted to advertising. See also Allan R. Pred, *Urban Growth and the Circulation of Information: The United States System of Cities, 1790–1840* (Cambridge, Mass., 1973).

[32] Walter J. Ong, *Orality and Literacy: The Technologizing of the Word* (London, 1982), p. 128.

[33] See Michael Calvin McGee's very useful analysis of "ideographs," in "The 'Ideograph': A Link between Rhetoric and Ideology," *Quarterly Journal of Speech* 66 (1980): 1–16.

[34] John William Ward, *Andrew Jackson: Symbol for an Age* (New York, 1955); Northrop Frye, *The Critical Path: An Essay on the Social Context of Literary Criticism* (Bloomington, Ind., 1971), p. 121. See also Northrop Frye, *The Stubborn Structure: Essays on Criticism and Society* (Ithaca, N.Y., 1970), pp. 30, 249–56.

opinion to subscribe to new partisan values by means of thematic "recurrence": the promotion of old republican rhetorical themes to serve new ends. Tocqueville observed that democratic citizens "will often have vacillating thoughts, and so language must be loose enough to leave them play. As they never know whether what they say today will fit the facts of tomorrow, they have a natural taste for abstract terms. An abstract word is like a box with a false bottom; you may put in it what ideas you please and take them out again unobserved."[35] Jacksonian editorials resurrected old republican themes and refashioned them to convey new values and serve new rhetorical ends.

In place of classical mythology, Jacksonian editors created folk myths around contemporary politicians, often providing them with historical staging. Historical allegories from classical times had often been used in legitimating a cause, but Jacksonian allegories were different. They drew upon historical folklore in creating a democratic political vernacular accessible to the ordinary voter and on intimate terms with him.[36] This was an age that celebrated Webster's ceremonial speeches, but it was also the age of nicknames and narratives, folk songs, poems, symbols, and slogans. Formality gradually retreated in the face of the familiar.

In the early nineteenth century, American editors had introduced deliberative questions in a demonstrative mode of discourse, so by mid-century legislators raised demonstrative questions of praise and blame in the deliberative setting of the legislative assembly, not for the ears of the other legislators but for the readers of the printed page. By 1850, newspapers printed important congressional and parliamentary debates verbatim. These debates attracted an attentive national audience that followed these events the way succeeding generations would follow sports playoffs.

In Britain the elimination of the stamp duty on newspapers in 1855, the extension of the franchise in the Second Reform Act of 1867, and the railroads, which by mid-century permitted overnight distribution of the metropolitan dailies, together created a

---

[35] Alexis de Tocqueville, *Democracy in America*, ed. J. P. Mayer and Max Lerner, trans. George Lawrence (New York, 1966), p. 450.

[36] Gustafson, *Representative Words*, p. 39.

national audience for the political press. By the middle of the 1860s outdoor rallies, mass assemblies, and addresses reinvigorated speechmaking in Britain. Instantaneous transmission of information permitted the national audience to learn of events and read speeches or debates within twenty-four hours. In an age that celebrated combativeness, editors portrayed Gladstone and Disraeli in gladiatorial contests, personifying the respective concerns of their parties.[37]

American editorials during the Civil War and afterward took on a muted form. American language, like American politics, seemed chastened by the excesses that led to war. The Civil War overshadowed the appeals to transcendent values. The war's aftermath seemed to offer less opportunity for hyperbole, but also less scope for the levity and familiarity characteristic of antebellum rhetoric. Secession, war, and Reconstruction created an atmosphere of crisis in politics and lent a sense of imperative to electioneering. Editorials often sought to build upon existing political allegiances rather than create new ones.[38] These editorials returned to a more formal, somewhat more remote, persuasive style in America. It might be called the *admonitory* style. Hortatory rhetoric was active, urging voters to mobilize; admonitory rhetoric was reactive, warning them of the consequences of political failure. If hortatory rhetoric was inventive; admonitory rhetoric was reiterative. Hortatory rhetoric was the language of political mobilization; admonitory rhetoric was the language of stable party competition. In an age that celebrated competitive individualism, admonitory rhetoric hailed the collective competition of team effort.

Hortatory rhetoric survived to a ripe old age in Britain, largely through the talents of "Old Man Eloquent." From the Midlothian Campaign of 1879 until his last general election in 1895, Gladstone inspired—and antagonized—voters with his moralistic appeals. In *Culture and Anarchy,* Matthew Arnold contrasted "right reason" with a persuasion more "natural" to the taste, which he

---

[37] Stephen Koss, *The Rise and Fall of the Political Press in Britain* (London, 1981), 1:121–66.

[38] See McGee, "Ideograph," pp. 12–14. For a discussion of the "legacy" of "liberty and equality," see Appleby, "The American Heritage—the Heirs and the Disinherited," in *Liberalism and Republicanism,* pp. 222–31.

termed "bathos." Gladstone may have epitomized what Arnold meant by "right reason." Peter Gay has observed that during the Midlothian tour Gladstone "used reason as much as pathos, statistics as well as orotund phrases, explanations no less than exhortation." On some deeper level, Gladstone's appeal "was erotic, as the relations of leaders to led must always be." Sublimated eros and unexpurgated bathos sum up much of late Victorian British rhetoric.[39]

The rise of the "independent" press and of "yellow journalism" brought on a more attenuated relationship between the American press and parties. The independent journals sought to provide "objective" news coverage that surmounted partisanship; the yellow newspapers appealed beyond partisanship to gain the widest circulation for their advertisers. The press began to conceive of itself as a neutral "medium" of information rather than as a partisan "organ" or "appendage." Newspapers in the United States and later in Britain came to perceive themselves as conveyors of information, "objectively" packaged. A new emphasis arose on "human interest" stories. Features on crime, "society," and sports achieved a new prominence. Politics began to be presented in a fashion emphasizing its entertainment value.[40]

Consistent with the new universalism of the independent press was a renewed emphasis on nationalism at the end of the century. The Spanish-American and the Boer wars reaffirmed the strength of nationalism. The mass circulation dailies of Hearst, Pulitzer, and Northcliffe used appeals to nationalism to attract a wide audience, and advertising revenues followed. After the Northcliffe Revolution and the innovations of Pulitzer and Hearst, the mass circulation dailies looked upon their readers more as consumers than as political participants.[41]

[39] Matthew Arnold, *Culture and Anarchy: An Essay in Political and Social Criticism* (Ann Arbor, Mich., 1965), especially pp. 150–62; Peter Gay, *The Cultivation of Hatred*, vol. 3 of *The Bourgeois Experience, Victoria to Freud*, (New York, 1993), p. 285.

[40] Michael E. McGerr, *The Decline of Popular Politics: The American North, 1865–1928* (New York, 1986), pp. 107–37; Michael Schudson, *Discovering the News: A Social History of American Newspapers* (New York, 1978), pp. 91–105; Alan J. Lee, *The Origins of the Popular Press in England, 1855–1914* (London, 1976), pp. 76–130. See also Koss, *Political Press*, 1:306–55.

[41] Koss, *Political Press*, 1:409–35.

Newspapers attached new prominence to visual appeals in the late nineteenth century in both America and Britain. American cartoons addressed themselves increasingly to workingmen. Thomas Nast's cartoons in *Harper's Weekly* in the 1860s and 1870s had targeted a middle class audience; in Walt McDougall's cartoons of the 1890s laborers were the medium and the message. Workingmen were the stock characters in the political engravings and cartoons of the late nineteenth century, and the captions addressed themselves to labor's interests. Print communications had incorporated oral devices at the end of the eighteenth century; at the end of the nineteenth century newspapers incorporated visual devices. The press used both approaches to communicate with a growing audience, in this way initiating and assimilating them into the political culture.[42]

The twentieth century has not seen the end of any of the forms of rhetoric described in this work. The task continued of initiating and assimilating ever larger political audiences by means of rhetorical innovation. As in the nineteenth century, one form of rhetoric might predominate and another might decline in popularity but none of these forms ever disappeared from editorials. If anything, the advent of television has given a new prominence to laudatory forms of persuasion. Political crises still call forth a burst of what Matthew Arnold called "fire and strength" until a new set of partisan values emerge and "bathos" reasserts itself.[43]

"The historian," writes J. G. A. Pocock, will "look for indications that words were being used in new ways as the result of new

[42] *Louisville Courier-Journal*, 22 October 1888.

[43] Arnold, *Culture and Anarchy*, pp. 150–62. See also John Zvesper, *Political Philosophy and Rhetoric: A Study of the Origins of American Party Politics* (Cambridge, 1977), pp. 6–10; Green, *Shaping Political Consciousness*, pp. 6–12. As Roger Chartier observes, "Every textual or typographic arrangement that aims to create control and constraint always secretes tactics that tame or subvert it; conversely, there is no production or cultural practice that does not rely on materials imposed by tradition, authority, or the market and that is not subjected to surveillance and censures from those who have power over words or gestures." Chartier, "Texts, Printing, Readings," p. 174. In times of crisis, as Lasswell noted, the language of the dominant forces within a democratic society veers towards the collectivist language of despotic regimes, while the forces seeking change in crisis are forced ever closer to a "limited repertoire of more or less unintelligible cries." Lasswell, *Language of Politics*, p. 36.

experiences, and were occasioning new problems and possibilities in the discourse of the language under study."[44] Words were being used in new ways for mobilizing an ever-expanding electoral universe. Electioneering language worked to transform the functional separation in deferential societies between "debate" and "result." It helped, however imperfectly, to transform the role of participants in the United States and Britain from a passive determinative capacity to an active deliberative one. Describing this transformation of politics, press, and language is not always a simple matter. As one of the first writers to treat parliamentary rhetoric in a more or less systematic fashion, William Gerard Hamilton remarked, "Rhetoric would be a very easy thing, if it could be contained in a rule. But *contrivance* is a main consideration in an orator; who must vary according to causes, conjunctures, occasions, and relations." This book has much to do with causes, conjunctures, occasions, and relations. It has not a little to do with contrivance.[45]

[44] J. G. A. Pocock, "Introduction: The State of the Art," in *Virtue, Commerce, and History: Essays on Political Thought and History, Chiefly in the Eighteenth Century* (Cambridge, 1985), p. 13;

[45] William Gerald Hamilton, *Parliamentary Logic* (1808; Cambridge, 1927), p. 69.

CHAPTER ONE

# Demi-Aristocratical Democracy:
# The Persistence of
# Anglo-American Culture, 1780–1799

In order to secure a seat in our august senate, 'tis necessary a
man should either be a slave or a fool; a slave to the people, for
the privilege of serving them, and a fool himself, for thus begging
a troublesome and expensive employment.
                                    —Robert Munford, *The Candidates*

A decade after the War for American Independence,
America and Britain still shared many elements of a common political culture. Political abstractions and institutions
may have altered but electioneering rhetoric in the Anglo-American world remained much the same. If the old political order in
America had disappeared, the old political expressions had not.
"The rhetoric of public interest changes very slowly," J. R. Pole
has observed. "Because people continue, with disarming simplicity,
to believe the words they utter, they imagine themselves to be
governed by the form described by a rhetoric belonging to the
past."[1]

On both sides of the Atlantic, the Neoclassical literary style still
exerted strong influence.[2] Classical schemes of rhetoric still held

[1] Pole, *Political Representation*, p. 46.
[2] Gustafson, *Representative Words*, pp. 96 and 169, n. 58. See also Linda K.
Kerber, *Federalists in Dissent: Imagery and Ideology in Jeffersonian America* (Ithaca,
N.Y., 1970); Robert Dawidoff, *The Education of John Randolph* (New York, 1979).

sway. Political discourse addressed to a mass audience was framed and laid out according to the dictates of classical theorists. Explicit distinctions between rulers and ruled persisted in the elite's dialogue with the audience.[3]

The governing elite believed that men of the right "character" could best serve the larger interests of the polity. According to Rhys Isaac, "Elections provided for the endorsement of the most eminent of the gentlemen to attend the legislature at the center of the province as custodians and revisers of the body of laws itself."[4] Character was the principal criterion by which to judge the would-be custodians' merit. Laudatory election appeals praised the man of virtue who furthered the interests of the whole society. The laudatory form stressed personal conduct over policy, "men" over "measures." Electors should confer office upon those candidates who would promote the larger interest over their own self-interest and without "preferment to faction."[5]

Classical rhetorical tradition categorized public speaking according to the speaker, audience, and occasion. Public speaking before a mass audience demanded epideictic, or demonstrative, rhetoric. In epideictic speeches Aristotle wrote, "you will develop your case mainly by arguing that what has been done is, for example, noble and useful. The facts themselves are to be taken on trust; proof of them is only admitted on those rare occasions when

---

[3] The distinctions between "rulers" and "ruled" were prevalent in colonial society. In the 1790s many vestiges of what Gordon Wood has described as "patronage" in colonial society remained. See Gordon Wood, *Radicalism,* pp. 63, 73, 229–43.

[4] Isaac, *Transformation of Virginia,* p. 113.

[5] Zvesper, *Political Philosophy and Rhetoric,* pp. 3–16, 31. See also Kenneth Cmiel, *Democratic Eloquence: The Fight over Popular Speech in Nineteenth-Century America* (New York, 1990), p. 43. On the subject of character, see J. G. A. Pocock, "Civic Humanism and Its Role in Anglo-American Thought," in *Politics, Language, and Time,* pp. 80–103. On the ideological influences on the American Revolution, see, for example, Bailyn, *Ideological Origins;* Buel, *Securing the Revolution;* Gordon S. Wood, *The Creation of the American Republic, 1776–1787* (Chapel Hill, N.C., 1969); Caroline Robbins, *The Eighteenth-Century Commonwealthman* (Cambridge, Mass., 1959); J. G. A. Pocock, *The Machiavellian Moment: Florentine Political Thought and the Atlantic Republican Tradition* (Princeton, 1975); Murrin, "Great Inversion,"; Rowland Berthoff, "Independence and Attachment, Virtue and Interest: From Republican Citizen to Free Enterpriser, 1787–1837," in *Uprooted Americans: Essays to Honor Oscar Handlin,* ed. Richard L. Bushman et al. (Boston, 1979), pp. 99–124.

they are not easily credible or when they are set down to someone else." Candidates grounded their appeals on generalities rather than specifics; on morality rather than policy. Speeches concentrated on the past and avoided reference to the future.[6]

Wooing the voters involved much more than formal rhetoric, however, and printed election appeals offer only part of the context. Late-eighteenth-century electioneering relied primarily on oral, not printed, forms of communication. In this way electioneering discourse was closely related to ritualized oral recitation of the printed word in the churches and the courts. The speaker demonstrated his understanding of authoritative written knowledge and communicated what Isaac calls "the customary and indispensable knowledge that had been stored within these writings from ancient times."[7] Polling often consumed several days; an election provided a festival atmosphere. Electors traveled from near and far to exercise their suffrage by voice voting.[8] In Britain, hustings were erected: these were wooden platform structures on

---

[6] Olivia Smith, *Politics of Language*, pp. 1–34; Cmiel, *Democratic Eloquence*, pp. 23–54; Aristotle, *De Rhetorica*, I.ix. In ancient times this style of rhetoric had been prescribed for political as well as ceremonial addresses to a mass audience. Eighteenth-century writers on rhetoric maintained that the epideictic style of rhetoric was most suitable for clergymen addressing their congregations. George Campbell of Aberdeen and Hugh Blair of Edinburgh universities were the most influential rhetoricians in late-eighteenth-century Britain and America, respectively. Campbell and Blair retained the Aristotelian categories in their own treatment of rhetoric, but as one might expect, the functional role of epideictic rhetoric had changed somewhat. George Campbell omitted in his *Philosophy of Rhetoric* any mention of secular addresses to a mass audience. See George Campbell, *The Philosophy of Rhetoric*, (London, 1776; Philadelphia, 1818), pp. 115–29. Hugh Blair, *Lectures on Rhetoric and Belles Lettres*, 2 vols. (London, 1783), 2:101–26. In America, however, Jonathan Witherspoon, Nicholas Boylston, and Samuel Phillips sought to establish better standards of rhetorical method and style on the eve of the Revolution. See Douglass Adair, "A Note on Certain of Hamilton's Pseudonyms," in *Fame and the Founding Fathers*, ed. Trevor Colbourn (New York, 1974), pp. 274–75; Charles S. Sydnor, *American Revolutionaries in the Making: Political Practices in Washington's Virginia*, 2d ed. (New York, 1965), p. 21.

[7] Isaac, *Transformation of Virginia*, p. 124.

[8] Robert J. Dinkin points out that viva voce voting continued in the middle states and in New England for state assembly and town elections. In many southern states, voice voting continued into the early nineteenth century. *Voting in Revolutionary America: A Study of Elections in the Original Thirteen States, 1776–1789* (Westport, Conn., 1982), pp. 101–3.

which speechmaking and polling took place. In America, a table
or perhaps a tree stump (thus "stump speech") formed the center
of the arena in which the electioneering ritual occurred. Candidates often delivered elaborate speeches before the electors and,
as in a courtship ritual, they frequently offered inverted expressions of deference to their would-be dependents.

In oral speeches and in newspaper advertisements political suit-
ors "humbly begged" constituents to vote for them, "treating"
them with refreshments or remuneration for the "honour of their
suffrages." A candidate might conclude by saying he was "pleased
to have the honor" of being his constituents' "obedient servant."[9]

The "friends" of a candidate often sponsored printed solicitations, implying with this word at least a personal connection
between the candidate and his supporters.[10] These solicitations
listed the reasons why a candidate or his "friends" thought he was
worthy of being elected to the legislature. Solicitations emphasized
such qualities as "independence," "integrity," and "fidelity."[11] They
assumed connections of personal, rather than political, interests
between candidates and electors.[12] References to a candidate's
political positions or even his principles were unusual.

In soliciting the electors, a candidate's address steered a course
between flattery and condescension: a candidate must present
himself without being either too ostentatious or too obsequious.
Candidates nearly always addressed the electors as "GENTLEMEN."
The candidate often made grateful allusions to "the partiality
shewn me" in previous elections for "the honour of your suffrages."
In this exercise in transposed deference, great pains were taken
to avoid transparent hypocrisy. The candidate might express his
wish that he would "merit the approbation" of his constituents.
Such sentiments displayed not so much the candidate's hypocrisy

[9] Ibid., pp. 78–89; Charles G. Steffen, *The Mechanics of Baltimore: Workers and Politics in the Age of Revolution, 1763–1812* (Urbana, Ill., 1984), pp. 89–99.

[10] Isaac defines "friend" in this context in colonial Virginia: "A 'friend' was a person, whether of higher, lower or equal station, related by the expectation of a mutual exchange of services." *Transformation of Virginia*, p. 113.

[11] James Madison, "James Madison's Autobiography," ed. Douglass Adair, *William and Mary Quarterly*, 3d ser., 2 (1945):199.

[12] Gordon Wood describes the evolution in the notion of "interest." *Radicalism*, especially pp. 71–77, 87, 89, 243–70.

as his appeal to objective criteria: a candidate's character or conduct showed whether he deserved the votes of his constituents.[13]
Whether the constituency was competitive and highly organized
or a rotten borough, the ritual preserved the fiction that political
honors depended on moral worth.

A typical British solicitation of this form appeared in the London
*Morning Chronicle* during the 1784 election, addressed to "the
Worthy Liverymen of the City of LONDON."

> Gentlemen,
> THE Dissolution of Parliament having given me an opportunity of
> aspiring to the high honour of representing my native place, permit
> me to solicit the favour of your Votes, Interest and Poll, (if necessary)
> to succeed to that important station.
> I hope that the long residence of my family amongst you, for near
> a century Liverymen of this City, and engaged in commerce, will
> have secured to them at least a character for independence and
> integrity, which I flatter myself neither my public nor my private
> conduct has in any degree diminished. If amongst the various
> candidates for your favours, you are pleased to distinguish me as
> one worthy of your confidence, I will execute the trust with a zealous
> attention to the principles of the Constitution, and endeavor to
> promote to the utmost of my abilities the commercial interest and
> prosperity of this metropolis.
>> I am, with great respect, Gentlemen,
>> Your most obedient and devoted servant,
>> SAMUEL SMITH, jr.[14]

American solicitations were very similar. Candidates used an
obsequious form with republican flourishes to address their constituents. The Jeffersonian *Aurora* published the following solicitation in 1796.

---

[13] John Adams, for example, in his *Defence of the Constitutions,* listed the "classical
virtues" as "prudence, justice, temperance and fortitude." *Works of John Adams,*
ed. Charles F. Adams (Boston, 1850–56), 6:206–7.

[14] *Morning Chronicle,* 29 March 1784. Smith said he would do the utmost to
"promote" the "interest" of the City of London. Cf. Burke's speech to his Bristol
constituents, which makes note of Burke's efforts on his constituents' behalf.
Edmund Burke, *Works,* 3:6, 50.

To the ELECTORS of the CITY & COUNTY OF PHILADELPHIA.

FELLOW CITIZENS,

SOME of my Friends have advised me to offer myself as a candidate for the office of a COMMISSIONER at the ensuing Election, and in obedience to their advice, as well as in conformity to my own inclination, I thus publicly solicit your suffrages. I do not mean to make a parade of what I will do, should I be so happy as to meet your approbation; for those who know me will believe that I will discharge the duties which will devolve upon me with fidelity, and those who do not know me will consider such protestations as the hackneyed professions of a man who is desirous of getting into office. While I am solicitous of avoiding such cant, I trust I shall not be charged with a want of respect for a public for whom I entertain the highest regard, and whose suffrages will confer a lasting obligation upon

HENRY SHRUPP[15]

Officeholder's good character sustained the health of government; elections could cleanse the body politic of vice and restore virtuous influences. "CYRUS" likened the system of elections to a healthy purgative. Writing in *The Connecticut Journal,* "CYRUS" described elections as an "irresistible power" which "pervades, invigorates and purifies every part of government." Elections infused "life, health and beauty into the most deformed and debilitated body."[16] Elections operated on "the prime interests and steady passions of our rulers, giving a salutary direction to the public measures," said the Philadelphia *Gazette of the United States.* God and the Constitution reposed a trust in the electors: to select the "most fit persons" for the national and state legislatures.[17]

"CURIUS," writing in the London *Morning Chronicle* in 1780, spoke similarly of the electors' weighty responsibility: "On the due exercise of this choice [of representatives] our happiness or misery, our glory or disgrace, our freedom or servitude entirely depends."

---

[15] *Aurora and General Advertiser,* 24 September 1796.
[16] *Connecticut Journal,* quoted in *Gazette of the United States,* 25 September 1790.
[17] Ibid.

"Our boasted liberty must perish," said CURIUS, "when once the people cease to be zealous in maintaining it."[18]

In a 1794 Independence Day oration in Connecticut, the Reverend John Lathrop of Boston's Old South Church described the basis for judging the suitability of candidates. "To determine whether a man is worthy of our suffrages, we must enquire, whether he is *a man of ability and information of virtue, stability and firmness; of pure republican principles; and his interest is united with those of his country.*"[19] In the *North Carolina Journal* in 1796, "Æneas" proclaimed that every man could aspire to "greatness and honor" in this "demi-aristocratical democracy." "Let him convince the people that he is a man of superior talents and they will confer a proper dignity upon him."[20]

In London, an editorial in the *Morning Chronicle* argued that the representative for the City of London "ought to be equally possessed of solidity of judgment, firmness of heart, and integrity of principle. . . ." He should "always act upon the good of his country in general, and of his constituents in particular." The worthy candidate would "sacrifice all selfish considerations to public ones, and be equally unseduced by the allurements of corruption, and unterrified by the clamour of the multitude."[21]

Electors should value a candidate's virtue rather than his verbal cleverness. "CIVIS," writing in a London political solicitation, asserted that "The true true [*sic*] patriot is he who preserves his virtue by his actions and not by his words alone." "A RE-DRESSER OF PUBLIC NUISANCES" made a similar point in describing "the *whining, whimpering* Address" of a London candidate that the writer contrasted with "the *manly sentiments* of your Burkes, your Lascelles, and your Onslows." The *Connecticut Journal* lamented the voters' preference for "men of artifice and the splendor of words to those whose political wisdom and experience have been proved."[22]

---

[18] *Morning Chronicle and London Advertiser,* 9 September 1780, 22 September 1780.

[19] "An Oration Delivered at Worcester, on the Fourth of July, 1794" (Worcester, Mass., 1794), quoted in *Gazette of the United States,* 18 September 1794.

[20] *North Carolina Journal,* 8 September 1796; *Gazette of the United States,* 18 September 1794.

[21] *Morning Chronicle and London Advertiser,* 9 November 1780.

[22] *Morning Chronicle,* 7 September 1780, 29 September 1780; *Connecticut Journal*

In London, the Whiggish *Morning Chronicle* counseled electors to act in a disinterested fashion at the polls. Voters should not insist upon "anything personally lucrative to themselves. . . ."[23] "The Tablet," published in the *Gazette of the United States,* declared that the people of the United States would "not be easily beguiled into a bad choice of rulers, because the public opinion is so well-informed as to be competent to decide upon the merit of characters." The "great mass of individuals know too well what promotes their own interest and safety, not to reprobate the idea of forming a legislature of weak and wicked men."[24]

By the middle of the 1790s, however, the rhetorical decorum began to disappear. With the violent passions aroused by the French Revolution, panegyric gave way to invective. This was certainly not the first appearance of harsh language. Verbal abuse had often surfaced earlier when tensions were high and when politicians sought popular consent on matters of overriding concern. As Gordon Wood has pointed out, however, in the gentleman's game of politics, these polemics were often highly personal, "a succession of individual exchanges between gentlemen who were known to one another, quickly becoming unintelligible to an outsider and usually ending in bitter personal vituperation."[25] After the French Revolution the invective did not subside: gradually it became less personal and more general, more obsessed with conspiracy and often verging on political paranoia.

The hortatory form of rhetoric that appeared on both sides of the Atlantic made much use of what Richard Hofstadter called

---

article quoted in *Gazette of the United States,* 18 September 1790.

[23] *Morning Chronicle,* 30 March 1784.

[24] *Gazette of the United States,* 10 November 1790. For an interesting analysis of "interest" in the context of patronage, and "interests" in the context of democracy, see Gordon Wood, *Radicalism,* pp. 71–89 and 243–70. Those who did get elected must necessarily be "far removed" from the "basest of mankind." *Gazette of the United States,* 3 November 1790. In "An Oration Delivered at Worcester, on the Fourth of July, 1791" (Worcester, Mass., 1791) Edward Bangs spoke on the theme "What Cannot a Wise Choice of Rulers and a Proper Confidence in Them . . . Perform!" (Worcester, Mass.: American Antiquarian Society, Early American Imprints Series). Reference to this speech is made in *Massachusetts Spy: Or The Worcester Gazette,* 7 July 1791.

[25] Gordon Wood, "The Democratization of Mind in the American Revolution," in *Leadership,* p. 69.

the "paranoid style" in American politics. Hortatory rhetoric took its inspiration in part from the Country partisans in the early eighteenth century. Speeches by British radicals John Wilkes and Horne Tooke found enthusiastic audiences in America as well as in Britain. Hortatory speeches were common on both sides of the Atlantic during the American Revolution.[26]

Yet the real conflict over Anglo-American political language came about not during the American Revolution but in the midst of the French Revolution. The language conflict was not merely a dispute over style; it also marked an unprecedented struggle between the rulers and the ruled. In its early stages that struggle on both sides of the Atlantic was remarkably similar; the results, however, were markedly different.

The press in the early 1790s in Britain and America betrayed more similarities than differences. Both the Pitt Ministry and the Adams administration created elaborate support systems for party "organs." The Pitt Ministry improved upon Walpole's system supporting friendly journals and repressing opposition papers. These policies inspired the Adams administration's subsidies for the Federalist press.[27]

The parties in power responded to the rhetorical challenge of their opponents by imposing repressive constraints on the press and on free expression, orchestrating a systematic attack on opposition journals, and skillfully promoting a network of pro-Ministerial newspapers. In counterattacking, the newspapers supporting Pitt and Adams imitated their adversaries: they adopted many of the tactics of hortatory rhetoric.

The moderate opposition, British Whigs and American Republicans, found themselves in a dilemma. Their officeholders and

---

[26] Richard Hofstadter, "The Paranoid Style in American Politics," in *The Paranoid Style in American Politics and Other Essays* (New York, 1965), pp. 3–40; also Gordon S. Wood, "Conspiracy and the Paranoid Style: Causality and Deceit in the Eighteenth Century," *William and Mary Quarterly*, 3d ser., 39 (1982): 401–41; James H. Hutson, "The Origins of 'The Paranoid Style in American Politics': Public Jealousy from the Age of Walpole to the Age of Jackson," in *Saints and Revolutionaries: Essays on Early American History*, ed. David Hall, John M. Murrin, and Thad W. Tate (New York, 1984), pp. 332–72.

[27] James Morton Smith, *Freedom's Fetters: The Alien and Sedition Laws and American Civil Liberties* (Ithaca, N.Y., 1956), p. 105.

editors had employed the same laudatory rhetoric in elections as the governing parties. Faced with the same threat of prosecution as the radical democrats, many moderate editors in the United States adopted a harsher rhetorical style. In Britain, on the other hand, successful prosecutions of leading Whig journals for seditious libel forced many British editors to abandon their overt opposition.

The radical democrats faced similar threats in both countries but with very different outcomes. In the early years of the nineteenth century, radical American editors gradually found themselves addressing the mainstream of public opinion. In Britain, on the other hand, continued repression forced many to emigrate to America or continue their publications extra-legally.

One of the most gifted British radicals who remained was Horne Tooke. Addressing the electors of Westminster, Tooke used the rhetorical scheme of antithesis in describing the political context, and employed the scheme of anaphora (repetition of the same phrase at the beginning of successive clauses) to emphasize his points. Both these devices were typical of hortatory rhetoric, especially in its most effective form: the speech delivered on the hustings. Tooke, a virtuoso performer of hortatory rhetoric, called upon the electors of Westminster to ask themselves

In the present cruel struggle between Liberty and Slavery, who are the persons starving for want of bread? To whom do the Ministry propose a substitute for bread? Who are the persons oppressed, beggared, dishonoured, vilified and ruined? Who are languishing in their gaols? ... Who are sent as felons to Botany Bay? Who are cast into dungeons and treated and tried as traitors? [Several persons cried out "*the People.*"] Mr. Tooke said, "It is true. It is so. It is we."[28]

[28] *Morning Post and Fashionable World,* 8 June 1796. Tooke was a truly original orator, pamphleteer, and lexicographer; he was also an ordained Anglican priest and habitual gambler. His principal work, titled *ΕΠΕΑ ΠΤΕΡΟΕΝΤΑ. Or, the Diversions of Purley,* 2 vols., 2d. ed. (London, 1798–1805), was both a political and a lexicographical work. See David Simpson, *The Politics of American English, 1776–1850* (New York, 1986), pp. 81–90; Olivia Smith, *Politics of Language,* pp. 110–53; Max Atkinson, *Our Masters' Voices: The Language and Body Language of Politics* (London, 1984), pp. 57–83, 105–11, 157–63.

Hortatory rhetoric often focused on conspiracy. According to "POLIO," the "Janus head of aristocracy" threatened to overpower the "fair face of Republicanism"; only the citizens could act to "prostrate the monster." His appeal concluded with a typical hortatory peroration:

> your country and your children—(Would you beget slaves!!) all nature call upon you at this portentous period by your exertions—by your virtue, to save the finest quarter of the globe from the worst of curses——slavery! Shall this great call be made in vain?[29]

The collision over the French Revolution raised the specter of external threats, internal conspiracies, and national ruin. At the same time editors continued personal attacks on the opposition, often in the form of antithetical contrasts. These often compared the character of two candidates, frequently concentrating on a specific virtue, such as "fortitude."

Party identification needed contrast and competition. Negative associations reinforced party solidarity: in articulating what they stood for, the parties had to accentuate what they stood against. Editors focused their readers' hostility by *ad personam* attacks against the leadership of the opposing party. As George Campbell had observed in his 1776 treatise on rhetoric,

> It would have been impossible even for Cicero to inflame the minds of the people to so high a pitch against oppression, considered in the abstract, as he actually did inflame them against Verres the *oppressor.* Nor could he have incensed them so much against *treason* and *conspiracy* as he did against Catiline the *traitor* and *conspirator.*[30]

A favorite *ad personam* attack contrasted one candidate's "firmness" and another's "weakness." Charles Simms, a candidate for presidential elector, accused Jefferson of "a want of firmness" for fleeing Richmond in 1781 at the approach of the British.[31] A letter in the *Gazette of the United States* proclaimed that only "firm and

---

[29] *Aurora,* 7 October 1796.
[30] Campbell, *Philosophy of Rhetoric,* p. 105.
[31] *Gazette of the United States,* 6 October 1796.

decisive" patriots could act as "inveterate foes of weak measures." "The energy of the true federalist," the letter continued, "will stamp the character of America with strong and manly features, calculated to beget the confidence of the people, and strike terror to the heart of France."[32]

"Phocion" wrote a series of letters for the *Gazette of the United States* contrasting the character and conduct of Jefferson and Adams. The *"governor of the antient dominion"* in a time of "real danger, dwindled into the *poor timid philosopher*" and thus "shamefully abandoned his trust."[33]

"Phocion" contrasted Jefferson's behavior with the conduct of "the spirited and truly patriotic HAMILTON." "Like the philosopher of Monticelli [*sic*], Hamilton had reasons to retire, with a large family and a dwindling fortune." With "a Roman spirit," however, he declared he would "remain at his post, as long as there was any danger of his country being involved in war."[34]

Anglo-American political culture split into hostile camps, each with real and imagined connections to belligerent powers abroad. Vehement rhetoric sometimes provoked physical violence. Polarized by different conceptions of liberty, foreign policy, and political economy, these disagreements reached the combustion point in the legislative chambers and the press, and on the streets. With a view of politics centered on character, partisans saw their adversaries as bad men engaged in evil pursuits.

[32] Ibid., 24 September 1796. Bentham classified this as an argument *ad metum.* See Jeremy Bentham, *Bentham's Handbook of Political Fallacies,* ed. Harold A. Larrabee (Baltimore, 1952). See also Albert O. Hirschman, *The Rhetoric of Reaction: Perversity, Futility, Jeopardy* (Cambridge, Mass., 1991), pp. 81–86; David Leverenz, *Manhood and the American Renaissance* (Ithaca, N.Y., 1990).

[33] *Gazette of the United States,* 8 October 1796. "Phocion" also said Jefferson "skulked away to a snug retreat" when it required the exertions and talents of the "wisest and bravest statesmen to keep the federal ship from foundering on the rocks." "Phocion" then pursued the metaphor of the ship of state, saying that Jefferson had abandoned "the old helmsman" Washington and left "others to buffet the storm." On the significance of the ship metaphor, see Fischer, *Revolution of American Conservatism,* pp. 10–12.

[34] *Gazette of the United States,* 25 October 1796. John Adams's manhood likewise benefited from Phocion's comparison with Jefferson. Adams's *"firm and steady* pursuit of his patriotic career" and his *"manly* and independent conduct at Paris in *negotiating the peace,* whereby *great advantages* were acquired," could "never be forgotten."

Partisans reached for that tool of constraint long available to curb critical editors: prosecution at the common law for seditious libel. Parliament passed the Sedition Act in 1795, after a mob attacked George III on his way to give the speech from the throne. Henceforward, writing, speaking, or publishing anything that could incite hatred against the King or His Majesty's Government would be punishable by banishment or transportation for seven years.[35]

The Sedition Act received a great deal of attention in the American press, particularly from the Federalists. The *Gazette of the United States* applauded them and reported American "Jacobins' " dismay. *Porcupine's Gazette*, edited by William Cobbett, published the statutes and the parliamentary debates in the summer of 1798.[36] The Adams administration modeled its response to American "Jacobins" on the Pitt government's measures. Rather than silencing a small radical minority, however, the prosecutions under the American Sedition Act stopped the publication of the most influential Republican newspapers.[37]

When in power, Republicans also engaged in repressive litigation. Dr. Benjamin Rush, a Republican, sued William Cobbett for libel in Pennsylvania. The alleged libel appeared in an article Cobbett had written criticizing Rush's practice of bloodletting. Cobbett fled to England in 1800 to avoid paying damages.[38]

---

[35] The Habeas Corpus Act 34 Geo. 3, c. liv suspended habeas corpus until repealed in 1801. The Sedition Act of 1795 etablished a licensing system for public meetings and empowered magistrates to disperse meetings at which seditious sentiments were uttered. 36 Geo. 3, c. viii. Stanley Elkins and Eric McKitrick make the point that there were ten times as many prosecutions for treason in Britain as in the United States in the 1790s. They argue that "radicals" in America "were beginning to organize the entire political class . . . in a new and unaccustomed way." *The Age of Federalism: The Early American Republic, 1788–1800* (New York, 1993), pp. 711–13.

[36] For an example of Cobbett's writing during this debate, see William Cobbett, "Detection of a Conspiracy," in *Peter Porcupine in America: Pamphlets on Republicanism and Revolution,* ed. David A. Wilson (Ithaca, N.Y., 1994), pp. 241–57.

[37] James Morton Smith, *Freedom's Fetters: The Alien and Sedition Acts and American Civil Liberties* (Ithaca, N.Y., 1956), p. 105; John C. Miller, *Crisis in Freedom: The Alien and Sedition Acts* (Boston, 1951), pp. 67–70.

[38] G. D. H. Cole, *The Life of William Cobbett,* 3d ed. (London, 1947), pp. 65–68; see also Cobbett, *Porcupine,* pp. 41, 228–30.

The violent feelings that accompanied the American Quasi-War with France in 1798 infected the partisan exchange between the *Gazette of the United States* and the *Aurora*. Cobbett, alias "Peter Porcupine," was an easy target for the *Aurora:*

> All the sluices of *English vulgarity,* the slang of the *English stews,* the *morose grossness* of the *English foot-soldier dialect* were constantly pouring forth in torrents . . . from the pen of the *noted English corporal Porcupine* . . . our sentiment surpasses pity, for it extends to *contempt,* a contempt excited by the *abject meanness* and *dastardly character* of the calumniator.[39]

Tory journals took up the cause of William Cobbett in America: the first-issue of the monthly *Anti-Jacobin Review* described Peter Porcupine's account of his libel trial in Pennsylvania. In explaining his emigration to America and his enlistment in the Federalist cause, Cobbett said he might wish that great warmth would be as "admissible in the cause of virtue, order and religion, as had been tolerated in the wicked course of villainy, insurrection and blasphemy." "Alas!" said the reviewer,

> Peter, at this time knew but little [of the] spirit and temper . . . of democracy and Jacobinism. He knew not, that the men who profess those principles are, for the most part, vindictive, malignant, oppressive and intolerant. . . . He knew not, it would seem, that those

[39] The attack concluded with a remarkable challenge: "Porcupine" was invited to call at the *Aurora*'s offices to meet the editor or the widow of the former proprietor, who "whether in petticoats or breeches will be ready to give him suitable satisfaction." *Aurora,* 5 November 1798. Newspapers reserved some of the harshest invective for opposing editors. The *Aurora* referred to "Phocion" as a "sniveling cur." Ibid., 3 November 1796. On the same day the *Gazette of the United States* called the *Aurora*'s editor, Philip Freneau, a "tool" of the Republicans. *Gazette of the United States,* 3 November 1796. The *Aurora* described the *Gazette*'s editor, John Fenno, as "this wiseacre" and charged him with being the "instrument" of the Federalists because he accepted a government printing contract. Fenno, said the *Aurora,* "received his education in England, and his modes of thinking are entirely English, no wonder he should suppose others capable of acting as he would if similarly circumstanced." *Aurora,* 3 November 1796, 11 October 1796.

whose duty it is to defend the laws often *sleep on their posts,* while their enemies are ever vigilant, active and alert.[40]

Dire warnings accompanied vivid descriptions of disaster resulting from an opposition victory. Juntos, Jacobin cabals, Democratic Societies, Associations, Washington Benevolent Societies, the Bavarian Illuminati: these conspiratorial groups frequently appeared in party newspapers in Britain and the United States. Newspapers made "Alarming discoveries!" They detected "Jacobin treachery" and proclaimed that "a daring and aspiring Tory faction must be disappointed." The *United States Oracle of the Day,* a Federalist paper, echoed a biblical warning against false prophets. The *Oracle* cautioned its readers to beware *"of those who wear sheep's clothing but within are ravening wolves."*[41]

These early attempts to fashion party appeals employed what Hofstadter called "Dionysian" rhetoric to castigate the opposition.[42] "Democrats" and "Aristocrats," "Jacobins" and "Tories" were common appellations in the United States for the opposition. These have at least some parallel in the subsequent dialogue of Anglo-American parties. The "Cave of Adullam," "Locofocos," and "Wooly Heads" are a few examples of the picturesque epithets that later parties fashioned for their opponents, yet the fierce rhetorical style of the early republic differed from the later rhetorical style. Language employed in the 1790s had a greater intensity than any in either country except on the eve of the Civil War. "Sedition," "treason," "villainy," and "turpitude" marked the designs of "atheists" and "tyrants." Their schemes were "vile," "base," and "malicious."

Hortatory rhetoric appeared threatening in its style, method, and intent. These rhetorical tactics gained readers and nurtured partisan loyalties. This prospect frightened those officials in the

[40] *Anti-Jacobin Review and Magazine; or, Monthly Political and Literary Censor,* vol. 1, no. 1, art. 1, July 1798, p. 10. The review described Cobbett as "having contributed to give a proper tone to the public spirit in America."

[41] Portsmouth, New Hampshire, *United States Oracle of the Day,* 13 August 1800. See Matt. 7:15 AV, "Beware of false prophets, which come to you in sheep's clothing, but inwardly they are ravening wolves."

[42] Richard Hofstadter, *The Idea of a Party System: The Rise of Legitimate Opposition in the United States, 1780–1840* (Berkeley, 1969), p. 130.

Pitt and Adams administrations whose minds linked the legitimacy of the political administration with the legitimacy of "the state."

In the United States, these views were not noticeable after the "Revolution of 1800." The incoming administration allowed the Sedition Act to expire and Republican journals replaced Federalist ones as the recipients of state patronage. Federalist journals found it necessary to discover a new base of support. Since many state governments in the commercialized Northeast remained in Federalist hands the journals survived. Moreover, they had resources from their greater connections with commercial interests: they gained financial support from commercial "subscribers" (i.e., patrons).

In Britain, press constraints and one-party dominance of Parliament permitted laudatory rhetoric's ascendancy in Britain until the end of the Napoleonic conflict.[43] Ironically, one of those who led the way for the reintroduction of hortatory rhetoric in Britain was none other than William Cobbett, a conservative in America who turned radical when he returned home to England, in a reversal of the usual emigration and political conversion patterns.

The expiration of the Sedition Act in the United States in 1801 removed the largest obstacle that inhibited the establishment of a new rhetorical style among Republicans and Federalists alike, and this new style quickly incorporated both hortatory rhetoric and the attention-getting devices of commercial advertising. American politics and political communication became salable commodities. The furious exchange between the American Federalist and Republican newspapers in the Quasi-War with France in 1798 and the election of 1800 proved that a new rhetoric of politics could sell issues and policies.

[43] State libel laws in the United States continued to hamper free expression of the press until the second decade of the nineteenth century. See Jeffrey Smith, *Printers and Press Freedom,* pp. 88–92; Levy, *Emergence of a Free Press,* pp. 304–7.

CHAPTER TWO

## Oral Speech on the Printed Page: Electioneering Rhetoric in the United States, *1800–1824*

> On the anniversary of our independence every city and almost every village of this Union resounds with formal discourses, strictly belonging to the demonstrative class of the ancients. . . . Our success in this department of literature has not been correspondent to our partialities in its favor.
> —John Quincy Adams, *Boylston Lectures on Rhetoric*

I n his lectures on rhetoric as Boylston Professor at Harvard in 1810, John Quincy Adams observed that if the American style of discourse did not compare favorably with that of Greece and Rome, nevertheless in the "art of mingling moral sentiment with oratorical splendor, modern eloquence has perhaps equaled that of the ancients."[1] This mixture of moral splendor and oral emphasis made a potent instrument for communicating with an enlarged electorate. The "Revolution of 1800" stimulated a dramatic expansion in electoral participation and required an accompanying change in political rhetoric.

The election of 1800 marked not only the victory of Jeffersonian Republicanism but also the triumph of the hortatory style of political rhetoric. The new style of political rhetoric exploited the

---

[1] John Quincy Adams, *Lectures on Rhetoric and Oratory* (New York, 1962), p. 252.

cadence and emphasis of oral communication, using emphatic punctuation such as exclamation marks, question marks, and dashes. Emphatic typography such as italics, boldface, and underlining also mimicked oral speech. Symbols, slogans, and graphic juxtapositions gave a visual presence to printed communication.

Hortatory rhetoric combined antithesis and invective with a practical, programmatic focus. The new style of persuasion laid particular stress on contrast: between Christianity and Atheism for the Federalists; between Monarchy and Republicanism for the Republicans. It also drew on the folk imagery of conflicts from the past: the American Revolution, the French Revolution, the English Civil War, and the "Norman Yoke."[2]

Printed communication began to take its cue from the sing-song meter of the huckster, and from the visual iconography of commercial symbols. The amount of space devoted to advertising increased exponentially; advertising revenue expanded proportionally.[3] The design, language, and layout of advertising changed the style and content of newspapers.[4]

The system of subsidies for Federalist newspapers instituted by the Adams administration fell like a rich prize into the hands of the Republicans in 1801. The act establishing the Department of State provided that the secretary would select newspapers in which to publish the laws and resolutions passed by Congress. While secretary of state in the early 1790s, Jefferson had himself used this patronage to reward such loyal Republican editors as Philip

---

[2] Christopher Hill, "The Norman Yoke," in *Democracy and the Labour Movement,* ed. John Saville (London, 1954), pp. 11–66; R. J. Smith, *The Gothic Bequest: Medieval Institutions in British Thought 1688–1863* (Cambridge, 1987), pp. 98–103; Simpson, *Politics of American English,* pp. 81–90; Cmiel, *Democratic Eloquence,* pp. 94–122; Daniel J. Boorstin, *The Americans: The National Experience* (New York, 1965), p. 308, and, more generally, pp. 277–324; also Daniel J. Boorstin, *The Americans: The Colonial Experience* (New York, 1958), pp. 271–340.

[3] See Donald R. Avery, "The Newspaper on the Eve of the War of 1812: Changes in Content Patterns, 1808–1812" (diss., Southern Illinois University, 1982), pp. 213–32. Avery observed that the mean amount of space devoted to commercial advertising in New England was 28 percent greater than in the South or the West.

[4] James M. Wood, *The Story of Advertising* (New York, 1958), pp. 87–111; Alfred Lee, *Daily Newspaper,* pp. 32, 60.

Freneau. In the late 1790s, Federalist Timothy Pickering used subsidies to establish a Federalist press network in coastal cities.

The incoming secretary of state in 1801, James Madison, recognized the value of press subsidies. By the time Madison had relinquished his position in 1809, he had established a Republican press network across the republic. The patronage machinery used to support the Federalist journals ironically provided the means for the Republicans to consolidate their electoral base.[5]

Beginning in 1801 the American press enjoyed thirty years of unequaled expansion. The number of newspapers quintupled; daily newspapers multiplied by two and a half times.[6] Commercial revenues sustained the rapid growth of the American press. As the commercial agrarian economy expanded, a growing number of households needed the commercial information provided for producers and consumers by the press.

The Jefferson administration promoted and shaped this expansion. Madison took care to support the best-established journals in the cities; the Republicans did not wish to squander government revenues on high-risk ventures. Madison encouraged the dissemination and republication of articles, letters, and editorial opinions across the network of party journals. This network flourished in the North, which had the fiercest party competition.[7] Federalist newspapers in northern cities survived and even expanded thanks to small groups of financial underwriters.[8]

[5] Culver Smith, *Press, Politics, and Patronage*, pp. 24–29, 42–48.

[6] Pred, *Urban Growth*, pp. 58–59, 80, 153; Richard D. Brown, *Knowledge Is Power: The Diffusion of Information in Early America* (New York, 1989), pp. 110–31; Alfred Lee, *Daily Newspaper*, pp. 711–14.

[7] New England had a rich oral tradition which encouraged public speaking on both sacred and profane topics. See Sacvan Bercovitch, *The American Jeremiad* (Madison, Wis., 1978); Perry Miller, "Moral and Psychological Roots of American Resistance," in *The Reinterpretation of the American Revolution 1763–1789*, ed. Jack P. Greene (New York, 1968), pp. 251–74; James M. Banner, *To the Hartford Convention: Federalists and the Origins of Party Politics in Massachusetts, 1789–1815* (New York, 1970), pp. 26–33.

[8] Culver Smith, *Press, Politics, and Patronage*, pp. 47–48. John Nicholas complained in a letter to Alexander Hamilton that there was a great need for a nationwide network of Federalist newspapers which would republish each other's material and correspond regularly. The Federalists, he wrote to Hamilton, "seldom republish from each other, while on the other hand, their antagonists never get hold of anything however trivial in reality, but they make it ring through all their

Conspiracy and the invidious motivations of the political opposition figured prominently in Jeffersonian rhetoric. The press created resonant epithets by using historical allusions. The Republican press depicted the Federalists as Tories; Federalists cast the Republicans as Jacobins. "The same old *tory faction* are now active to divide the people, and to destroy the happiness of our country," said the Boston *Independent Chronicle*. "*FREEMEN OF BOSTON!*" cried another appeal in the *Independent Chronicle*. The "enemies to our common good are a faction made up of the shreds and patches of those unextinguished *Tories* who were, perhaps, too kindly permitted to return to the bosom of a country that they would have sold to the tyrant of the hour!"[9]

Occasionally, the historical perspectives of Federalists and Republicans clashed, generating tremendous heat in the process. In one such case, the Portsmouth, New Hampshire *Federal Address* referred to the struggles of the British against Napoleonic "tyranny," a common theme in the Federalist press. No free government existed in Europe, said the *Federal Address*, "but in the land of *our forefathers*, and *THEY* are compelled to defend their freedom and independence by sacrifices the most painful, and by exertions of which the cause of liberty alone is worthy, and which can be achieved by those only who know its value."[10]

The reaction from the Boston *Independent Chronicle* was as fierce as it was predictable; it drew on an alternative view of the land of the forefathers:

> OUR forefathers and the forefathers of the addressers, if they are Americans, were persecuted, scourged and exiled by this very government! Our forefathers fled from the tyranny and persecution of this government, crossed the Atlantic and settled in the wilderness of America. . . . The whole history of *our* forefathers, their whole lives and sufferings, afford abundant proof that *they* never thought it a free government.[11]

---

papers from one end of the continent to the other." Nicholas to Hamilton, 4 August 1803, Papers of Alexander Hamilton, Additional Manuscripts, shelf 18, bins 22–23, reel 20; Library of Congress.

[9] *Independent Chronicle*, 5 November 1804.

[10] *Federal Address*, quoted in the *Independent Chronicle*, 19 March 1807.

[11] *Independent Chronicle*, 19 March 1807.

Displaying partisan positions or quotations on a series of vaguely defined "issues" dramatized the parties' differences. These contrasts presented the favored party's position to the greatest advantage while the opposition received the worst treatment possible. Frequently these appeared framed by slogans that stereotyped—inevitably with great distortion—the party's positions. A newspaper editorial often urged its readers: "*Look on this picture!—And on this!*" These appeals relied on graphic recognition as well as recognition of the line from *Hamlet.*[12]

One antithetical comparison introduced examples of Jefferson's hypocrisy. The *Boston Gazette* juxtaposed some of Jefferson's conciliatory expressions with excerpts from a vituperative election pamphlet written by James Callender.

"*Thou* HYPOCRITE, *out of thine own mouth will I condemn thee!*"

**'LOOK HERE!'**

| **Upon this picture** | **and on this.** |
|---|---|
| *Pamphlet paid for by Mr. Jefferson* | *Speech of Mr. Jefferson when he was sworn in as Vice President* |
| CONSTITUTION | CONSTITUTION |
| The Federal Constitution was crammed down the gullet of America | I might here proceed and with the greatest truth declare my zealous attachment to the *CONSTITUTION* of the United States. |
| | *Speech of Mr. Jefferson at his installment.* |
| FEDERAL ADMINISTRATION | FEDERAL ADMINISTRATION |
| Under the old confederation, matters never were, nor could have been so wretchedly conducted as under the successive MONARCHS of *Braintree and Mount Vernon.* | But would the honest patriot, **in the full tide of successful experiment,** abandon a Government which has so far kept us *free and firm?* |

[12] *Hamlet*, 3.4.53–54. Hamlet addresses the Queen after killing Polonius and compares his father and his uncle: "Look here upon this picture, and on this, / The counterfeit presentment of two brothers." Other quotations from Shakespeare include: "Merciful Heaven, / Thou rather with thy sharp and sulphurous bolt / Splits the unwedgeable and gnarled oak / Than the soft Myrtle." *Measure for Measure*, 2.2.114–17.

*Mr. Jefferson's Inaugural Speech*

WASHINGTON

For years together the Grand Lama of
federal adoration, the immaculate
Divinity of Mount Vernon, approved
the *blackest* measures.

WASHINGTON

Without pretensions to that high
confidence you reposed in our first and
greatest revolutionary character . . .
destined for him the *fairest* page in . . .
the volume of *faithful* history

*Jefferson's Speech before the Senate
when sworn in Vice-President.*

ADAMS

"This hoary-headed incendiary bawls
out to arms." "Alas, he is not an object
of more envy, but of compassion and
*horror.*"

ADAMS

And no one more sincerely daily prays
that no accident may call me to the
higher and more important functions
of which the constitution *eventually*
devolves upon his office.

We have now done with these extracts. Here's

Such an act
That blurs the grace and blush of modesty
Calls virtue, hypocrite—
and sweet religion
Makes a rhapsody of words.

The contrast ended with a quotation from the gospel of Luke.
"*And he that was called* JUDAS *drew near unto Jesus to kiss him. But
Jesus said unto him,* 'JUDAS *betrayest thou the Son of man with a kiss.*' "[13]
The Republican press reacted to such comparisons by questioning Callender's integrity. "CALLENDER *versus* CALLENDER" was one

[13] *Boston Gazette,* 2 September 1802. The comparison begins with an allusion
to two passages from the Bible: Matt. 7:5 AV, "Thou hypocrite, first cast out the
beam out of thine own eye," (see the very similar Luke 6:42) and Job 15:6 AV,
"Thine own mouth condemneth thee, and not I: yea, thine own lips testify against
thee." The last quotation is abridged from *Hamlet,* 3.4.40–48. Hamlet is addressing
the Queen. The full quotation is: "Such an act / That blurs the grace and blush
of modesty, / Calls virtue hypocrite, takes off the rose / From the fair forehead
of an innocent love / And sets a blister there, makes marriage vows / As false as
dicers' oaths, O, such a deed / As from the body of contraction plucks / The
very soul, and sweet religion makes / A rhapsody of words." The reference to
Judas is from Luke 22:47–48 AV.

such effort: juxtaposed quotations condemned the journalist's own inconsistency and hypocrisy in his sudden switch from Republican to Federalist.[14] Steadiness of principle had become an important standard for judging officeholders and editors, a standard that only achieved wide currency in the press as political "principles" became clearly identified.

In "JEFFERSON AGAINST JEFFERSON" the Federalist *Boston Gazette* used the same technique against the incumbent president. In this case, the charge of inconsistency turned on Jefferson's opinions about the inherent inferiority of African Americans, a subject on which he was notoriously inconstant, saying one thing in the *Notes on Virginia* and another to Benjamin Banneker.

| **Jefferson's Notes on Virginia** | **Extract from Jefferson's Letter to Banneker.** |
|---|---|
| The . . . Blacks . . . mixture with other colors has been observed, by every one and *proves their inferiority.* | I rejoice that Nature has given to our Black brethren talents *equal* to those of the Whites, and that the appearance of want of them is *owing merely to the degraded condition of their existence, both in Africa and America.*[15] |

A similar juxtaposition compared both real and reputed positions of John Quincy Adams and William Eustis in their race for a seat in the U.S. House of Representatives.

| **Principles and Measures advocated & professed by JOHN Q. ADAMS** | **Principles and Measures professed and pursued by Doctor EUSTIS.** |
|---|---|
| 1. Those who are tired of the republican form of government, and are prepared for a revolution. . . . | 1. Those who prefer the Constitution of the U.S. as it now stands to a hereditary monarchy, with a king and order of nobility. |
| 3. Those who believe a public debt to be a public benefit. . . . | 3. Those who believe the peace of the country is more secure when it owes little or nothing.[16] |

[14] *Aurora,* 7 October 1802.
[15] *Boston Gazette,* 11 November 1802.
[16] *Independent Chronicle,* 28 October 1802.

One Republican newspaper's first page was printed to resemble a ledger sheet and under the names of the party candidates were the words

**PROFIT**               and               **LOSS**

What should we gain in Sullivan? ... We should gain a man [who will] by his ... own exertions cherish science, literature, commerce, agriculture, arts & manufactures and make the State as famous for these blessings as for the pure Republicanism he would stamp on it.

What should we lose in **STRONG?** ... We should lose a man who in the course of his administration has done nothing to advance the glory of the State. Let science, literature, commerce, agriculture, arts & manufactures attest this truth. . . .[17]

Antithetical contrasts premised on moral values had to construct a framework of party principles clearly enough to make them amenable to contrast. Party principles gradually became values for their own sake, not because they derived from a moral hierarchy. "We can distinguish between *black* and *white*—but do not believe that a *grey* party can exist long," said an *Aurora* editorial entitled, "PRINCIPLES, AND NOT MEN."[18]

"PRINCIPLES, AND NOT MEN" was also the title of an editorial in the Boston *Independent Chronicle,* which linked the Jeffersonians' principles to the Mayflower Compact and the American Revolution.

It was the principle of the Tories and the Addressors of Gov. Hutchinson and Gen. Gage; men who, from want of penetration or fortitude, would have bartered away for a shameful security and the quiet practice of *their* law, and *their* gospel, all the natural rights and social privileges which our ancestors had held in fee simple, from the first moment of their landing on Plymouth Beach, until the time when the holy spirit of insubordination and insurrection to an

[17] Ibid., 1 April 1805.
[18] It was only later, at the end of the early republican period, as political values became distinctly separable from moral values in the public mind, that the idea of "principle" began to have connotations antithetical to "party." In the Jacksonian period, antitheses between "a man of principle" and "a man of party" became quite common.

established government, became a burden to God & man. But it was not the principle of the "Whigs," as they were then called, for want of some better appellative. For the Whigs knew the principle *they* contended for, was to be found in the reason and nature of things; and they therefore had it inscribed in the first *moment* of their *union,* by the pen of JEFFERSON.[19]

By the end of Jefferson's second administration, principles and policy had became thoroughly intermixed. Unity on these matters seemed essential to the Republicans but difficult to achieve. Federalists attacked Republican "despotism of party."[20] This familiar phrase took on a totally new sense: not "usurpation" by a "faction," but the tyranny of party solidarity, which required conformity on every point, not just the most essential ones. In this context, the operative word in "despotism of party" was no longer "party" but "despotism."

. We sincerely wish that party zealots would reflect, that to convict a man of stupidity or crime, is not the most winning method to recall him from error or from vice. Let us also avoid *despotism of party.* Let us not be offended if a friend whose general sentiments are just, and whose heart is pure, unfortunately entertains peculiar opinions upon minor points.[21]

Defending the need for uniformity, Republicans drew an analogy between party unity and gravitational force. United political action, once denounced as a corrupting influence, appeared as a fundamental natural force, upon which depends all order in the universe.

Nothing so certainly indicates the dissolution of a nation or party as want of union. The adhesive power is as necessary to political as moral or physical existence. In the physical world, destroy the power of adhesion, and all matter would fly off in millions of small particles,

---

[19] *Independent Chronicle,* 26 March 1801.
[20] Fischer, *Revolution of American Conservatism,* p. 64; for a description of the negative attributes of parties, see Hofstadter, *Idea of a Party System,* pp. 12–3.
[21] *Boston Gazette,* 9 November 1812.

and lose itself in the immensity of space.—This power then is absolutely necessary to the excellence also of party.[22]

Not only axioms, but slogans and symbols appeared more frequently after the War of 1812. Sometimes they graced the masthead of a newspaper; other times they ornamented—and exaggerated—contrasts of party positions. In 1816, the Republican *New Hampshire Patriot* displayed on its front page a picture of an eagle side-by-side with a picture of a crown. Above the Republican eagle was the slogan "VIGILANCE AND LIBERTY, ECONOMY AND NATIONAL PROSPERITY." Printed above the supposedly Federalist crown were the words, "EXPENSIVE GOVERNMENT AND ROYALTY, ENERVATION AND SLAVERY."

According to the text appearing beneath the symbols, Republicans favored: "Moderate salaries, no unnecessary Taxes, no shackles to freedom, no arbitrary restraints on the rights of conscience, manful resistance to all foreign encroachments, a flourishing treasury, 'free trade and no impressments.' " Federalists allegedly preferred "Exorbitant salaries, 'PERPETUAL Direct Taxes,' a sedition law to abridge the liberty of speech and the press, 'law religion' [i.e., an established church] that shall compel all denominations to support the 'standing order,' submission to foreign insults, a continually accumulating national debt—in fine, a government with all the tinsel and trappings of monarchy."[23] While this editorial linked Federalism with royalty and slavery, it devoted greater space to Federalist policy. "Treachery," "subversion," and "conspiracy" assumed less importance than "salaries," "taxes," and "law religion."

A Federalist mock epitaph, mixing invective with attacks on Republican policy, appeared in 1808:

*Monumental Inscription*

To perpetuate to posterity a melancholy recollection of the evils produced
     by a DEMOCRATIC MAL-ADMINISTRATION, and for the purpose of
exposing the arts and the wickedness of UNPRINCIPLED DEMAGOGUES,

---

[22] *Independent Chronicle*, 12 November 1812.
[23] Concord, *New Hampshire Patriot*, 27 October 1816.

the following BEACON is erected, by way of counterpart and contrast to
the elegant inscription which appeared in the Columbian Centinel, at the
close of the federal administration in 1801.

**On the Fourth of March next,**
**WILL EXPIRE**
**To the joy of every native AMERICAN, who has**
**his Country's good at heart,**
**And to the morbid chagrin of Presidential**
**Parasites, Sycophants, and**
**Office-holders, The**
**DEMOCRATIC ADMINISTRATION**
**of the**
**GOVERNMENT OF THE UNITED STATES:**
**Conducted by**
**A JEFFERSON;—a MADISON,**
**a GALLATIN, et id genus omne;**
AEt. 8 Years.

ITS DEATH
Was occasioned by an inherent principle of
Mortality, which would have alone
eventually extinguished the
VITAL SPARK,
Had it not been accelerated by foreign Intriguers
and domestic Traitors;
Who have been cherished and nurtured by their
great FOSTER FATHER,
The drift of whose wretched policy has been
To Loosen the UNION—
Annihilate the CREDIT—Endanger
the PEACE—Suspend the PROSPERITY—Tarnish the HONOR—and
Destroy the FELICITY
OF HIS COUNTRY[24]

Lighthearted political exchanges prevailed after the War of
1812. Irony replaced vituperation; opprobrium gave way to ridi-

[24] *Boston Gazette,* 3 November 1808. Funerary iconography appeared in Paul
Revere's broadside against the Boston Massacre and in the "Coffin Handbill"
sixteen years after the publication of this display appeared in the *Boston Gazette*
in 1808.

cule. "Wonderful Disclosures" supplanted "Alarming Discoveries!" "Johnny Jump-Ups" (i.e., Republicans eager for war with Britain) replaced "Jacobins."[25]

Editors increasingly preferred slogans to slander. Federalists searched around for a new sobriquet as their fortunes waned. In Delaware, where party loyalty was very stable, metaphors showed a great deal of experimentation. The "Friends of Peace" carried with it connotations not only of opposition to "Mr. Madison's War," but also positive associations for the numerous and powerful Quaker community in Delaware. Quakers had previously cast their votes for the Republicans. At the end of the war, Federalists frequently referred to themselves as the "Washington" party, which identified them with their only truly popular partisan. Delaware Republicans spent much time ridiculing the title. They contrasted the sayings of Washington on foreign policy, frugal government, and Republican principles with those of the more extreme Federalists. Republicans adopted the name of "American" party on one occasion in Delaware, and the Federalist press busily absorbed itself in distinguishing the opposition from "Americanism."[26]

Editors increasingly appreciated the benefits of courting specific interests and distinguishable constituencies. Federalists wooed Delaware Quakers; Republicans courted New Hampshire Baptists. Republicans cultivated Pennsylvania's immigrants, denouncing "scurrilous lies" of the Federalists against immigrants, which they gleefully recounted in detail. Republicans reassured manufacturers in Delaware of firm support.

Targeting particular religious constituencies became a favorite method of gaining support, as in an appeal addressed "TO THE PEOPLE CALLED QUAKERS." The appeal tacitly acknowledged the legitimacy of "party purposes" by not attacking them directly; it asserted the primacy of the moral tenets of Quakerism and reminded its readers that in a conflict between religious obligation

[25] This did not occur until after the War of 1812. In June 1812 the Baltimore *Federal Republican*'s offices were sacked and its editor was severely attacked. See Steffen, *Mechanics of Baltimore*, pp. 244–47; also Paul A. Gilje, "The Baltimore Riots of 1812 and the Breakdown of Anglo-American Mob Tradition," *Journal of Social History* 13 (1980): 547–64.

[26] *Independent Chronicle*, 28 October 1802.

and party demands, the former must rule those who were honest and righteous. "The stronger must the conviction be," said the *Aurora*, "of your apostacy or hypocrisy, should you, for party purposes, give your aid willingly to measures, as contrary to your own convictions."[27]

The Republicans had employed ironic appeals as early as 1800 in support of Jefferson, such as one in the *Aurora*, which not only satirized the Federalists' reasons for opposing Jefferson, but also castigated the excesses of the Puritans, the Federalists' presumed ancestors. This kind of satire assumed the audience understood the arguments of both parties. The word "imperious" was probably a double-entendre intended to imply the Federalists' subservience to British imperial policy. Republicans reminded Philadelphia Quakers and Catholics who the author of Virginia's Statute of Religious Freedom was.

IMPERIOUS REASONS

WHY

**THOMAS JEFFERSON**

SHOULD NOT BE ELECTED PRESIDENT

OF THE UNITED STATES.

1. He was the Author of the Declaration of Independence.

2. He was the Author of the Laws which abolished tithes in Virginia.

3. By him also was an established privileged church, to the exclusion of other modes of worship abolished in Virginia.

4. Through this conduct of his, so much at variance with the English system—A quaker can go three times into Virginia without being hanged.

5. By his odious pursuit of religious toleration, the Roman Catholics have been suffered to build churches in that State.

6. But the most important Reason of all appears in the Boston Centinel, *That if Mr. Jefferson had been Secretary of State, the British Treaty never would have been ratified.*[28]

Another ironic appeal appeared in 1814, in the *Boston Gazette*, which displayed on its front page a drawing of a fully rigged ship with the caption, "The Strong and well-governed ship Massachusetts." The name of the Federalist gubernatorial candidate was

[27] *Aurora*, 29 September 1808.

[28] Ibid., 13 September 1800.

Caleb Strong. "GALLANT MEN AND TRUE!" it continued, "ARE YOU A FARMER? . . . Do you prefer Taxes to Crops——Assessors and Tax-Gatherers to good customers for your butter and cheese?

> Do you like to have Congress *Mortgage your Estates* against your will, for fifty years to come? If you do, do not vote for STRONG, for he is opposed to all these things. ARE YOU A MERCHANT? . . . Do you sigh for steady sales and steady markets? If you *do*, vote for a man who prefers "Magnanimous moderation" to "indiscriminate opposition." ARE YOU A MECHANIC? Do you like rusty tools?——Do you wish to slumber over your forge or your work bench? no employ and high prices of everything you eat, drink and wear?——Why *don't vote* for STRONG, his paternal heart bleeds when he sees his country *suffering in this manner.* . . . ARE YOU A SAILOR? . . . Do you prefer *an old skillful Pilot,* who has commanded the GOOD SHIP Massachusetts many a long year . . . or will you choose a Fresh hand that [a]s soon as he gets in . . . will say *'bout ship* and head right onto the gerrymander breakers.[29]

Federalists referred epithetically to their only popular partisan in slogans and iconography. One slate of candidates proclaimed itself the "WASHINGTON FEDERAL REPUBLICAN NOMINATIONS." Symbolism also figured prominently in election campaigns. Masonic symbols and references to Revolutionary War battles undoubtedly courted both Freemasons and veterans of the Revolution. The *Boston Gazette* published an appeal in the Massachusetts election of 1816 under the headline:

**WASHINGTON & STRONG!**

**BROOKS & SARATOGA!**

*FOR MASSACHUSETTS*[30]

Newspapers appealed in serious and lighthearted fashion to occupational interests. In the appeal excerpted below, the *Boston Gazette* struck a familiar tone, using puns in courting specific occu-

---

[29] *Boston Gazette*, 27 March 1814.
[30] Ibid., 14 March 1816.

pations. This "ADDRESS TO THE ELECTORS OF ALL TRADES AND PROFESSIONS" included Butchers, Bakers, Blacksmiths, Coopers, Blockmakers, Sailors, Clock and Watch makers, Dyers, Hatters, Lawyers, Soap-Boilers, Shoe-Makers and Rope-Makers.

### BUTCHERS.

THE butchers are doubtless patriotic, for they *cleave* to the people, and no set of men ever *shed more blood* for the good of the public than they. It is therefore requisite to address to them but a very few *loins* requesting their attention to the ensuing election, for if our good Governor should not be elected, it would be *lamb* entable indeed.[31]

The great changes wrought in American political language in the years after the War of 1812 were quite noticeable to members of the older generation.[32] On November 1, 1816, the *Alexandria Gazette*, a Federalist newspaper in Virginia, published a letter by Henry Lee, Jr. of Westmoreland County, son of "Light Horse Harry" Lee and half-brother of Robert E. Lee. In an unsuccessful bid for office, Lee declared himself to be a candidate for the U.S. House of Representatives, using a rhetorical style long out of fashion in New York and New England.

FELLOW CITIZENS—I DECLARE myself a candidate for the honor of representing you in the next Congress. As I am activated by no sordid motive, I shall not attempt, by pretensions, to glide into your confidence, or to over-reach your good sense. I profess what I feel, a desire to advance your welfare, an ambition to be distinguished

---

[31] *Boston Commercial Gazette*, 1 April 1819. Sean Wilentz, *Chants Democratic: New York City and the Rise of the American Working Class, 1788–1850* (New York, 1984), p. 92.

[32] Character was still the basis for old-fashioned solicitations, which continued to be published even in Philadelphia newspapers as late as 1820, and quite commonly south of the Mason-Dixon Line. See, for example, a solicitation by John Vallence, published in the Philadelphia *Union*, 13 September 1820. "BELIEVING that my character is generally known to my fellow-citizens, I trust it will not be considered presumptuous in offering myself to your consideration as a candidate for the office of COUNTY COMMISSIONER. . . ."

by your preference, and a devotion to the free principles of our
constitution.

Between my competitors and myself, judge as citizens of our common
country, not as members of adverse parties. I ask no more. If you
inherit the freeborn spirit of your fathers; if your bosoms beat with
the pure patriotism which created this Republic, and by which alone
it can be preserved—you will extend this justice to me and discharge
this duty to your country.[33]

Lee closed by saying that the "best way to prevent evil is to
renounce its course." Party spirit, he said, "is the source of all our
woes." He advised his readers to open their eyes and their hearts
to the public good. In choosing men for representatives, they
should seek the services of the most worthy candidate.

In contrast to this very traditional appeal, an editorial appeared
in the New York *Courier* four days later including Lee's letter
verbatim, undoubtedly because it epitomized a style of election
appeal that had disappeared from New York politics. The latter
passage reveals the extent of change that rhetorical styles had
undergone in the North in a decade and a half of strenuous
party competition.

Fie, Fie, Mr. Lee! how dare you, federalist that you are, think the
national debt too large, the taxes too heavy and the corruption too
extensive? Accusations of this sort [are] only to be made against
the Tory Administration, and the British Ministry. But against the
Republican cabinet in Washington—it is really too impudent. You
should reflect, sir, that the saints cannot err and that democracy
"can do no wrong," that one man may steal a horse while another
is hung [sic] for looking over a fence. "Principles, not men" is the
democratic motto—aye, sir, principles—principles—the democrats
never abandon principles for men, all which is proved fairly and
clearly by their attachment to the principal and interest of the
national debt. And this, sir, though a miserable pun, is a very serious
and abiding fact. No—Mr. Lee the funeral has gone by. You will not
gain your election, be your concern for your country ever so great.[34]

---

[33] *Alexandria Gazette,* 1 November 1816.
[34] *Courier,* 27 October 1816.

This piece eulogizes the concerns of the earlier generation for principles above party, for men over measures. Yet even while extolling these virtues, the Federalist editor of the *Courier* was speaking another language, a language that had more in common with the language of Jacksonian democracy.

The *Courier* editor used bitter sarcasm to point up Republicans hypocrisy. He satirized a common refrain in northern Republican newspapers, which had castigated high debt and heavy taxes as English, and by extension, Federalist, vices. He referred to the Republican "saints," knowing that the Republican press was busily deifying Jefferson in the same fashion that the Federalists had canonized Washington. "Principles, not men" was the motto he spoke of disparagingly, and it was indeed the emphasis of policy over personality that distinguished late Jeffersonian electioneering rhetoric from the laudatory discourse of the older generation of Federalists and Republicans. The *Courier* found itself caught up in emphatic language as much as its opponents, even as it mourned the dying political culture of the Founders. The funeral procession had indeed gone by for Henry Lee and his generation. Their language attracted attention only as an anachronism.

"We have resumed in these United States," said John Quincy Adams in his Boylston lectures on rhetoric in 1810, "that particular style of speaking, which was so customary among the Greeks and Romans, but which in the island of Great Britain seems to be almost entirely unpracticed."[35] The American speaking style had made its way to the printed page; in Britain the hortatory style was forced underground. Even as John Quincy Adams observed the importance of classical models for epideictic speech, American political rhetoric was already moving away from such models of public address. Party newspapers had already developed many elements of the "Jacksonian" campaign in the first two decades of the nineteenth century. Sloganeering, symbols, party nicknames, debate over internal policy, targeted appeals to a wide range of interests: all these features of the Jacksonian political culture appeared before the War of 1812. Opprobrious and vituperative language had waned well before the "Era of Good Feelings." The

---

[35] John Quincy Adams, *Lectures on Rhetoric and Oratory*, p. 236.

detailed contrasts, however, the attacks on policy matters, the ridicule evident in the party press showed that partisan contentiousness still existed at the end of the War of 1812 and in the post-War period.

The two parties became increasingly associated with specific policies. Members of the electorate could more easily identify their interests with those of the party. The organizations targeted and courted specific constituencies within the electorate, and members of these groups responded with affiliation and support. The party press no longer appealed to vague moralisms veiled in abstractions but instead began to advocate political "principles." Party newspapers moved from irrational charges of conspiracy to equally irrational but more popular and effective techniques for eliciting mass support: symbols and slogans. The rhetorical form of communication changed irrevocably in America from laudatory to hortatory appeals, framed in the cadence and emphasis of the spoken language, which emerged to serve a deliberative purpose. Parties in this way created new loyalties: allegiances to parties as institutions and not merely as embodiments of virtue, loyalties to specific policies and not merely to republicanism, loyalties from specific constituencies to specific parties. These loyalties combined to create a stronger bond of identity between politicians and participants.

## Reform Agitation under
## Repressive Constraints:
## British Rhetoric, 1800–1832

If your cause is too bad, call in aid the party: if the party is bad,
call in aid the cause. If neither is good, wound the opponent.

William Gerard Hamilton, *Parliamentary Logic*

T he long Tory ascendancy from Pitt the Younger through
Lord Liverpool and the Duke of Wellington marked a
period of solid intransigence against change in many
forms: against suffrage agitation, repeal of the Test and Corporation Acts (which discriminated against Nonconformists), Catholic
emancipation, and parliamentary reform. "Stasis," a word meaning
both "stagnation" and "civil strife," is a term that effectively sum-
marizes early nineteenth-century Britain.[1] The contrast between
change and continuity is nowhere better illustrated than in the
political language employed by the British press during the elections of the pre-Reform period.

Unlike the United States in the early nineteenth century, where
the press expanded dramatically, Britain had a press that remained
tightly constrained in circulation, advertising policy, and matters of

---

[1] The Oxford English Dictionary, 2d ed., defines "stasis" as (1) "Inactivity;
stagnation" and (2) "Party Faction, civil strife." For an elaboration of this idea,
see Asa Briggs, *The Age of Improvement* (London, 1959), p. 190; W. R. Brock, *Lord
Liverpool and Liberal Toryism, 1820 to 1827* (London, 1967), pp. 26–46.

expression, thanks to the survival of the stamp tax, the advertising duties, and continued vigorous enforcement of the Sedition Act. The stamp duty made the purchase of newspapers prohibitive for an English workingman, who had to read the newspapers in coffeehouses. In 1829 the *Westminster Review* estimated that thirty people read a single copy of a London newspaper. Prohibitive taxes on advertising insured that newspaper proprietors could not use revenues from commercial sources to lower their costs and expand circulation.[2]

Uninhibited criticism of the government appeared only in the illicit, partly underground, "unstamped" press. Foremost among the editors of the unstamped journals was William Cobbett, formerly the editor of the *Gazette of the United States*. Cobbett, accustomed to the American practice of politics and journalism, grew restive under the Tory ministry in Britain and launched his *Political Register* as a cheap publication for the workingman.

Parliament reacted to the threat of cheap newspapers in 1819 by passing the Newspaper Stamp Duties Act, which extended the stamp tax to pamphlets and other publications. The purpose of the act, according to Arthur Aspinall, was to destroy the cheap newspapers and pamphlets published by the Radicals. Previously, only newspapers had been subject to a four pence tax. Until 1819, Cobbett published his *Political Register* as a series of open letters, claiming his publication was a pamphlet and subject only to a three shilling tax per edition. Henceforth, all pamphlets containing remarks on any matter of church and state were considered newspapers.[3] The Whigs meanwhile grew somnolent after many years in opposition and with many restraints on free expression. The institutional role of the minority party nonetheless changed in these years. The idea of a Loyal Opposition emerged in the 1820s. The Whigs' support of Queen Caroline against the unpopu-

---

[2] "Weekly Newspapers,"*Westminster Review* 10 (April 1829): 478; see also "Newspaper Press," in ibid. (January, 1829): 216–37.

[3] The law (60 Geo. 3, c. 9) applied to any pamphlet printed for sale at an interval of less than twenty-six days and sold for less than sixpence before the tax. See Aspinall, *Politics and the Press*, pp. 57, 42–60; E. P. Thompson, *The Making of the English Working Class* (London, 1963), pp. 451–71; Cole, *Life of Cobbett*, pp. 237–41.

lar George IV showed that the Opposition could exploit public opinion for parliamentary advantage.[4]

Political conflict over reform begot a conflict over political language: conservatives and reformers clashed in Parliament and in print over the form of language appropriate to parliamentary debate. William Gerard Hamilton, in *Parliamentary Logic*, treated parliamentary rhetoric in a morally neutral fashion, disinterestedly explaining the most effective way to win a point in deliberative debate. Jeremy Bentham quarreled with Hamilton's concentration on rhetorical means and his disregard of political ends. Bentham treated Hamilton's work and the contemporary political language as a symptom of the moral degeneration rife in a corrupted and unreformed Parliament. Bentham's *Handbook of Political Fallacies* is a manual of argument, demonstrating the many specious assertions maintained by opponents of reform.[5]

Parliamentary conflicts notwithstanding, political rhetoric in the stamped press remained wedded to continuity. On its placid surface, British electioneering rhetoric differed markedly from the rhetorical style developing in the United States. The stamped press reverted to the laudatory form of rhetoric. Lacking serious competition, the Tory press had little incentive to adopt another kind of language.[6] Whig papers meanwhile found themselves under legal pressure: partisan invective had landed some Whig journalists in jail.[7] Such attacks on the ministry as the Opposition published they often disguised as commentary from another source. The Opposition papers expressed less than enthusiastic support for Whig leader Charles James Fox and what support there was frequently appeared in pseudonymous letters.

Laudatory rhetoric prevailed in the stamped press; unstamped journals preserved the hortatory style. William Cobbett ended his American career in 1800 and returned to Britain as a Tory editor.

---

[4] Aspinall, *Politics and the Press*, pp. 306–11; Cole, *Life of Cobbett*, pp. 247–54.

[5] William Hamilton, *Parliamentary Logic*, pp. 70–88; Bentham, *Handbook*, p. 5.

[6] J. C. D. Clark, *English Society, 1688–1832: Ideology, Social Structure, and Political Practice during the Ancien Regime* (Cambridge, 1985), p. 199.

[7] The Libel Act of 1799 (39 Geo. 3, c. 79) was amended and the penalties mitigated slightly in 1811 (51 Geo. 3, c. 65). See Aspinall, *Politics and the Press*, pp. 39–40.

Cobbett illustrates Louis Hartz's point that even American conservatives are liberals elsewhere: the former Federalist soon became a leading journalist of the radical reform movement. He denounced what he called "The Thing": the "rotten part of the constitution." Cobbett proved instrumental in preserving hortatory rhetoric in British journalism.[8]

Whigs and Radicals alike cast themselves in opposition to all things associated with George IV. When in 1820 the king sought to obtain a bill of divorce in Parliament from Queen Caroline, public opinion and the Whig Opposition rallied behind the queen. The king's profligacy contrasted unfavorably even with his consort's questionable conduct. Queen Caroline enjoyed extraordinary popularity, especially in London. Opposition newspapers, which previously had been afraid of criticizing the Government, now took great pleasure in publishing the most graphic details of royal adultery.[9]

Religious tensions surfaced again at the end of the 1820s as Parliament debated repeal of the Test and Corporation Acts and Catholic emancipation. Moreover, the Irish question, so often tied to religious issues, stood out in the discourse of the 1820s. The old cry of "No Popery" and the division of Parliament into anti-emancipation "Protestants" and pro-emancipation "Catholics" sharpened political antagonisms very clearly. The whole question of Catholic emancipation may have accelerated the influence of British public opinion on Parliament. Every major politician of necessity made known his opinion of Catholic emancipation and took responsibility for his position.[10] Public opinion made itself felt as never before on this critical constitutional issue.

The public, whether represented or unrepresented, found themselves caught up in the question of parliamentary reform by 1830. The unreformed Parliament had a bewildering variety of franchise regulations. There were the "rotten boroughs": Old Sarum had no inhabitants. "Potwalloper" boroughs such as Preston had almost

---

[8] Michael Brock, *The Great Reform Act* (London, 1973), p. 43. Cole, *Life of Cobbett,* pp. 106–45, 270–85, 350–71.

[9] Aspinall, *Politics and the Press,* pp. 306–11; Piers Brendon, *The Life and Death of the Press Barons* (London, 1982), p. 41.

[10] Michael Brock, *Great Reform Act,* p. 56.

universal male suffrage. Manchester, the second largest city in England, had no representatives whatsoever in Parliament. Advocates of Reform called for a redistribution of parliamentary seats to reflect the vast demographic changes of the previous century. They urged uniform franchise restrictions for borough and county electors. The British press was obsessed with the Reform question for most of two years. At the end of the agitation, Reform was achieved and politics reverted to quiescence. This did not last long. After the passage of the Reform Bill, public opinion exerted a powerful external leverage on the machinery of government. Politics and political language in Britain would never be the same.

As the American and French Revolutions had altered the political side of British journalism, the industrial revolution affected the economic side.[11] Steam presses allowed newspapers to print a run with two or three times as many copies as the old manual presses. *The Times* was the first newspaper to use steam power in printing in 1807. The way *The Times* used this technological advantage reveals much about early-nineteenth-century British journalism.[12] Rather than using steam presses to widen circulation, as American newspapers later did, *The Times* jealously sat on its printing and papermaking patents, meanwhile catering to its relatively small elite audience. *The Times* employed its technological monopoly preemptively, insuring that no other British journal would threaten its dominant voice.[13] Thanks to its position, *The Times* did not need government subsidies and did not always support the government. *The Times* supported reforms in the period immediately after Peterloo,[14] thereby enhancing its reputation as a weathervane of public opinion. Appearing sensitive to public opinion and "above the partisan fray," *The Times* enjoyed the confidence of elite readers of all political persuasions.[15]

---

[11] The circulation of the dominant journal, *The Times*, expanded threefold. See James Moran, *Printing Presses: History and Development from the Fifteenth Century to Modern Times* (London, 1973), pp. 101–11; Colin Clair, *A History of Printing in Britain* (London, 1965), pp. 205–14; *History of "The Times"* (London, 1952), 1:109–19.

[12] Moran, *Printing Presses*, pp. 106–10; Clair, *Printing in Britain*, pp. 101–11.

[13] Brendon, *Press Barons*, pp. 37–40, 48–49; Koss, *Political Press*, 1:46–47.

[14] Koss, *Political Press*, 1:312–17; *History of "The Times,"* 1:234–54.

[15] "It floats with the tide; it sails with the stream," said William Hazlitt in "The

Several new Tory journals began publication in this period: the *Sun* and *John Bull* adopted a less elitist tone than *The Times* and found themselves nearly self-sufficient. Among the Whig newspapers, the *Morning Chronicle* retained its position as the principal organ of the Opposition.[16] The unstamped press had two periods of growth. The first occurred from 1815 to 1819, between Waterloo and Peterloo. The second period of growth came during the agitation preceding Reform, from 1827 to 1832. The unstamped press was already agitating for reforms that the Chartists would adopt a few years later.

Electioneering speeches often displayed conflicting notions of parliamentary representation. The Tories praised candidates for their "independence"; the Radicals heralded nominees for their "attachment to principle." Contested elections in the unreformed Parliament were relatively infrequent; contests were often in large boroughs with less restrictions on voting. One such seat was Westminster, where, for example, radical candidates routinely pledged their support for various political "principles," usually very broadly construed. Tory candidates proclaimed their "independence," justifying their refusal to commit themselves to any future policy by defending virtual representation.

The Tories generally relied on the moral caliber of the prospective legislator and in the best Burkean tradition trusted him to make appropriate choices for the nation. The Radicals, on the other hand, insisted upon more concrete assurances, including specific pledges on policy. The *Morning Chronicle,* in a fashion characteristic of the Whigs, took a mediating position in 1802 between the strict accountability demanded by the Radicals and the untrammeled independence championed by the Tories. "The candidate who professes to reject the *sense* of his Constituents, ought at least to prove that he has some of his own."[17]

The *Sun* assiduously praised candidates who cherished the liberties of the people but maintained their independence. Alderman

---

Periodical Press," *Edinburgh Review* 38 (May 1823): 364; quoted in Koss, *Political Press,* 1:46.

[16] Aspinall, *Politics and the Press,* pp. 85–102, 183–285; Koss, *Political Press,* 1:48.

[17] *Morning Chronicle,* 8 July 1802.

Curtis of the City of London, "loved the People, he loved their Liberties, and venerated the Constitution; but he felt it his duty to declare, that though he would at all times preserve their independence, he should also maintain his own; he never would set up his own opinion against that of the whole Nation; but he would go into the House *unshackled*."[18]

As the Tory press regularly applauded "independence," they vilified their opponents for their subservience to "faction." The *Sun* declared that Sir Francis Burdett's party of Radical Whigs wanted "to introduce ruin, under the pretensions of reform." If elected, Burdett would not consider himself obliged to the voters "because he will be forced into the situation by the arts of a junto of which he is at once the dupe, the instrument and the pretended idol."[19] Tory newspapers frequently depicted Burdett as the instrument of a Radical conspiracy dedicated to subverting the Constitution; the prime mover behind this conspiracy was Horne Tooke. In a letter to the Whiggish *Morning Chronicle*, "HOLOFERNES" likened "PARSON HORNE" to the Old Man of the Sea. "He never quits those he gets *into his hands till he stifles them; he has rendered this Island famous for the number of people he has been the death of.*"[20] The *Sun* attacked Burdett again in the 1812 election. In this appeal, however, the newspaper castigated Burdett for his own "defamation" of the government, which, in keeping with the Tory view of popular election rhetoric, it dismissed as a "heap of hackneyed jargon," appealing to "the lowest order of the mob." "During the life of HORNE TOOKE, it was generally supposed that much of the Baronet's violence was to be imputed to the counsels of that hoary Apostle of Faction." Burdett, however, needed "no incitement or instruction in the science of political defamation."[21] The *Sun* wondered whether Burdett would introduce to Britain "the *system* of the French Revolution and the *Guillotine*," or "a *military despotism*."[22]

---

[18] *Sun,* 16 July 1802.

[19] Ibid., 14 May 1807.

[20] *Morning Chronicle,* 13 May 1807.

[21] *Sun,* 8 October 1812.

[22] Ibid. Burdett had quoted the line from Hamlet, "Look on this picture and on this!" The *Sun* noted that he introduced "a short parody on Hamlet's comparison between the two brothers, and therefore, we may conclude, by applying to him

After the Napoleonic Wars, Tory papers recognized that British society was in a state of unrest. The 1818 election exhibited a rhetoric more anxious than any election for twenty years. Tory journals tried rallying the electors to the cause, castigating the opposition with allegations of conspiracy. "The CAUSE OF THE COUNTRY is really at stake on this occasion," said the *Sun*, "for if the JACOBINS, that is the *Burdettites*, were to succeed in Westminster, they would raise their heads throughout the united Empire, and in due time level all distinctions, and bury THE THRONE AND THE ALTAR and every vestige of our glorious Constitution under *Universal Suffrage*, the meaning of which is UNIVERSAL RUIN!!!"[23]

An appeal set in large type in the *Sun* reminded electors of how they should cast their votes. Tory journals assumed that voters should draw their lessons by extrapolating from past and present experience to the future.

MEMENTOS FOR ELECTORS
BEFORE THEY ENGAGE THEIR VOTES.
REMEMBER,
That you belong to a Country unequaled in modern
times for Wealth, Power, Prosperity and Glory.
REMEMBER,
That, being one of its National Guardians, you are
bound as far as you are able, to transmit it in
the same state to posterity.
REMEMBER,
That it has been raised to this high state under
the Constitution which it now has, and which was
settled at the glorious Revolution in 1688.
REMEMBER,
... That to destroy the Constitution, which
under Providence, has made us what we are, is to
destroy ourselves.
REMEMBER,
That those men who boast the loudest of their
honesty are not often the most honest.

---

what JUNIUS said of his late political Preceptor, "the Gentleman deals in *fiction*, and naturally appeals to the evidence of *the Poets*."

[23] Ibid., 24 June 1818.

REMEMBER,
That Liberal Education, respectable connections,
independent circumstances, and clear character,
are pledges of honesty which cannot often fail,
and are better than all professions.[24]

Conservatives urged their audiences to examine their representatives' past behavior; Radicals counseled their readers to consider the future. Drawing from his familiarity with the American rhetorical idiom, William Cobbett urged his readers to consider future policy rather than past performance in rendering their decision. A universal electorate would need to ask the question all deliberative bodies must consider: "What is to be done?" Addressing his readers as "FRIENDS AND FELLOW-COUNTRYMEN," he proposed to give his opinion about "*what ought to be done* in case of any event, which would overthrow the Borough mongers and their System." The system, Cobbett said, "*must* come down of itself in a few years"; it might "be pushed at almost any hour. Be ready; be *steady;* be *just;* be firm; and England will again see happy and glorious days."[25]

In the year leading up to Peterloo, the language of Radicals and Conservatives diverged as they had in the 1790s. This divergence appears very clearly in the *Sun*'s glossary of Radical slogans juxtaposed with Conservative definitions, published in 1818.

SKETCH
OF AN
ELECTION VOCABULARY
necessary to be understood at the present period

| *Words* | *Their true Meanings* |
| --- | --- |
| Universal Suffrage | Jacobinical Republicanism |
| Annual Parliaments | Annual Botheration |
| Triennial D[itt]o. | Not much better |
| Corruption of Parliament | Supporting the constitution |
| Reform of Parliament | Jacobin Ascendancy |
| Ministerial Tyranny | Upholding the Government |
| Oppression | Enjoying the most just Laws |
| Restoring the Constitution | Making a new one |

[24] Ibid., 4 June 1818.
[25] *Cobbett's Political Register*, 29 August 1818.

| | |
|---|---|
| Borough-mongering | Taking the Constitution as it is |
| Freedom of Election | Mobbing your Opponents |
| Freedom of the Press | Publishing Sedition & Blasphemy |
| Friends of the People | Makers of Mischief |
| Independent Men | Slaves to the People |
| Slaves | Their lawful Rulers |
| Enlightening the People | Telling them Lies |
| Right | Wrong |
| Wrong | Right |
| Catholic Emancipation | Protestant Captivity[26] |

Henry Hunt, a Radical candidate for a Westminster seat in 1818, declared himself a firm believer in pledging commitments on constitutional reforms. He urged his supporters to consider these when they cast their votes. "My course is plain and direct, and disdains all subterfuge or studied moments of speech—Universal Suffrage and Annual Parliaments, and . . . opposition to all laws that have a tendency to curtail the Liberties of the People, and oppress and starve the Poor."[27]

The state of the nation did not appear nearly as grave to the *Sun* in 1820 as it had in 1818. The *Sun* described the 1820 election as "a kind of general Saturnalia." George Canning made much of this happy contrast in an election speech in Liverpool.

What was the situation of the country in November 1819? Do I exaggerate when I say that there was not a man of property who did not tremble for his possessions? that there was not a man of retired and peaceable habits who did not tremble for the tranquillity and security of his home? that there was not a man of orderly and religious principles who [did] not fear that those principles were about to be [pulled] out from under the feet of succeeding generations? Was there any man who did not fear that the Crown was in danger? . . . Is there a man of peace and tranquillity who does not feel his domestic tranquillity to have been secured? Is there a man of moral and religious principles who does not look forward with better hope to see his children educated in those principles? Who does not look

[26] *Sun,* 9 June 1818.
[27] *Cobbett's Political Register,* 13 June 1818.

with renewed confidence to the revival and re-establishment of that moral and religious sense which had attempted to be obliterated from the hearts of mankind?[28]

William Cobbett published a rebuttal to Canning in his *Political Register*. According to Cobbett, Canning had begged the deliberative question.

> You boldly protest against the necessity of *any change;* and yet we clearly perceive, that you do not think, that things can go on in this present way, and that you see a *crisis* of some sort or another at hand. In the contest of the Manifesto you *congratulate* your audience on the complete restoration of order, confidence, reverence for the laws, and a just sense of the legitimate authority of the parliament. And yet, you conclude with an earnest and sober invocation to that same audience to "see that the *time is come,* at which *the decision must be taken, for,* or *against* the *institution of the British Monarchy!*" The struggle, then, is not over, it seems! There is yet, even in your opinion, a trial of struggle to be made; a crisis to come.[29]

Cobbett concluded with a reference to "time." For Cobbett, as for most of his Radical contemporaries, "time" looked backward at the present from the future. "History," he said, would note the Government's failure to destroy democracy. For Cobbett, "history" meant *future* history: succeeding generations' perspective on contemporary actions would be the final judge. Future "history" would evaluate the forces that constrained the present and determined the future. "*Time* must be the arbiter," he said in his concluding sentence to Canning. The advocates of change, he felt, had nothing to fear from the forces of time. Canning's speech implied that Conservatives drew their assurance from the present's resemblance to an idyllic past. They dared not look to the future for comfort. Time would favor the advocates of change, since, as he said in conclusion to Canning, "they do not fear the arbiter and you do."[30]

---

[28] *Sun,* 18 March 1820. Cannings speech is quoted from the *Morning Herald,* 29 March 1820.

[29] *Cobbett's Political Register,* 8 April 1820. Cobbett accused the British Government of attempting to destroy "the last remaining democratic government": the government of the United States.

[30] Ibid., 25 March 1820, 8 April 1820.

By the time of the 1826 election, Tories felt sufficiently confident of success that they once again published laudatory appeals, even in contested metropolitan elections. In the City of London election for example, the *Sun* spoke glowingly of potential candidates of "high character" from the City; the *Sun* also recognized that an urban representative must speak for specific interests. "Whiggism and Radicalism are so completely out of fashion, and their remaining votaries so few and so insignificant, that we are convinced, if other men of high character, great commercial consequence, and practical knowledge, had been induced to step forward, the character of the City would be redeemed."[31]

The Whig press made recommendations in a similar fashion, even on the verge of the Reform struggle. The Whiggish *Leeds Mercury* endorsed Henry Brougham in the 1830 election. The *Mercury* praised his virtue and talent; like the *Sun* it also appraised how well he could serve Yorkshire's interests. Brougham's accomplishments were "so various and eminent as to perplex the writer who would describe them; but his distinguishing characteristic is the directness and energy with which he has devoted himself to objects of *real and high utility*." A county "so immense in extent and population, so important in its landed, manufacturing, commercial and shipping interests . . . should be represented by a man inferior to none and first among the Commons of England."[32]

In other constituencies, the Reform controversy revived hortatory rhetoric. The Tory *Standard* fiercely attacked Sir Francis Burdett as "the lick-spittle baronet" and John Cam Hobhouse as the "fawning parasite" of Burdett.[33] The Whiggish *Morning Herald* attacked opponents of reform as Wellington's "sycophants who, for their own selfish purposes, applaud his errors, and cheer him on measures subversive of the welfare of the country . . . [they] the worst enemies of his fame."[34] The Whiggish *Morning Chronicle* raised the image of aristocratic parasitism, referring to "a set of titled mendicants" oppressing the "people of property" by means

---

[31] *Sun*, 13 June 1826.
[32] *Leeds Mercury*, 17 July 1830.
[33] London *Standard*, 29 July 1830.
[34] *Morning Herald*, 30 July 1830.

of "what is called *virtual* representation." "The salvation of the country depends on the protection of the productive classes from the fangs of the Aristocracy."[35]

More prescient members of the Government and the aristocracy were learning a lesson. "You have no idea how the wise and the unwise of all parties croak; for the spirit of the lower classes is of a most alarming description," said Lady Georgina Stuart-Wortley at the conclusion of the 1830 elections. The spirit of the unenfranchised lower classes might be contained; the mood of the electors was another matter. In the elections of 1830 the electors rendered a harsh judgment on incumbents of all persuasions: "Protestants" and "Catholics," pro-Reform radicals and anti-Reform ultras. A static political culture gave way under increased pressure. The lid on political communication came unfixed, and vehement language reappeared.[36]

Electioneering rhetoric in the early nineteenth century maintained a focus on the character and conduct of worthy candidates for Parliament. Editors nevertheless came to terms with other concerns of a candidate as well. Editorials turned their attention to representing the range of interests within a single constituency; candidates took greater note of specific economic concerns and promised to devote special attention to them.[37]

The resurgence of the Whig Opposition at the end of the 1820s revitalized political debate within Parliament; the controversies over Catholic emancipation and Reform spread beyond the halls of Parliament. Constitutional crises forced these issues into the public arena and stasis no longer described the natural order of society. As Asa Briggs noted, resisting change "was itself a form of action." The *Birmingham Argus* issued an obituary notice on May 1, 1829 lamenting the passage of Catholic emancipation. It may also serve as an epitaph for the unreformed regime.

[35] *Morning Chronicle,* 14 August 1830.
[36] Lady Georgina Stuart-Wortley to her mother, the Countess of Harrowby. Harrowby MSS, lxii, f. 271; Michael Brock, *Great Reform Act,* pp. 106, 93.
[37] This, of course, had been true even of Burke; see his "Speech at Bristol," *Works,* 3:6–7. See also Pole, *Political Representation,* pp. 488, 492–99, 534–35; W. R. Brock, *Lord Liverpool,* p. 34.

Died, full of good works, deeply lamented by every HONEST BRITON, MR. CONSTITUTION. His decease took place on the 13th of April in the year of our Lord 1829, at the House of the *Incurables*.[38]

The obituary expressed the tension between the old order and the new discourse; even as it mourned the passage of emancipation, it did so with concrete metaphors, the emphatic typography and contrived devices of a reinvigorated hortatory rhetoric. This evidence of stubborn resistance to change appeared in a provincial paper in a growing industrial city. Henceforward, the most radical reformers and their most determined adversaries would employ hortatory rhetoric with equal facility.

[38] Charles, C. F. Greville, *A Journal of the Reigns of King George IV and King William IV*, ed. Henry Reeve (London, 1874), 2:29; Asa Briggs, *The Age of Improvement* (London, 1959), p. 194; Clark, *English Society*, pp. 349–420; *Birmingham Argus*, 1 May 1829.

# CHAPTER FOUR

# Creating a National Audience:
# Jacksonian America, 1828–1860

Here's the Sewer! Here's some of the twelfth thousand of the New York Sewer! Here's the Sewer's exposure of the Wall Street Gang, and the Sewer's exposure of the Washington Gang, and the Sewer's exclusive account of a flagrant act of dishonesty committed by the Secretary of State when he was eight years old; now communicated, at a great expense, by his own nurse. . . . Here's the Sewer, here's the Sewer! Here's the wide-awake Sewer, always on the look-out; the leading Journal of the United States, now in its twelfth thousand, and still a-printing off. Here's the New York Sewer!

—Charles Dickens, *Martin Chuzzlewit.*

Martin Chuzzlewit's steamboat was "overrun by a legion of these young citizens," wrote Dickens, "before she tied up at the wharves in New York." Dickens's novel testifies to a bold new style of political language that asserted itself in the Jacksonian press. Echoing forth in the cries of the newsboys, this language must have seemed alien and offensive to many British observers, accustomed to more decorous language on the other side of the Atlantic.

What in the Jacksonian newspapers offended Dickens and his compatriots? Not the shouts of newsboys, whose British counterparts were equally vociferous, or the prurient subject matter that the *Sewer* and its sister journals, the *New York Rowdy Journal,* the

*Peeper, Family Spy, Keyhole Reporter,* the *Plunderer,* and the *Stabber* treated as suitable subjects for publication. More salacious reports appeared in the pages of *The Times* during the Queen Caroline affair.

Dickens seemingly took offense at American newspapers' tendency to use titillation as a tool of persuasion. The *Sewer* did not concern itself with questions of state or commerce. The newspaper boasted instead of its "exclusive" revelations about the political and economic élite. Dickens implied that these reports of moral failings were irrelevant, trivial, and perhaps libelous.[1]

The emergence of a mass-circulation press profoundly affected the language of politics. The new mass-communications enterprises became known as the "penny papers." The "penny press" had its beginnings in New York, but quickly spread to other cities. A new type of assertive entrepreneur began to seize control of the urban press and assumed an unprecedented degree of political autonomy. James Gordon Bennett of the *New York Herald,* one such entrepreneur, masterminded the first successful independent mass circulation daily. He was more concerned with selling newspapers than with expressing an opinion on politics.[2]

Bennett's lack of concern with party politics was more typical of press barons fifty years later. More representative at least in his commitment to party politics was the other giant among the New York publishers: Horace Greeley. Concealed beneath his eccentric demeanor and his missionary zeal for reform causes was shrewd commercial acumen. He developed an effective rhetorical style and could portray events and issues in a way that made sense to a mass audience.[3]

---

[1] On the matter of sensation as a tool of persuasion, see F. R. Leavis, *The Great Tradition: George Eliot, Henry James, Joseph Conrad* (London, 1948), p. 29.

[2] Isaac Clark Pray, ed., *Memoirs of James Gordon Bennett* (New York, 1855), pp. 89–213. Bennett was unusual in announcing his complete independence of party politics, a policy he soon abandoned. He announced in the inaugural edition of the *New York Herald* that the paper would be "the organ of no faction or COTERIE, and care nothing for any election or any candidate from president down to a constable." *New York Herald,* 6 May 1835. See also James L. Crouthamel, "James Gordon Bennett, the *New York Herald,* and the Development of Newspaper Sensationalism," *New York History* 54 (1973), pp. 294–316.

[3] Horace Greeley, *Recollections of a Busy Life* (New York, 1868); James Parton, *The Life of Horace Greeley* (New York, 1855); Glyndon G. Van Deusen, *Horace Greeley:*

Greeley used sensational language in new ways for political persuasion; his *Log Cabin* and later his *New-York Tribune* aroused popular interest in questions of policy. The Whig editor in his national edition created a vast new audience and helped break down the remaining boundaries between demonstrative and deliberative discourse. His newspaper proved a formidable instrument of mass persuasion.

The *Log Cabin*'s breathless tone bears a strong resemblance to Dickens's fictional New York *Sewer*. In this case, at least, art imitated life.

THE EXTRA LOG CABIN Is now published, and for sale at this office. It contains a fine PORTRAIT OF GEN HARRISON; A FULL REFUTATION OF THE WHITE SLAVERY SLANDER, also of the falsehood that Congress refused a Vote of Thanks to Gen. Harrison for his Bravery and Conduct in the War, with Engravings of the GOLD MEDALS which were voted him by Congress; engravings of OLD FORT DEFIANCE and FORT MEIGS; the Battle-Guards of WAYNE'S VICTORY, TIPPECANOE and THE THAMES, with full authentic accounts of the several Battles and other Military Operations in which Gen. Harrison has been engaged, Gen. Harrison's LETTERS TO BOLIVAR, SHERROD WILLIAMS, JAMES LYONS, &c.&c.—the whole forming a compendious and eloquent record of the CHARACTER, SERVICES, PRINCIPLES and OPINIONS of General Harrison, and a conclusive refutation of the malignant slanders which have been uttered against him.[4]

As is clear in the above example, newspapers in the Jacksonian era often mimicked oral speech. The typographical devices, slogans, antithetical contrasts, emphatic punctuation, and the epithets that characterized the party dialogue in the Jeffersonian era appeared in all parts of the Union in the Jacksonian period. Jacksonian discourse adopted the emphatic tone of Jeffersonian hortatory rhetoric, refined symbolic iconography in politics, and

---

*Nineteenth Century Crusader* (Philadelphia, 1953); Richard Kluger, *The Paper: The Life and Death of the New York Herald Tribune* (New York, 1986), pp. 13–30; Donald A. Ritchie, *Press Gallery: Congress and the Washington Correspondents* (Cambridge, Mass., 1991), pp. 35–51.

[4] New York *Log Cabin*, 11 July 1840.

distilled complex policy discussions into simple alternatives for mass persuasion.

Where Jacksonian rhetoric differed from Jeffersonian language was in its intimacy and its accessibility. Office seekers acquired nicknames; hack writers scrutinized lives for telling facts (or fictions) about politicians. These telling facts were not necessarily scandalous, as Callender's allegations about Jefferson and his "slave concubine" Sally Hemmings had been. The political universe was too large for the bitter invective based on intimate knowledge that characterized eighteenth-century rhetoric. Neither were the telling facts necessarily true. Rather they were details that brought a politician to the level of the ordinary voter's scrutiny. William Henry Harrison and his fictional log cabin is only the most famous example. The more remote the politician, the more imperative it was for him to reveal such telling examples of his ordinariness: Daniel Webster took great pains to remind voters of his own log-cabin boyhood (less fictional than Harrison's but still stretching the truth).

Jacksonian rhetoric conveyed intimacy in its tone as well. Editors gradually abandoned the constraints of formality in favor of familiarity. Rhetoric became more conversational and editors framed their appeals in folk diction and idiom. This made the language more accessible. Appeals often addressed their audience directly: the "Coffin Handbill" addressed itself to the "Gentle Reader." Jacksonian rhetoric marked the successful creation of a democratic vernacular. Dramatic punctuation, capitalization, and italics signaling abrupt changes in cadence and emphasis reappeared, along with new typographical symbols borrowed from commercial advertising, such as pointing hands, which had become by this time the standard signal to "Look at this!" Log cabins, liberty poles, cornucopias, laurel wreaths, and the Stars and Stripes adorned the mastheads of party newspapers. These symbols had achieved some consistency by 1840: in that year the log cabin ornamented the mastheads of Whig newspapers from Maine to Mississippi.

Early Jacksonian election appeals often used emphatic slogans as well. Some slogans celebrated the candidates, such as "Tippecanoe and Tyler Too!" Other slogans endorsed policy, such as "Equal Rights and No Monopoly!" or "Fifty-Four Forty or Fight!" These slogans were not very different in style from those of the Jeffersonian period, even if they contained more programmatic substance.

Political nicknames, on the other hand, had less programmatic substance but they became far more important. Jeffersonians coined nicknames for *parties* (e.g., the "Washington Party" or "The Friends of Peace"). Jacksonians invented nicknames for the candidates *themselves*; a practice inconceivable to partisans raised in a more deferential political culture. For those American presidential candidates who were military heroes, these nicknames often linked them with military exploits. Thus Andrew Jackson became "Old Hickory," William Henry Harrison became "Old Tip," Zachary Taylor became "Old Rough and Ready," while "Old Fuss and Feathers" was Winfield Scott; John C. Frémont was "the Pathfinder."[5] Coined on the battlefield, these names were resurrected by the press during presidential "campaigns." Even politicians who lacked any military credentials had nicknames. Henry Clay became "Harry of the West," James K. Polk became "Young Hickory," and Martin Van Buren became "The Little Magician" or alternatively, "Old Kinderhook," the source of the slang expression "O.K." This testifies to the importance of political nicknames for American colloquial speech. Nicknames reinforced the mythical lives of Jacksonian political figures.[6]

Jacksonian election discourse could not impart the sense of crisis characteristic of Jeffersonian rhetoric. Fundamental questions of government, sovereignty, and foreign relations no longer divided the electorate. Struggling to provide a sense of presence in their language, Jacksonian polemicists created stirring myths around

[5] On presidential nicknames and nicknames in general, see Walt Whitman, "Slang in America," *North American Review* 141 (November 1885): 433–34, reprinted in *Specimen Days, Democratic Vistas, and Other Prose*, p. 368.

[6] Allen Walker Read has done exhaustive research on this matter. See his "The First Stage in the History of *O.K.*," *American Speech* 38 (February 1963): 5–27; "The Second Stage in the History of *O.K.*," *American Speech* 38 (May 1963): 83–102; "Could Andrew Jackson Spell?" *American Speech* 38 (October 1963): 188–95; "The Folklore of *O.K.*," *American Speech* 39 (February 1964): 5–25; "Later Stages in the History of *O.K.*," *American Speech* 39 (May 1964): 83–101; "Successive Revisions in the History of *O.K.*," *American Speech* 39 (December 1964): 243–67.

the lives of conventional politicians; they dressed contemporary disputes in the costume of historical allegories.[7]

Historical folklore can strike a chord in collective memory that will resonate for many generations. The "Norman Yoke" and the English Civil War were already venerable examples of historical folklore; the American Revolution became another. Americans had employed historical allegories rhetorically before, particularly classical ones. They served a legitimating function (e.g., Washington as Cincinnatus). Classical allegories, however, lost much of the audience, and Jacksonian editors employed historical folklore with a democratic audience to serve the same ends more effectively.[8]

Editors borrowed an imperative tone from the past by invoking the appropriate historical stage setting. Normans and Saxons, Cavaliers and Cromwellians, Loyalists and Patriots, and Jacobins and Tories fought as rhetorical mercenaries in battles that the Jacksonian parties no longer had the idiomatic weaponry to engage in themselves. The Democratic press characterized the struggle of the Jacksonians against the Bank of the United States as a conflict of democracy against aristocracy.[9] Whigs made their policy of a protective tariff analogous to the Revolutionary patriots' economic nationalism; they proclaimed the Democrats' free-trade policy was akin to American Toryism. In the years before the Civil War editors invoked the American Revolution and rejected their opponents' Revolutionary claims repeatedly in election appeals.

A striking change in the imagery of electioneering rhetoric took place in the Jacksonian era. In the Jeffersonian era political rhetoric concentrated on the ideological conflict between Federalists and Republicans. In the Jacksonian period political rhetoric

[7] Frye, *Critical Path*, pp. 120–21.

[8] Howe, *American Whigs*, pp. 69–95; Meyers, *Jacksonian Persuasion*, p. 209; Garry Wills, *Cincinnatus: George Washington and the Enlightenment* (Garden City, N.Y., 1984); Paul K. Longmore, *The Invention of George Washington* (Berkeley, 1988); Ward, *Andrew Jackson*; Catherine L. Albanese, "Our Father, Our Washington," in *Sons of the Fathers: The Civil Religion of the American Revolution* (Philadelphia, 1976), pp. 140–64; especially 144; Barry Schwartz, *George Washington: The Making of an American Symbol* (New York, 1987), p. 7.

[9] See Louis Hartz, *The Liberal Tradition in America: An Interpretation of American Political Thought since the Revolution* (New York, 1955) pp. 89–113.

created a figurative dimension of struggle. Jeffersonian ideological conflict had never been entirely accessible to the larger American audience. Jacksonian figurative struggles, however, such as the "Bank War," or "the Battle of the Giants" (i.e., the Webster-Hayne Debate), provided resonant symbols for the larger audience.[10]

If the Jacksonian era witnessed the rise of familiarity, it was also marked the apogee of rhetorical formality. This was the golden age of stylized American oratory: the "godlike" Daniel Webster, Henry Clay, and Edward Everett delivered highly ornamented demonstrative speeches on ceremonial occasions. Yet even formal discourse was more accessible: Webster successfully elaborated the budding democratic mythology that now supplanted allusions to classical history and mythology. Deliberative speeches had become popular oratory.[11]

Appeals proved more effective among this democratized audience if the protagonists came forth from American history rather than from classical history or mythology. Democrats, "Whigs," Nullifiers, Free-Soilers, temperance advocates, nativists, and Republicans—all laid exclusive claim to lineal descent from the Founders. The new persuasion recast the lives and events of the previous generation to suit the immediate occasion. Jacksonians struggled to seize the American Revolutionary mythology and exploit it for a single political interest.[12]

Political "heroes" struggled against impersonal forces embodying malevolent purposes, such as the "Monster Bank" or the "Slave Power." Impersonal enemies make appeals to fear (argument *ad metum*) more effective. If apostrophe is a form of personification,

---

[10] Kenneth Burke, *Rhetoric of Motives*, pp. 204–5.

[11] For a discussion of ceremonial orations, see Meyers, *Jacksonian Persuasion*, p. 6; Kathleen Hall Jamieson and David S. Birdsell, *Presidential Debates: The Challenge of Creating an Informed Electorate* (New York, 1988), pp. 49–51; Paul D. Erickson, *The Poetry of Events: Daniel Webster's Rhetoric of the Constitution and the Union* (New York, 1986).

[12] On the invention and elaboration of tradition, see Eric Hobsbawm, "Introduction: Inventing Traditions," in *The Invention of Tradition*, ed. Eric Hobsbawm and Terence Ranger (Cambridge, 1983), p. 5; Victor Turner, "Religious Paradigms and Political Action: Thomas Becket at the Council of Northampton," in *Dramas, Fields, and Metaphors: Symbolic Action in Human Society* (Ithaca, N.Y., 1974), pp. 60–97; Alice Gérard, *La révolution française: Mythes et interprétations, 1789–1970* (Paris, 1970).

this was anti-apostrophe. In the "Bank War," Jackson clashed with Nicholas Biddle, not with "The Bank." Democrats made the threat of the Bank more vivid by calling it "the very Monster."[13] At the same time, a monster is a figure, an invention. Perhaps conjuring up an adversary in fantastic form makes victory seem more attainable.[14]

Figurative conflict remained at the center of public attention, until literal conflict over slavery achieved such overriding importance that it displaced historical allegories and mythic exploits. Staged as historical pageantry that combined celebration, declamation, and often demagoguery, electioneering rhetoric frequently preserved its centrality at the cost of its veracity. Not coincidentally, the word "rhetorical" began to have negative connotations.[15]

The "Coffin Handbill," first published in 1825 and an early example of Jacksonian hortatory rhetoric, conveyed its message through typographical devices and illustrations. Entitled "A BRIEF ACCOUNT OF SOME OF THE BLOODY DEEDS OF GENERAL JACKSON," the handbill displayed six coffins with the names of six militiamen executed for desertion after the Battle of New Orleans. A figure of Jackson, holding a sword cane, with the cane/sheath in one hand and a sword in the other, stood over another figure. "Gentle reader," the caption said, "it is for you to say whether this man who carries a sword cane, and is willing to run through the body of any one who may presume to stand in his way is a fit person to be our next President—to be the ruler of a peace loving People."[16]

[13] Meyers, *Jacksonian Persuasion*, pp. 10–14, 101–20.

[14] This is Thomas Leonard's point in his observations about Thomas Nast's "monsters." "To see one's fears exaggerated beyond what one dared to imagine works against fright." *Power of the Press*, pp. 115–16.

[15] The *Oxford English Dictionary*, 2d ed., gives one definition of "rhetorical" as "composed or expressed in artificial or extravagant language." The first instance the OED2 lists where the adverb "merely" appears dismissively with the word "rhetorical" occurs in America in 1852. The quotation is from Harriet Beecher Stowe, *Uncle Tom's Cabin: Or Life Among the Lowly*, "If these words had been spoken by some easy, self-indulgent exhorter, from whose mouth they might have come merely as pious and rhetorical flourish."

[16] MSS Broadside Collection, Library of Congress. For an earlier example of funerary iconography, see Paul Revere's broadside after the Boston Massacre in 1770, reproduced in Baumgardner, *American Broadsides*; Cobbett used the coffin as an attention-getting device in Britain during the 1830s, as is noted below.

The emphatic typography in the "Coffin Handbill" helped condemn Jackson's conduct. The verbs "exterminate" and "destroy" and the coffins arrayed around the page offered a grisly vision. The picture of Jackson running a man through with a concealed weapon emphasized the disingenuousness, capriciousness, and violence of Jackson's temperament. The attack on Jackson's character and conduct echoed an earlier style of invective but in this example visual imagery and emphatic typography assisted the reader's judgment.[17]

The Washington *Globe* presented a very different image of Andrew Jackson. Jackson "shed his blood in the war of independence; he had won imperishable renown by his defence [sic] of New Orleans; and he had been raised by a grateful and just people to the highest office in the world." Jackson in the Democratic *Globe* was the "savior" of his country. The *Globe* invoked the American Revolutionary struggle against "aristocracy," to lend legitimacy to the Democratic party and to Jackson's struggle against the Bank. The Bank was "the germ of an American nobility, an instrument to enable the aristocracy of England to . . . bring these States into a dependence on the British Isles, not less degrading and more fatal to their interests than their colonial condition." Nicholas Biddle had on the Fourth of July "presented himself to our Chief and demanded a surrender." Jackson had done "as our fathers did in 1776; [he] asserted the right of our people to freedom, and of our States to independence." This would be hailed as a "*second Declaration of Independence*," which "true Whigs" would "support with no less ardor and self-devotion than their fathers did the first."[18]

For the Democratic press, Nicholas Biddle personified the danger of a "monied aristocracy." The *Globe* said Biddle was "the MONARCH whom the monied aristocracy have chosen to manage, with undivided effect, the instrument of their power." For the opposition press, however, Jackson loomed as an equally menacing

---

[17] For an explanation of the effect of Jackson's character on his fellow politicians, see Robert Wiebe, *The Opening of American Society: From the Adoption of the Constitution to the Eve of Disunion* (New York, 1984), pp. 35–66, 235–37; see also Howe, *American Whigs*, pp. 69–95.

[18] *Globe* (weekly ed.), 12 July 1832.

figure. "It is our solemn conviction," said the *Gazette of the United States,* "that the re-election of General Jackson is fraught with the most awful dangers to the Republic, the destruction of the institutions upon which the liberties of the people, the pecuniary prosperity and permanency of the Union rest." The *New York Commercial Advertiser* denounced Jackson for his claim to "a DISPENS-ING POWER" over the law. Such a pretension had "not been exercised with impunity, even in the British monarchy, except in despotic times."[19]

The Whigs and Democrats struggled over the Revolutionary legacy. The name "Whig" itself showed careful attention to historical significance: "Whigs" supported the American Revolution. The Whigs were the "patriots"; they called the Democrats "Tories." That did not prevent the Democratic press from calling American Whigs "the aristocratic party."[20]

The American Revolution provided useful historical analogies for Jacksonians, but the Bible provided a moral context for political persuasion. The richest biblical analogy in the repertoire of the Jacksonians was the scriptural parallel that likened the Bank to the Beast in the Book of Revelation. The Washington *Globe* first published an editorial entitled "THE MONSTER REELING." Democratic journals throughout the Union reprinted it.

New Hampshire warned the Bank Monster in March not to attack the Hero and Patriot, whom the people had placed at the head of our government.

Heedless of the warning, he reared his twenty-six heads, and armed his hundred hands to persuade, and awe, and alarm the American people into submission to his power and ingratitude to their benefactor.... He broke loose upon Philadelphia, outraged patriotism, trampled upon virtue, perverted religion, bought the venal; frighted the weak, and with a crown upon his tallest head

[19] Ibid., 26 July, 1832; *Gazette of the United States,* 23 October 1832; *New-York Commercial Advertiser,* 3 November 1832.

[20] *Boston Post,* 24 October 1836; also 26 October 1836, 1 November 1836, 14 November 1836. See also Philip Hone, *The Diary of Philip Hone, 1828–1851,* ed. Allan Nevins (New York, 1927), 1:85.

inscribed with *"Terror and Corruption,"* marched in triumph through the streets of a conquered city.[21]

Darker accusations, reminiscent of earlier hortatory rhetoric, alleged that opponents performed secret rituals and practiced idolatry, blasphemy, or blatantly sacrilegious behavior. 'JACKSON BLASPHEMY,' denounced Jackson supporters for irreverence.

> All hail! Jackson, the greatest of Lords,
> To whom we dedicate our lives and our swords:
> All hail!
> To what power compare we that greatest deed,
> Whose bloody fame flies with boundless speed
> *Great Jackson, all hail!*
> Jesus had not such portentous fame!
> When founding a great religion with his name:
> *Great Jackson, all hail!*[22]

"Does it not behoove every citizen," asked the *New-York Commercial Advertiser,* "to save our institutions from the irreverent hands of those base profligates, who have essayed to overthrow the sacred ark of our political faith?" Democrats, said the *Commercial Advertiser* some weeks later, had pledged themselves "in favor of making the MILITARY IDOL *entirely independent both of Congress and the Supreme Court!*" The Democratic press responded with their own accusa-

---

[21] *Globe* (daily ed.), 17 October 1832. The relevant passage from Revelation reads as follows: "AND I stood upon the sand of the sea, and saw a beast rise up out of the sea, having seven heads and ten horns, and upon his horns ten crowns, and upon his heads the name of blasphemy." Rev. 13:1 AV. The *Globe* editorial has echoes not only of biblical imagery but of classical mythology: the Hundred-Handers of Greek creation myth and also the infant Hercules. "And here comes the young giant, Ohio with her Herculean club, and repeats the blow of her elder sister [Pennsylvania], making the monster reel with death-like dizziness."

[22] MSS Broadside Collection, Library of Congress. The religious imagery of the broadside is not unique: "The ministers of our holy religion are invoked to enter into the strife; . . . and introduce the inexorable and tyrannic reign of a golden Idol under the name and influence of the mammoth Bank." Washington *Globe* (daily ed.), 15 October 1832. See Dan. 3:4–5 AV, "Then an herald cried aloud, To you it is commanded, O people, nations, and languages . . . ye fall down and worship the golden image that Nebuchadnezzar the king hath set up." See also *New-York Commercial Advertiser,* 6 November 1832.

tions of sacrilege. "In their drunken, hard-cider carousals, they have made a mockery of the most sacred forms of the Christian church . . . and have even gone so far as to administer the holy sacrament of the Lord's supper, '*in the name of Old Tip!*' "[23]

More lighthearted attacks were also common in the Jacksonian press. Satire made its way into political rhetoric, mimicking, for example, a theatrical advertisement almost perfectly except for its placement in the newspaper. The following appeal relied on its readers' recognition of *A Midsummer Night's Dream.* "Nick Bottom" was Nicholas Biddle, president of the Bank of the United States.

### FEDERAL THEATER.
Grand and attractive entertainment, consisting of extracts
from Shakespeare's celebrated drama of

### MIDSUMMER-NIGHT DREAM.
with alterations and improvements adapted to the Federal Stage
and to the peculiar powers of THE MOST

### SPLENDID ACTORS IN THE UNION, entitled
*Calm Summer-Morning Dream,*
A SUBLIME SPECTACLE OF
*SOLITARY GRANDEUR!*
got up at great expense, with splendid scenery and decorations,
under the supervision of
*"The Committee of Public Safety."*
☞ The committee have the pleasure of announcing that they
have engaged, as STAGE MANAGER, the illustrious *President
of the Society for the Confusion of Useful Knowledge,* who will play the
part of
☞ **NICK BOTTOM, THE WEAVER** ☜
for this season only.[24]

---

[23] *New-York Commercial Advertiser,* 4 October 1832, alluding to 1 Sam. 5:1 AV, "And the Philistines took the ark of God, and brought it from Ebenezer unto Ashdod." Second quotation from *New-York Commercial Advertiser,* 2 November 1832. Democratic reply from *Boston Post,* 1 October 1840.

[24] *Boston Post,* 11 November 1836. The mock notice parodies the Society for the Diffusion of Useful Knowledge.

Shakespearean allusions often appeared in newspapers without any reference; despite expanding circulation newspaper readers had some familiarity with the plays. The Washington *Globe* made a Shakespearean allusion concerning Biddle, Clay, and Webster in 1832, likening them to "the witches in Macbeth, dancing around the bubbling cauldron," while "the Man of the People," Andrew Jackson, would "dissipate all their machinations into thin air."[25]

Other Shakespearean allusions appeared in the following condemnation of Daniel Webster, which appeared in the *Richmond Enquirer.* "Mr. Webster's Worcester speech *out-Herods Herod.* . . . He denounced the whole Tariff system in 1824, not only as mischievous, but unconstitutional—and now supports it in all its excesses. . . . *Shame, shame, where is thy blush?*"[26] The *Boston Post* combined a Shakespearean and a biblical allusion: "The snake, though scotched, is not killed—it hissed at JACKSON, but its fangs could not reach him: . . . the reptile can never regain that Eden its iniquity has forfeited."[27] Milton was another author for whom editors displayed an occasional partiality. Reference to *Paradise Lost* appeared in an editorial published in the Washington *Globe:* "The evil spirit of toryism which, / 'Squat like a toad close to the ear of Eve.' "[28]

[25] *Globe,* 18 October 1832, alluding to *Macbeth,* 1.3.79–81. "Banquo: The earth hath bubbles, as the water has, / And these are of them. Whither are they vanished? / Macbeth: Into the air; and what seem'd corporal melted."

[26] *Richmond Enquirer,* 26 October 1832. See *Hamlet,* 3.2.14–15, "I would have such a fellow whipped for o'erdoing Termagant; it out-herods Herod: / pray you, avoid it," and 3.4.82–84, "O shame! where is thy blush? / Rebellious hell, / If thou canst mutine in a matron's bones." Herod, like Termagant (supposedly a Saracen god), was a loud and boisterous character in traditional nativity plays. See also Matt. 2:7–8 AV.

[27] *Boston Post,* 3 October 1848, alluding to *Macbeth,* 3.2. 13–15. The *Oxford English Dictionary,* 2d ed., defines "scotch," citing *Macbeth:* "To inflict such hurt upon (something regarded as dangerous) that it is rendered harmless for the time." "We have scotched the snake, not kill'd it: / She'll close and be herself, whilest our poor malice / Remains in danger of her former tooth."

[28] *Globe* (daily ed.), 18 October 1832. The line is adapted from Milton, *Paradise Lost,* IV. 788–90, 799–800, "*Ithuriel* and *Zephon,* with wingd speed / Search through this Garden, leav unsearcht no nook, / But chiefly where those two fair Creatures Lodge, / . . . / In search of whom they sought; him there they found / Squat like a Toad, close at the eare of *Eve.*"

Newspapers used literature as one form of political entertainment, and also began to exploit events themselves for their entertainment value. The invention of the telegraph in 1844 and its use by journalists created a new imperative for the rapid transmission of events. The news headline on the front page followed soon thereafter. As the news headline grew more important, the political masthead grew less so; the emphasis on political opinion gave way to accentuating events themselves instead of filtering events through the lens of opinion. Using events themselves as persuasive instruments gained favor as a rhetorical strategy toward the end of the Jacksonian era.[29]

The *Boston Post* used an arresting variety of typographical layouts in headlines, not to emphasize the paper's political opinions but to display the importance of a desired outcome: the election of Lewis Cass as president. The *Post* created a sense of momentum by publishing early state election returns and reinforced its message of the inevitability of a Democratic triumph.

**DEMOCRACY
TRIUMPHANT!**

**CASS AND BUTLER
CERTAIN TO BE ELECTED!!**
We have not only triumphed in the October elections, but the
Summer elections have all resulted in our favor. The
following states have held elections with a result favorable
to democracy:—
**OHIO
IOWA
MAINE
INDIANA
GEORGIA
ILLINOIS
MISSOURI
WISCONSIN
PENNSYLVANIA
SOUTH CAROLINA**

[29] Alfred Lee, *Daily Newspaper,* pp. 491–507; Schudson, *Discovering the News,* pp. 34–35.

**Giving Electoral Votes** 1 1 6
In **OHIO,** where the whigs claimed 1 5,000 majority, we have gained
**Two Members of Congress!**
**Elected TEN Senators to the Whigs FOUR!**
**A Majority of the House of Representatives**
**And have the POPULAR VOTE of the State!**
In MAINE we beat the whig candidate for Governor by
*22,000 PLURALITY!!*
We have in the Legislature
*A LARGE MAJORITY!*
IN INDIANA, where the Taylor men expected a victory, we
SWEPT THE BOARD!
Our popular majority is over
**7,000!**
In ILLINOIS the democracy made
**A CLEAN SWEEP!**
Our popular majority is
**10,228!**
In MISSOURI, ever true Missouri, we
**CARRIED EVERYTHING!**
BY A POPULAR MAJORITY OF
*15,352!*
In little ARKANSAS there was a most awful
*SKINNING OF COONS!*
The election resulted in favor of CASS and BUTLER by upwards of
**5,000!**
In SOUTH CAROLINA the Legislature is favorable
to CASS and BUTLER, and so are
**All but One of the Congressmen!**[30]

In the age of instantaneous communication, American campaigning became simpler, cruder, and more inclined to bombast.[31] Instantaneous communications permitted greater participation by

---

[30] *Boston Post,* 7 November 1848.

[31] Even newspapers lacking telegraph connections to the Northeast caught the contagion for instantaneous communications. Some Journals used flag signals (also called the "telegraph"); others used relays of horses. The New Orleans *Daily Picayune* published a jockey mounted on a galloping horse, trumpeting "NEWS!!" just below the masthead. The headline proclaimed the news was "Seventy-Two Hours Ahead of the Mail." On "bombast," or "spread-eagle" style see Cmiel, *Democratic Eloquence,* pp. 64–65.

the voters, however, in debate as well as result. The boundaries between demonstrative and deliberative rhetoric diminished in the 1850s. Shorthand transcription of congressional debates allowed verbatim publication in the newspapers. Attention focused as never before on speeches in the halls of Congress.[32] Members of Congress began to deliver speeches primarily intended for the eyes of newspaper readers rather than the ears of their fellow legislators. Prompted by the sectional crisis and abetted by instantaneous communication, acrimonious congressional debates drove a moral wedge ever deeper into the national consciousness.[33]

In the 1830s and 1840s, hortatory electioneering rhetoric addressed deliberative questions; in the 1850s, hortatory rhetoric invaded Congress, the state legislatures, and debating societies. Legislators' speeches adopted the emphatic tone, vivid imagery, panegyric, and invective of hortatory electioneering. Thanks to instantaneous communication, these fierce exchanges found their way into the newspapers the following day. Exhortation helped to stimulate public interest in the congressional debate over the extension of slavery; it also provoked violent reactions against those who used it, including Thomas Hart Benton, Jonathan Cilley, Charles Sumner, and Owen Lovejoy. Exhortation made an impact on members of Congress and, what is more important for electioneering, on the public.

Charles Sumner went well beyond the bounds of Victorian propriety in his 1856 speech "The Crime Against Kansas." He illustrated his philippic against slavery and popular sovereignty with allusions and personal attacks deeply offensive to his opponents—and some of his allies—in the Senate.[34] Sumner's address was loaded with sexual imagery. Sumner likened the imposition of slavery on Kansas to "the rape of a virgin Territory." He spoke of slavery as a "great Terrestrial Serpent . . . coiled about the whole land." He said of Senator Andrew P. Butler of South Carolina that Butler had "chosen a mistress . . . [who] though polluted in the

---

[32] Ritchie, *Press Gallery*, pp. 30–32; Culver Smith, *Press, Politics, and Patronage*, pp. 206–32.

[33] Meyers, *Jacksonian Persuasion*, p. 209; Leonard, *Power of the Press*, pp. 63–96.

[34] David [Herbert] Donald, *Charles Sumner and the Coming of the Civil War* (New York, 1960), pp. 282–93.

sight of the world, is chaste in his sight—I mean the harlot Slavery."
Sumner's colleagues were not altogether surprised when Representative Preston Brooks of South Carolina attacked the Massachusetts
senator with a cane.[35]

The altercation between Sumner and Brooks illustrates the
deeper conflict between the old norms of congressional discourse
and the new. Brooks and his uncle, Senator Butler, took courtesy
between members for granted. Deliberative language provided for
orderly debate and facilitated compromise. For Brooks and Butler,
the norms of behavior looked inward; they centered on legislative
decorum. Sumner, on the other hand, was a newer breed of senator. Sumner's norms of behavior looked outward; they centered
on transcendent values. Sumner had been at his desk, franking
copies of his "Crime against Kansas" speech when Brooks attacked
him. Sumner's foremost interest was the good opinion of his constituents. His immediate audience was only incidental. Hortatory
language promoted vivid invective. Butler served merely as a conve-
nient foil to illustrate Sumner's attack. Butler and his generation
addressed fellow senators; Sumner and the younger generation of
northern politicians addressed the next day's newspaper readers.

Sometimes newspaper editors improved on the speeches. William H. Seward's "Irrepressible Conflict" speech, delivered in 1858,
figured prominently at the end of that year's congressional campaign. The *New-York Daily Tribune* rearranged the speech to suit
the purposes of its editor. According to the *Tribune*, Seward

---

[35] Ibid., pp. 293–97; *Congressional Globe*, 34th Cong., 1st Sess., 19–20 May 1856,
Appendix, pp. 529–44. Sumner's "Crime Against Kansas" speech may be found
in pamphlet form; see *"The Crime Against Kansas," Speech of Hon. Charles Sumner,
of Massachusetts. In the Senate of the United States, May 19, 1856.* (New York, 1856).
The speech was published at the *New-York Tribune* by Greeley and McElrath. Page
citations derive from this pamphlet, pp. 2, 3. See Kenneth Burke's description
of sexual imagery and political rhetoric, "The Rhetoric of Hitler's Battle," in *The
Philosophy of Literary Form* (Baton Rouge, La., 1967), p. 195. See also Leonard,
*Power of the Press,* pp. 84–85. Richard Henry Dana, Jr. wrote to Charles Sumner
in the summer after the assault, "When Brooks brought his cane in contact with
your head, he completed the circuit of electricity to 30 millions!" Richard Henry
Dana, Jr. to Charles Sumner, July 1, 1856, Charles Sumner Papers, Harvard
University, quoted in William E. Gienapp, *Origins of the Republican Party, 1852–1856*
(New York, 1987), p. 300. Gienapp argues that the caning of Sumner precipitated
Republican victories in the 1856 election.

"arraigned the Democratic party as the great ally of the Slave Power."[36] Seward did not use this phrase or many others the paper attributed to him. Greeley adjusted the themes of the speech to match familiar themes of the *Tribune.*

One of the most electrifying speeches delivered in Congress at the end of the sectional crisis was a philippic given in 1860 by Representative Owen Lovejoy of Illinois, entitled "The Barbarism of Slavery." Lovejoy's elder brother Elijah was a minister and anti-slavery editor in Alton who had been killed by a hostile mob. Like his brother, Owen Lovejoy had been a minister. The younger Lovejoy had preached for nearly eighteen years to the Hampshire Colony Congregational Church in Princeton, Illinois. He shared his elder brother's ability to define his opponents in vivid descriptive language, to refute their political positions by reductio ad absurdum, to state his own political argument plainly in vivid metaphors and compelling analogies. He brought that style of moral allegorizing to the floor of Congress.[37] Lovejoy had debated with Stephen Douglas in 1854 at Princeton, Illinois and had spoken for Lincoln at Freeport and Ottawa in the Lincoln-Douglas senatorial campaign of 1858. At Ottawa, Lovejoy "divested himself of his cravat and collar, opened his vest and shirt, and went at it." One reporter concluded that he "never listened to a speech so full of eloquence and magnetic power."[38] General Thomas W. Hyde recalled Lovejoy's at the 1860 Republican convention in Chicago:

> I remember best the powerful speeches of Owen Lovejoy, the greatest stump orator I ever heard. He would hold spellbound for two hours at a time nine thousand people in this vast hall, tearing his coat off and then his vest and cravat in the excitement of his invectives

[36] *New-York Daily Tribune,* 26 October 1858.

[37] On Elijah Lovejoy see Henry Tanner, *The Martyrdom of Lovejoy: An Account of the Life, Trials, and Perils of Rev. Elijah P. Lovejoy* (Chicago, 1881); Merton L. Dillon, *Elijah P. Lovejoy: Abolitionist Editor* (Urbana, 1961); Ruth E. Haberkorn, "Owen Lovejoy in Princeton, Illinois," in *Illinois State Historical Society Journal* 36 (1943): 291–99; George V. Bohman, "Owen Lovejoy on 'The Barbarism of Slavery,' April 5, 1860," in *Antislavery and Disunion, 1858–1861: Studies in the Rhetoric of Compromise and Conflict,* ed. J. Jeffrey Auer (New York, 1963), p. 120.

[38] Both quotations appear in the (Springfield) *Illinois State Journal.* See *Illinois State Journal,* 24 August 1858.

against slavery, though never alluding to the fact that but a short time before his brother had been shot by a pro-slavery mob.[39]

Unlike the Wigwam speech in Chicago, the "Barbarism of Slavery" address in Congress was somewhat extemporaneous.[40] He wrote to Lydia Maria Child that his speech was inspired by instinct: "I poured on a rainstorm of fire and brimstone as hot as I could." He wrote his wife, "I believe that I never said anything more Savage in the pulpit or on the stump." The "Barbarism of Slavery" speech caused an immediate sensation; Lovejoy told his wife that Washington buzzed "like a hive of bees when struck."[41] As Lovejoy knew, such a speech delivered in Congress could make a national reputation. Ten major newspapers printed the entire text of his speech. Horace Greeley hailed the speech and announced that he would order a large printing for the 1860 Republican campaign.[42] Before he had reached the middle of his "Barbarism of Slavery" address, Lovejoy was interrupted by Representatives Pryor of Virginia and Barksdale of Mississippi, the latter "shouting and flourishing a heavy cane."[43] What was it that provoked such a violent reaction?

Lovejoy filled his speech with learned allusions, but they did not provide its exceptional power. According to one critic, Lovejoy's greatest resource was his use of analogies. His analogies served as secular parables, conveyed in the same form as evangelical

[39] Thomas W. Hyde, *Following the Greek Cross; or, Memories of the Sixth Army Corps* (Boston, 1894), p. 3.

[40] The text of "The Barbarism of Slavery" may be found in a pamphlet, *"The Barbarism of Slavery," Delivered in the House of Representatives, April 5, 1860* (Washington, D.C., 1860). See also *Congressional Globe*, 36th Cong., 1st Sess., April 5, 1860, Appendix, p. 205.

[41] Letter from Lovejoy to Lydia Maria Child, in possession of George V. Bohman. Letter from Owen to Eunice Lovejoy, April 6, 1860, in Lovejoy MSS, William L. Clements Library, University of Michigan, Ann Arbor, both letters quoted in Bohman, "Lovejoy on Barbarism," pp. 116–17.

[42] Leonard, *Power of the Press*, p. 95; Bohman, "Lovejoy on Barbarism," p. 120. In the South, however, only Robert Barnwell Rhett's *Charleston Mercury* printed the entire text, with the editor's admonition that his readers should pay attention to every word and "put it away in a pigeon-hole for perusal." *Charleston Mercury*, 17 April 1860.

[43] *New-York Daily Tribune*, 7 April 1860.

homiletics.[44] Owen Lovejoy made particularly effective use of domestic analogies; in the most extended example in the 1860 speech, he likened the union of free and slave states to a troubled marriage. The wife in Lovejoy's parable represents the South. She has a wart or mole on her hand; she becomes so obsessed about it that she demands it be transferred to each of her daughters. The husband, who symbolizes the North, refuses to allow his wife to graft this deformity onto the hands of his daughters, that is, the territories.[45] In this parable, with its elements of the grotesque as well as the absurd, Lovejoy created a powerful indictment. Lovejoy may have hoped to upset some squeamish Victorians with this analogy, and perhaps provoke his opponents. In his peroration, Lovejoy invoked a historical parallel to the American Revolution certain to offend Southerners by conferring the Founders' devotion to liberty on future rebellious slaves. He predicted that in the future "some Marion will be found, calling his guerrilla troops from the swamps and everglades of South Carolina; and Patrick Henry will reappear in the Old Dominion, shouting, 'Give us liberty, or give us death!' "[46]

For Lovejoy, Illinois constituted a rhetorical proving ground. For another Republican, Illinois also provided an opportunity for delivering a more subdued form of exhortation Abraham Lincoln's use of allegory had much in common with Owen Lovejoy's. One observer, F. B. Carpenter, who came to know both Lovejoy and Lincoln, was struck with the similarity of their language. "Lovejoy had much more of the agitator, the reformer, in his nature," said Carpenter, "but both Lovejoy and Lincoln drew the inspiration of

[44] Bohman, "Lovejoy on Barbarism," pp. 124–25, n. 38, 123–24.

[45] The allegory of the domestic tension between husband and wife may have been inspired by James Madison, who wrote a very similar allegorical fable in the early 1820s. The fable only came to public attention in the 1850s. See Drew R. McCoy, *The Last of the Fathers: James Madison and the Republican Legacy* (New York, 1989), pp. 274–76. Lincoln used a similar domestic analogy in the First Inaugural: "A husband and wife may be divorced, and go out of the presence and beyond the reach of each other; but the different parts of our country cannot do this." Abraham Lincoln, *Complete Works*, ed. John G. Nicolay and John Hay (New York, 1905), 6:181.

[46] *Congressional Globe*, 36th Cong., 1st Sess., April 5, 1860, Appendix, p. 207.

their lives from the same source." Their "modes of thought and illustration were remarkably alike."[47]

John Hanks recalled that Lincoln kept *Aesop's Fables* and the Bible "always within reach," reading them frequently. William Herndon, Lincoln's law partner, said that these sources furnished Lincoln with the "many figures of speech and parables which he used with such happy effect." Charles Sumner observed more condescendingly that when Lincoln spoke, "the recent West seemed to vie with the ancient East in apologue and fable. His ideas moved, as the beasts entered Noah's ark, in pairs."[48]

Herndon described Lincoln's voice as "shrill, piping and unpleasant." As Lincoln understood, however, the effectiveness of a public speaker no longer relied more than incidentally on the quality of his voice. In the debates with Douglas, Lincoln did not direct his speeches to his immediate audience but instead to a reading public, who would digest his rhetoric the following day in the newspapers. Douglas played to the crowd; Lincoln deliberately addressed an audience beyond his immediate listeners. In the twentieth century, conventional wisdom holds that in the televised debates between Richard Nixon and John F. Kennedy in 1960, Nixon "won" the debates on the radio, while Kennedy "won" on television. In a similar fashion, Douglas may have "won" on the platform in the towns of Illinois, but Lincoln "won" the debates as they appeared in print.[49] In the verbatim transcription of the

[47] F. B. Carpenter, *Six Months at the White House: The Story of a Picture* (New York, 1867), p. 2.

[48] Hanks and Herndon's comments are from William H. Herndon, *Life of Lincoln* (Cleveland, 1942), p. 39. Sumner is quoted in Gunderson, "Lincoln's Rhetorical Style," p. 85.

[49] On the question of who "won" the Lincoln-Douglas debates, the author consulted with Harold Holzer, who concurs with this opinion (personal e-mail correspondence, 15 October 1994). Having watched the C-SPAN reenactments of the Lincoln-Douglas debates broadcast through the summer and fall of 1994, this author was struck by the different impression Douglas conveys in speaking to a "live" audience. Had the Lincoln-Douglas debates been televised, perhaps Douglas would have "won." For a detailed description of Lincoln as an orator, see Herndon, *Life of Lincoln*, pp. 331–33; also Abraham Lincoln, *Selected Writings and Speeches of Abraham Lincoln*, ed. T. Harry Williams (Chicago, 1934), pp. xlviii-xlix. In the wake of his defeat, Lincoln busied himself with correcting, restoring and editing his verbatim transcripts of the debates, clipped from the newspapers, which he then carried with him to Ohio to the Republican leadership there when

debates, the notations indicate that Douglas prevailed with the immediate audience. Douglas's rhetorical strategy was "agonistic": he hoped to gain a tactical advantage. Lincoln, on the other hand, understood that the act of public speaking merely provided a dramatic setting for written mass communication.[50]

The synthesis of the oral speaking tradition with print culture realized in Lincoln its enormous persuasive power. Abraham Lincoln had mastered the art of delivering a written address, fabricated and communicated primarily as a written document, but sustaining the dramatic presence of a spoken oration.

Lincoln's familiarity with the Bible and his practice of the law inspired his most important contribution to political communication: his ability to convey a damning indictment in a simple parable. Lincoln's parables were not Lovejoy's elaborate allegories. In Lincoln's parables the actors had proper names and familiar tasks, and their impact was immediate, formulating in concrete terms what would otherwise have been an abstract moral indictment of his opponents. Lincoln's talents as a raconteur of off-color stories perhaps enabled him to create parables more persuasive than Owen Lovejoy's.[51]

Lincoln made effective use of one such parable in the "House Divided" speech at Springfield (and the title of the speech itself is a biblical reference to Mark 3:25 AV and Matt. 12:25 AV). He asserted that a deliberate conspiracy existed among

---

he returned to working for the Republican Party in 1859. Herndon, *Life of Lincoln*, pp. 364–65. For a comprehensive treatment of the issues of the Lincoln-Douglas debates, see David Zarefsky, *Lincoln, Douglas, and Slavery: In the Crucible of Public Debate* (Chicago, 1990); also Harry V. Jaffa, *Crisis of the House Divided: An Interpretation of the Issues in the Lincoln-Douglas Debates* (Garden City, N.Y., 1959).

[50] Kenneth Burke, *Rhetoric of Motives*, pp. 52–53; Zarefsky, *Lincoln, Douglas, and Slavery*, pp. 239–43; "The Ottawa Debate," in *An Analysis of Lincoln and Douglas as Public Speakers and Debaters*, ed. Lionel Crocker (Springfield, Ill., 1968), pp. 189–90; Marvin G. Bauer, "Persuasive Methods in the Lincoln-Douglas Debates," in *Analysis of Lincoln and Douglas*, ed. Crocker, pp. 64–74; Jamieson, *Presidential Debates*, pp. 49–56, 67–68; Forest L. Whan, "Stephen A. Douglas," in *A History and Criticism of American Public Address*, ed. William Norwood Brigance (New York, 1943), 2:777–827.

[51] On what Garry Wills calls Lincoln's "revolution in style," see Wills, *Lincoln at Gettysburg: The Words That Remade America* (New York, 1992), pp. 148–74.

Stephen Douglas, Franklin Pierce, Roger Taney, and James Buchanan to insure the triumph of slavery in the Union. He formulated a parable with familiar references, likening this grand conspiracy to the collaboration of a group of carpenters raising a mill or a barn.

> When we see a lot of framed timbers, different portions of which we know have been gotten out at different times and places, and by different workmen—Stephen [Douglas], Franklin [Pierce], Roger [Taney], and James [Buchanan] . . . [w]e feel it impossible not to *believe* that Stephen and Franklin and Roger and James, all understood one another from the beginning, and all worked upon a common *plan* or *draft* drawn before the first lick was struck.[52]

Lincoln used the familiar hortatory theme of conspiracy to convince his audience that all the evidence fit together. As a lawyer, Lincoln delivered trial summations before a jury; the conspiracy parable helped convict northern Democrats of collusion in the minds of Republican voters.[53]

The press played an enormous role in stimulating the interest of the voters of Illinois and the Union at large in the Lincoln-Douglas debates. Newspapers in Illinois and the *New-York Tribune* published verbatim transcripts of the debates. Newspapers covered the debates from Charleston and New Orleans and from all over the North. Each debate became a stage setting for the enactment of familiar political language and rituals. The announcements in the press that accompanied each of the debates acted to "set off" and in many cases decode the more arcane disputes of the debates themselves. They conveyed the issues in a more familiar political vernacular.

---

[52] Springfield, *Illinois State Journal*, 17 June 1858, transcript of original nomination speech delivered on June 16, 1858. At Ottawa, Lincoln substituted the word "blow" for "lick." Ibid., 24 August 1858.

[53] Donald Zarefsky has explored the conspiracy argument in one chapter of *Lincoln Douglas, and Slavery*, pp. 68–110; see also Zarefsky, "Conspiracy Arguments in the Lincoln-Douglas Debates," *Journal of the American Forensic Association* 21 (1984): 63–75. Gustafson has observed that Lincoln defines principles "not by precept but by dramatic action." *Representative Words*, p. 385.

*The Great Debate*
BETWEEN
**LINCOLN AND DOUGLAS**
*AT OTTAWA, AUGUST 21, 1858*
**Twelve Thousand Persons Present!**
The Dred Scott Champion Pulverized!!!
**Great Republican Demonstration in the Evening!!**
POWERFUL SPEECH OF HON. OWEN LOVEJOY!
**BONFIRES——TORCH-LIGHT PROCESSION—GREAT
ENTHUSIASM![54]**

Just before the 1858 election, the *Illinois State Journal* published
a final appeal for a rally of Republicans. This newspaper appeal
combined the substantive and the symbolic aspects of the Republican campaign in hortatory form in its references to Henry Clay
and to refutations of Toryism and Abolitionism.

**COME ONE, COME ALL!**
**OLD WHIGS OF SANGAMON,**
Will you not turn out and give your old CHAMPION, ABE
LINCOLN, the "tall Sucker," a hearing for yourselves. Hear
him, and you will be satisfied that the charge of
**NIGGER EQUALITY**
is as false against LINCOLN, as the charge of
*Toryism* and *Abolitionism* was against CLAY[55]

In the Cooper Union speech in New York, Lincoln attempted
to seize from the Democrats the legacy of the Founders on the
question of slavery. He argued that Republican policy on slavery
in the territories was consistent with the intentions of the framers
of the Constitution. Speaking of the Founders' opinion of slavery,
Lincoln said, "As those fathers marked it, so let it again be marked,
as an evil not to be extended. . . ." Lincoln urged his listeners to
keep faith with the slave states in the spirit of the Founders. "Let

---

[54] Springfield, *Illinois State Journal*, 24 August 1858.
[55] Reported from a "Correspondent of the Press and Tribune." *Illinois State Journal*, 21 October 1858. See also Robert W. Johannsen, *Lincoln, the South, and Slavery: The Political Dimension* (Baton Rouge, La., 1991). For the significance of Henry Clay, see Zarefsky, *Lincoln, Douglas, and Slavery*, pp. 198, 156–60, 227–28.

all the guarantees those fathers gave it, be, not grudgingly, but fully and fairly maintained."[56] The speech used the authority of the Founders to sanction the policies of the Republicans. Although Lincoln addressed a deliberative question, he exploited the symbolic authority of the Founders to inspire and mobilize his listeners. Lincoln won the rhetorical contest over which party would claim the legacy of the Founders. After the election he would invoke the Founders' authority to save the Union.[57]

Lincoln's speech marked a transition point in American electioneering rhetoric. Lincoln's debates with Douglas had been punctuated with much of the good-natured familiarity characteristic of Jacksonian rhetoric. But Lincoln's Cooper Union speech and all his subsequent speeches struck a much more somber tone. The election of 1860 marked a retreat from familiarity. Hortatory rhetoric had created—and now divided—a national audience. Editorials reminded their readers of their duty in time of crisis. By the time of the 1860 election, even the *Charleston Mercury* began publishing hortatory manifestoes. For all the fire-eating reputation of its editor, Robert Barnwell Rhett, the *Mercury* usually adhered to decorous electioneering even in the late 1850s. In the fall of 1860, however, the *Mercury* published a different style of appeal. At this time of crisis, said the *Mercury*, South Carolina needed "firm and unflinching men" to "preserve, defend and protect the sacred honor and dignity of South Carolina." The *Mercury* alluded to the "Irrepressible Conflict" speech of William Seward. It warned that the "irrepressible, higher law conflict, is about to be visited upon us through the Black Republican Nominee. . . . '*Put on your*

---

[56] Address at Cooper Institute, February 27, 1860, in Lincoln, *Complete Works,* 5:293–328.

[57] Wills makes this point eloquently in *Lincoln at Gettysburg*, especially pp. 121–47. George B. Forgie, *Patricide in the House Divided: A Psychological Interpretation of Lincoln and His Age* (New York, 1979), deals extensively with Lincoln's appropriation of the Founders. See also Michael Kammen, *A Season of Youth: The American Revolution and the Historical Imagination* (New York, 1978), pp. 56–58. Douglas also sought to appropriate the legacy of the Founders. See Zarefsky's discussion of the historical argument, *Lincoln, Douglas, and Slavery*, pp. 141–65; Wil A. Linkugel, "Lincoln, Kansas, and Cooper Union," *Speech Monographs* 37 (1970): 172–79; Michael C. Leff and G. P. Mohrmann, "Lincoln at Cooper Union: A Rhetorical Analysis of the Text," *Quarterly Journal of Speech* 40 (1974): 346–58.

*swords and buckles—the foe, the foe, is nigh.*' " Elect such men, "in whose hands the honor of the State will be safe—*your endeared homes—your patriotic altars—your wives and children—*may be protected and saved from ruin."[58]

The Jacksonians successfully refined a hortatory form of persuasion that promoted political identification in a mass audience. They created a rhetorical style that conveyed the legitimacy of the Founders to their successors. Jacksonian and antebellum editors struggled to monopolize the legacy of the Founders for partisan purposes. Editors used what Michael McGee has called "ideographs": political slogans or labels that encapsulate ideology in political discourse. In the case of the Jacksonian Democrats, the dominant ideograph was "Equal Rights!"[59] The Whigs and the Republicans emphasized the Founders' jealous regard for "Liberty": Lincoln's speeches marked only the culmination of these efforts.[60] In the wake of Lincoln's election, secessionists hailed another legacy of the Revolution: "Independence." "Liberty" and "Independence" once inseparable, now became irreconcilable.[61]

On the eve of another great war in 1913, Lord George Curzon delivered the Rede Lecture at Cambridge University. Curzon took it upon himself in this lecture to find the modern counterpart of Pericles' "Funeral Oration." Curzon did not choose a single example but instead chose three "supreme master pieces" of modern parliamentary eloquence: they were William Pitt's toast after the

[58] *Mercury*, 8 October 1860. See Ralph T. Eubanks, "The Rhetoric of the Nullifiers," in *Oratory in the Old South, 1828–1860*, ed. Waldo W. Braden, et al. (Baton Rouge, 1970), p. 53. This persistent emphasis on honor indicates the South still exhibited characteristics of Peter Burke's definition of honor culture. *The Historical Anthropology of Early Modern Italy: Essays on Perception and Communication* (Cambridge, 1987), pp. 13–14, 223.

[59] McGee "Ideograph," pp. 1–16. McGee defines "ideographs" as slogans which function as the building blocks of an ideology. Zarefsky refers to them as "the incipient propositions by which ideological content is developed in rhetorical discourse." *Lincoln, Douglas, and Slavery*, p. 229. On the importance of "Equal Rights" for Jacksonians, see Rodgers, *Contested Truths*, pp. 39, 74–79.

[60] Wills, *Lincoln at Gettysburg*, especially pp. 98–117.

[61] See McGee's discussion of changes in the relationship between ideographs, in "Ideograph," pp. 13–14. On the contest between "liberty" and "equality," see Appleby, "The American Heritage—the Heirs and the Disinherited," in *Liberalism and Republicanism*, especially pp. 222–31.

victory at Trafalgar, and two speeches by Abraham Lincoln: the Gettysburg Address and the Second Inaugural.[62]

Curzon made an important observation on the rise of a new democratic style of rhetoric, which he identified with Lincoln. Should a man in England "arise from the ranks of the people, as Abraham Lincoln from the back-woods of America, a man gifted with real oratorical power, and with commanding genius, I can see no reason why he should not revive in England the glories of a Chatham or a Grattan." His "triumphs might be less in the Senate than in the arena; his style might not be that of the classics of the past. But he might by reason of his gifts sway the destinies of the State, and alter the fortunes of an empire."[63]

Lincoln succeeded in swaying the destinies of the state. As Tocqueville had observed, the impressive power of a great orator in a democratic society lies in the fact that he speaks to the whole nation: "This heightens both his thought and his power of expression."[64] By means of the mythic and religious imagery in his Gettysburg and Second Inaugural speeches, Lincoln nearly dispensed with forensic argument, linking the cause of Union to the workings of a transcendent authority.[65]

In the two dozen years separating Andrew Jackson's retirement from Abraham Lincoln's first inauguration, politicians and editors had created a powerful new political language. The language

[62] George Nathaniel Curzon, Marquis of Curzon, *Modern Parliamentary Eloquence*, The Rede Lecture (Cambridge, 1913).

[63] Ibid. Martin Van Buren, when an aspiring politician eighty-four years earlier, made an observation similar to Curzon's. In a small notebook he scribbled a set of unrelated maxims in pencil. One was a reflection on the force of opinion. "Those who have wrought great changes in the world never succeed by gaining over chiefs; but always by exciting the multitude. The first is the resource of intrigue and produces only secondary results. The second is the resort of genius and succeeds in transforming the face of the universe." Martin Van Buren, "notebook of miscellaneous notes on constitutional history, conversations with [Philip S.] Markley and Gen. Jackson in regard to alleged political intrigues to keep Clay as secretary of state, political maxims, etc." Van Buren Papers, Microfilm Reel 8, Library of Congress. Quoted also in Arthur M. Schlesinger, Jr., *The Age of Jackson* (Boston, 1945), p. 51; Jamieson and Birdsell, *Presidential Debates*, p. 65.

[64] Tocqueville, *Democracy in America*, p. 469.

[65] Wills, *Lincoln at Gettysburg*, pp. 99–117; James M. McPherson, "How Lincoln Won the War with Metaphors," in *Abraham Lincoln and the Second American Revolution* (New York, 1990), pp. 93–112.

enlisted the loyalties of Americans in parties and political institutions. Figurative partisan conflict prefigured real combat: the rhetorical battle over the Revolution reduced the grounds for compromise in a real war for the Union. That war in time would also become an important subject for new mythmaking.[66]

[66] Waldo W. Braden, *Abraham Lincoln, Public Speaker* (Baton Rouge, LA., 1988), p. 75; K. Burke, *Rhetoric of Motives,* pp. 21, 46.

# CHAPTER FIVE

# Parliamentary Reform and
# the Repeal of Constraints
# on Expression, 1832–1855

As if the Senate was intended
For nothing else but to be mended

—Samuel Butler, *Hudibras*

The First Reform Act initiated the transformation of Parliament to a more broadly representative institution. Parliament hardly transformed itself into a democratic assembly in 1832, however, and continued to show some resistance to change, as did the parties, the press, and political rhetoric in the Age of Reform. The period between the First Reform Act in 1832 and the repeal of the newspaper stamp duty in 1855 was an age of institutional innovation that nevertheless reinforced old habits of political behavior.

The British press in the 1830s was in a state of transition. The agitation for Emancipation, Reform, and Free Trade stirred many journalists into political independence, yet many newspapers still relied on partial subsidies from the parties. The rhetoric of post-Reform politics reflected this confusion. Laudatory rhetoric dominated electioneering even after the First Reform Act in 1832. The Reform debate, the influence of the unstamped press, religious controversies, and the Anti-Corn Law agitation stimulated the revival of hortatory electioneering.

Statutory constraints limited the growth of the press in Britain, as Edward Lytton Bulwer pointed out in a speech to the Commons in 1832. Bulwer called upon Parliament to repeal the "taxes on knowledge": the stamp duty, the paper duty, and the tax on advertisements. Bulwer made a series of revealing comparisons of the press in Britain and the United States. A U.S. newspaper sold for the equivalent of one and a half pence on the average, whereas in Britain the cost was seven pence. Every town in the United States with ten thousand inhabitants possessed a daily newspaper. In New York City alone, twelve daily newspapers published 1,456,416 untaxed advertisements in one year. In the same year all four hundred papers in Britain and Ireland published only 1,020,000 advertisements. An advertisement of twenty lines in a London paper if published daily for a year, would cost £202 16*s.*, whereas in New York the same advertisement would cost only the equivalent of £6 18*s.* 8*d.* A reformed Parliament, Bulwer argued, must reduce the influence of the five or six journals that enjoyed a monopoly of political coverage. If their influence was not reduced, Governments might depend too much on the most influential newspapers for support. These journals might otherwise succeed to the magnate's influence in the unreformed Parliament.[1]

The First Reform Act in 1832 and an initial reduction in the 1830s of the "taxes on knowledge" helped cause a fundamental change in political discourse.[2] Editors directed more attention to specific "communities." Liberals and Conservatives focused their most effective appeals on confessional groups. Religious identification in the broadest sense of belonging or not belonging to the Church of England, seems to have formed the most durable cleavage within the electoral universe.[3]

---

[1] *Hansard Parliamentary Debates,* 3d ser., vol. 115 (June 22, 1832), pp. 630–31.

[2] The restrictions on the press were substantially reduced in the 1830s. Restrictions on newspapers had been eliminated in 1825 (6 Geo. 4, c. 119). The tax on pamphlets was ended in 1833 (3 & 4 Will. 4, c. 23). Also in 1833, the advertisement duty was reduced to 1s. 6d. (3 & 4 Will. 4, c. 23). Banishment as a punishment prescribed under the Seditious and Blasphemous Libels Act was abolished in 1830 (11 Geo. 4 and 1 Will. 4, c. 73).

[3] J. P. Parry has pointed out that both parties wooed the Whig-Liberals, cross-pressured between their political sentiments and their religious loyalties on the

Other partisan appeals called upon collective memory and historical analogies. Editors subjected foreign policy to historical treatment because of its susceptibility to a moral gloss. The Tories' need to balance stability often conflicted with the Whigs' desire to foster liberty. The Whigs accused the Tories of collaboration with tyrants on the Continent. The Tories, on the other hand, alleged that the Whigs conspired with European radicals and revolutionaries. Whigs and Radicals attacked the foreign policy of Wellington. The Tories claimed Whigs' support of the July Revolution in France smacked of "Jacobinism." Whig journals devoted much attention to the moral dimension of foreign and colonial policy. The *Leeds Mercury* advised its readers to consider carefully how a Tory Government ought to act for the *"moral and religious improvement* of West Indies labourers?"[4]

The Reform Bill debate and the Tamworth Manifesto stimulated discussion of the question whether the Government should embark on a wide range of domestic reforms. In 1834, two years after the First Reform Act, the Tory leader Sir Robert Peel announced to his constituents in the borough of Tamworth a program of cautious policy innovation. For the first time a parliamentary leader felt obliged to address a deliberative question before a mass audience. Politicians and editors had hitherto

---

issues of the funding of the Irish Catholic college at Maynooth, Church of Ireland endowments, religious education, and Irish Church disestablishment. See J. P. Parry, *Democracy and Religion: Gladstone and the Liberal Party, 1867–1875* (Cambridge, 1986), pp. 16–46. For a discussion of liberal Anglicanism and its internal tensions, see Richard Brent, *Liberal Anglican Politics: Whiggery, Religion, and Reform, 1830–1841* (Oxford, 1987), pp. 19–64. For a discussion of religious influences on voting behavior, see Kenneth Wald, *Crosses on the Ballot: Patterns of British Voting Alignment Since 1885* (Princeton, 1983), pp. 162–201.

[4] *Leeds Mercury*, 20 December 1834. Slavery was a salient issue in the 1830 election as well; see Charles C. F. Greville, *The Greville Memoirs, 1814–1860*, ed. Lytton Strachey and Roger Fulford (London, 1938) 2:30. On anti-slavery appeals, see James Walvin, "The Propaganda of Anti-Slavery," in *Slavery and British Society, 1776–1846* (London, 1982), pp. 49–68; Seymour Drescher, *Capitalism and Anti-slavery: British Mobilization in Comparative Perspective* (London, 1986); Christine Bolt and Seymour Drescher, *Antislavery, Religion, and Reform: Essays in Memory of Roger Anstey* (Folkestone, England, 1980). Richard Brent describes the internal tensions within the anti-slavery movement between Anglicans and Nonconformists in *Liberal Anglican Politics*, pp. 252–300.

courted public opinion on a moral basis. Voting was a spiritual and patriotic obligation rather than self-interested behavior. The Whiggish *Morning Chronicle* still spoke of the "sacred duty" of electors to discharge their franchise in 1835. Tamworth was a fundamental step away from laudatory electoral politics in Britain because it dispensed with retrospective scrutiny. Thenceforward, prospective assessment gradually eclipsed retrospection.[5] Peel demanded "the most unconstitutional thing that can ever be imagined," said the *Leeds Mercury*. He hoped the people would give the Ministry "not an implicit confidence but a fair trial."[6]

Before Tamworth, even the Radicals often framed their appeals in retrospective terms. One London Radical on 1834 proclaimed that "a constituency could not have half so substantial a pledge of a man's future as the pledge of his past conduct . . . and if a man's conduct could not be trusted, it was in vain in trusting his words." *The Times,* in its brief Whiggish phase, also praised retrospective scrutiny. The people are "neither ungrateful nor capricious, whatever their Conservative libelers say to the contrary." Their knowledge and understanding of their "friends" was guided by "an unerring instinct." Those whom "they have once supported, and who never betrayed them, they will never betray or desert."[7] The *Standard* conveyed the Tory view of the elector's role in the political process: "Every man has a tribunal in his own breast" called "into active and authoritative exercise" when an elector acted in his political capacity. The day would come, said the *Standard,* when each elector would think "a No Tory cry or a Reform cry, or a No Church cry, a sorry plea for having done his best to prostrate the altars of the deity by aiding a contingent of blacklegs and swindlers."[8]

After Tamworth, politicians and editors appealed increasingly to the electors' self-interest. Such appeals were often condemned

---

[5] *Morning Chronicle,* 7 January 1835. Peel adopted "new language" towards the Reform Bill between its passage and Tamworth; see Lawrence Peel, *A Sketch of the Life and Character of Sir Robert Peel* (London, 1860), pp. 258–59.

[6] *Leeds Mercury,* 20 December 1834; *The Times,* 18 December 1834.

[7] The London Radical is quoted in *The Times,* 10 December 1832; subsequent quotations are from ibid., 19 November 1832.

[8] London *Standard,* 8 January 1835.

as "pledging." Virtual representation in Parliament presumed a Member would bring superior judgment and moral perspective to bear upon legislation without interference from uninformed constituents. Pledging seemed an unwarranted limitation on virtual representation. Extracting pledges from many candidates might bind Parliament without allowing for contingencies. As *The Times* stated it, a candidate pledged "chin-deep" was unworthy of confidence. Such a candidate would "take the mob for his preceptors." This would stultify the "ancient, wise and invaluable arrangement of the public business," established to guard against "headlong impulse and precipitancy." Any candidate "who voluntarily puts a gag in his own mouth and a chain upon his own free agency must be an improvident blockhead."[9] In a letter to *The Times*, "CONSERVATIVE" bemoaned Reform candidates who "pledged themselves to oppose the present Ministry without reference to their Measures." *The Times* blamed party spirit. "It is virtually saying that the interests of the community at large should be sacrificed at the shrine of party." To "CONSERVATIVE," a representative acted as the supporter and protector of his community's interests. "Party spirit" had Bolingbrokian connotations: the letter questioned whether anyone pledged to oppose a Government on strictly partisan terms was acting "in the spirit of true patriotism."[10]

A candidate who refused to pledge himself proclaimed his "independence"; the term's connotations depended very much on the context. According to R. D. Rees, there were many varieties: "independence from an aristocratic patron, independence of the ministers; of parliamentary connections"; it could also connote independence of the electors themselves. An independent might be one who possessed a "private income large enough to allow a candidate to win his seat by his own efforts and to ignore mercenary inducements."[11]

The controversy over pledging and independence faded away as the norms of candidate behavior changed. Religious conflicts

---

[9] *The Times,* 27 November 1832

[10] Ibid., 5 January 1835.

[11] R. D. Rees, "Electioneering Ideals Current in South Wales, 1790–1832," *Welsh Historical Review* 2 (1965): 236.

proved more durable: those between Anglicans and non-Anglicans reinforced party cleavage lines for most of the nineteenth century. This passage from the *Leeds Mercury* epitomized the Whig reaction to "Church and King" appeals long favored in Tory election contests.

> The cry which the Tories are raising, to answer their purposes at the Coming Election is—"*The Church is in danger!*" This is the bugbear with which they are trying to frighten members of the Establishment, in the hopes of making them run and hide their heads in the lap of Toryism . . . This was the cry which was raised at intervals during a hundred and thirty years, whenever it was proposed to repeal the odious Test and Corporation Act[12]

This Whiggish historical gloss was familiar to partisans. Tales of historical excesses and injustices reappeared many times in many forms for over a century. Whig newspapers exploited these ancient injuries in a regular fashion.[13]

In a similar style the Conservative *Standard* linked Radical candidates with the excesses of the French Revolution. "The motto of Hobhouse and Bailie," said the *Standard,* is " 'No Church.' " There is but one step further; but though we tremble to write it, it is an inevitable step, that step which was taken in the French Revolution. From 'No Church,' men pass inevitably to 'no God.'[14] *The Times* advised electors to withhold their support from candidates who would not publicly avow "the religious and political connections of this Protestant state." Voters must set their faces "like a flint" against "political atheism." The same issue of *The Times* published an advertisement with explicit scriptural references.

> CHRISTIAN ELECTORS! Almighty God hath declared "righteousness exalteth a nation, but sin is a reproach to any people."—Prov. xiv.34.

[12] *Leeds Mercury,* 13 December 1834.

[13] According to Parry, "Wherever it appeared in Europe and North America between the 1780s and 1914, the liberal movement took the form of an assault on the influence wielded by allegedly exclusive and corrupt régimes. These régimes were condemned because of their intimate alliance with particular religious agencies, the discrimination enforced between favoured and unfavoured religions, and the penalties of the unfavoured." Parry, *Democracy and Religion,* p. 16.

[14] London *Standard,* 6 January 1835.

Judge then whether they who disregard the Divine Word can be fitting legislators for our country. The blessing of God they cannot expect. Choose therefore "men such as fear God: men of truth, hating covetousness." Exod. xviii.21. "Meddle not with them that are given to change." Prov. xxiv.21.[15]

Religiously directed appeals, for Whigs and Conservatives alike, tapped a durable set of shared values and defined an adversary in a tangible fashion. Whigs focused moral indignation on Tory intolerance and abuses by the Church of England, Wales, and especially Ireland. Conservatives attacked Erastians, Nonconformists, and Radicals who subverted the beliefs and independence of the Established Church.[16] By exaggerating the invidious motives of the adversary and by using hyperbolic language, these appeals created a sense of urgency.

Partisan appeals built upon this confessional cleavage, exploiting collective historical memories of Anglicans and non-Anglicans alike. A typical editorial described first a grievance, usually one that had existed over a very long time. These appeals clearly, if not always accurately, identified the perpetrators of historical grievances and linked them with contemporary political adversaries. The *Morning Post* saw the struggle in the 1835 election as one between "Monarchy and Republicanism." The *Post* charged that "the 'Liberal' Holy Alliance" was laboring to overthrow anything that opposed the establishment of "a furious democracy." If every Dissenter "from the high-flown Calvanist [*sic*] to the cold-hearted Unitarian" combined with these democratic "infidels," then the "wolves" would "devour each other."[17]

Conservative, Whig, and Radical appeals obliquely exploited class antagonisms[18] and often traced a consistent theme of wrong-

[15] *The Times*, 6 January 1835.

[16] Boyd Hilton, *The Age of Atonement: The Influence of Evangelicalism on Social and Economic Thought, 1795–1865* (Oxford, 1988), p. 203–51; Parry, *Democracy and Religion*, pp. 16–25.

[17] *Morning Post*, 8 January 1835.

[18] Asa Briggs, "The Language of Class in Early Nineteenth-Century England," in *Essays in Labour History*, ed. Asa Briggs and John Saville (London, 1967), pp. 43–73; also Stedman Jones, "Rethinking Chartism," in *Languages of Class*, pp. 90–178.

doing. The *Leeds Mercury* published the following diatribe condemning the intrigues of "the Aristocracy" against "the People."

> It is the TORY ARISTOCRACY declaring war against THE PEOPLE OF ENGLAND! . . . *Will the daring experiment succeed?* YES—IF THE PEOPLE WILL ALLOW IT,—IF the garrison should sleep, and let the enemy carry their citadel by *coup de main,*—IF the thundering of the "Great Captain" at their gates make them shiver and quake: *in that case* he will march in *sword in hand,* and treat them as they deserve!—NO—*If the People are true to themselves,* if British electors are MEN,—if the Reformers of England, Scotland and Ireland joining hands, and swearing *indissoluble union* till the common enemy is vanquished tell the KING, from all their cities, towns and villages that they are *true to the cause which has made his reign glorious and send such Representatives as will use the same language in Parliament.*[19]

*The Times* itself employed the Whiggish theme of resistance to oppression when it championed Reform in 1832. "Reform will achieve a victory or suffer a defeat,—when liberty must triumph, or be trampled in the dust,—when you shall dare to record your votes in favor of freedom against oppression, or prove you still remain the slaves of custom." *The Times* almost seems to have adopted the militant tone of Cobbett in this passage: "Tyrants shall look on and tremble, when they see united freemen,—not tamely possessing rights—but actively using them in the best interests of humanity, by nobly supporting a single man struggling to be free—fighting his own and their battle—opposed by a host in arms against him."[20]

Militant rhetoric persisted throughout the 1830s, particularly in the unstamped press. In the 1830s the "great unstamped" played a very significant role in extending political information to the unenfranchised classes. The unstamped editors proved instrumental in changing the dominant form of political discourse, and in their journals hortatory rhetoric reached its apogee.

Parliamentary reform agitation gave Cobbett and Henry Hetherington the opportunity to resume their unstamped journals. Heth-

---

[19] *Leeds Mercury,* 22 November 1834. The "Great Captain" is Wellington.
[20] *The Times,* 8 December 1832.

erington's *Poor Man's Guardian, Cobbett's Weekly Register,* and the *Working Man's Friend,* among others, sought to disseminate political news to working-class readers. For Radicals like Cobbett and Hetherington, the source of political inspiration lay in Jacksonian America.[21] The unstamped journals often cited the Jacksonian Democrats as a model for action in their struggle for "Equal Rights" and against "Aristocracy." American editorials sometimes appeared verbatim in the unstamped newspapers, such as this editorial appearing in the *Poor Man's Guardian,* lifted directly from the New York *Mercantile Advertiser.*

> The Janus headed opposition are fighting to perpetuate a monied aristocracy, an odious monopoly, which threatens to subvert our liberties and dissolve the union.

> Fellow Citizens!—Shall General Jackson, the true and tried friend of the people, be your President; or shall the Bank of the United States make us the slaves of a purse-proud aristocracy? Fellow-citizens, hurry to the polls, and let your votes decide.[22]

Hetherington's *Poor Man's Guardian* not only emulated, but defended the "declamatory" style of political language employed by the Jacksonians in America. The *Poor Man's Guardian* launched a vehement attack on *The Times* for its disparaging description of "the declamatory style in which the American politicians indulge."

> So it is "*declamation*" to rouse the citizens of America to defend their rights—their liberties—their lives—the happy independence of their wives and children—every thing dear to human nature, from the relentless grasp of monied aristocracy—"*declamation!*" to guard the Republican youth of America from the fangs of that class ... "*declamation!*"—to expose those enemies of God and man, that have in all countries and in all ages combined with priestcraft for the enslavement of mankind!—Oh! fellow countrymen! had you but studied the history of usurers, as we have, you would soon see that it is to this class that we owe the destruction of all popular gov-

---

[21] E. P. Thompson, *Making of the English Working Class,* pp. 728, 751; also Cole, *Life of Cobbett,* pp. 388–406.

[22] *Poor Man's Guardian,* 8 December 1832.

ernments, and the assassination of all philanthropists since the beginning of the world.[23]

The Conservatives responded to the hortatory rhetoric of the Radicals. Their rhetoric sought to redirect some of the Radicals' vehemence back on themselves by depicting them as "Revolutionists" or "Destructives" and by castigating the Whigs as untrustworthy. "What must we call those Whigs," asked *The Times* in 1835, "who coalesce with revolutionists whom they before hated and resisted," in the hope that "through such a foul combination they may regain possession of Downing Street?" *The Times* relied on the king to do his duty. As long as an "atom of kingly power exists," said *The Times*, "the Destructives never can get possession of *office*."[24] The Whiggish *Globe* responded that "the title of Destructives would soon cease to be dreaded by Reformers, and that we should see the most moderate politicians putting forth their claims to support in election addresses as *Rational Destructives*." The name of "*Revolutionist* seems to obtain preference with our Tory friends as a less digestible designation for all Reformers."[25]

*The Times* referred to a large body of "malignants" who composed "the dregs—numerous and copious we acknowledge them to be—of those who call themselves the *Dissenting Body*." These "agitating Dissenters" were distinguished from the religious Dissenters, the former being "restless, ambitious, pushing, babbling termagants." The unprincipled agitation which beset the country was the work of these Nonconformists. "Those assuming the pet name of Reformers" would "trample the church under the hoof" of the

---

[23] Ibid. As late as 1835, the *Poor Man's Guardian* was using the traditional Shakespearean quote to introduce an antithetical comparison, "Look on this Picture! . . . And on this!" On the influence of the United States on the British, see David Paul Crook, *American Democracy in English Politics, 1815–1850* (Oxford, 1965); Henry Pelling, *America and the British Left, From Bright to Bevan* (London, 1956), pp. 1–4; Koss, *Political Press,* 1:55; Patricia Hollis, *The Pauper Press: A Study in Working Class Radicalism of the 1830s* (Oxford, 1970), p. ix; Stanley Harrison, *Poor Man's Guardians: A Record of the Struggle for a Democratic Newspaper Press, 1763–1973* (London, 1974), p. 79; Joel H. Wiener, *The War of the Unstamped: The Movement to Repeal the British Newspaper Tax, 1830–1836* (Ithaca, N.Y., 1969), pp. 211–13.

[24] *The Times,* 1 January 1835.

[25] London, *Globe,* 10 January 1835.

"voluntary principle" and would "reconstruct for William IV the same scaffold on which King Charles fell." *The Times* linked these radicals with the Puritan Roundheads and admonished "the people" to refrain from acting "with that fickle love of alteration with which the Puritans are accused in *Hudibras*—'As if the Senate was intended/For nothing else but to be mended.' "[26] *The Times* also invoked the specter of Revolutionary France. "The substitution of a voluntary principle for an established Church and in politics, of a savage republic for a constitutional monarchy, are the avowed idols," of the Radicals, "these breathing nuisances."[27] The *Standard* was more vehement in its effort to link Whigs and Radicals with the French Revolution. "We know what the French Revolution did to a whole people; but we know, also, that the shopkeeper class, who were the authors of that Revolution, were the most grievous sufferers by it." The *Poor Man's Guardian* published an equally shrill defense of the French Revolution entitled, "VINDICATION OF ROBESPIERRE'S MEMORY FROM THE CHARGES OF CORRESPONDENTS.— THE FRENCH 'TERRORISTS' PROVED TO HAVE BEEN REAL FRIENDS OF CIVILIZATION AND THE PEOPLE."[28]

Controversy over free trade in the 1840s revived the popular debate over policy. Along with confessional divisions, the conflict over repeal of the Corn Laws introduced hortatory appeals into the protectionist and free trade debate. At the same time, the Anti-Corn Law League formulated deliberative questions for a mass audience.[29] In the Corn Law controversy, the parties found it necessary to address themselves to a single issue: free trade.

Older themes intruded into the contest, however, and partisan editors found themselves in increasingly heated exchanges. "THE CRISIS HAS COME!" exclaimed the *Cambridge Independent Press* on the eve of the 1841 election. The approaching contest was more

---

[26] *The Times*, 17 December 1832.

[27] Ibid.

[28] London *Standard*, 6 January 1835; *Poor Man's Guardian*, 22 December 1832.

[29] Norman McCord has referred to the League as "one of the first examples of a recurring feature of modern political life, the highly organized political pressure group with its centralized administration and its formidable propaganda apparatus." Norman McCord, *The Anti-Corn Law League, 1838–1846* (London, 1958), pp. 163, 187.

important than any event since "the great revolution of 1688." The present struggle, according to the *Globe,* was not one of personal ambition or a party contest; "it is a fight for life or death between the people and monopolies."[30] If the Conservatives were to gain power, said the *Cambridge Independent Press,* the "white ensign" of "political regeneration" would no longer wave but would be replaced by the "black flag of Tory misrule and oppression" which would fly over "our crushed and prostrated liberties." Sir Robert Peel would revive "the worn-out remnant of Bourbon tyranny," Don Miguel of Portugal "would gloat over fresh atrocities." King Carlos of Spain would "shed more blood in anticipation" while the "autocrat of Russia and the despot of Austria" would "boast of a connecting link with English principles and English freedom."[31]

The rhetorical call to duty sometimes emphasized both a "sacred" obligation and a partisan obligation. The *Standard* framed this election appeal with references to individual responsibility.

Let men remember what are the interests at stake, and dependent upon every elector's *individual* conduct, and the *individual* conduct of every one who can by fair and honourable means influence an election. It is never to be forgotten that in such cases . . . all electors have an equal right, an equal weight and an equal duty. Let them remember the interests at stake are the commerce of the country, the national honour, the happiness of the poor, and the *Protestant Reformed religion.* The decision of London is all-important to the country elections and therefore, let the Londoners do their duty.[32]

Deliberative questions, set off by a juxtaposition of policy positions, came into favor in the free trade controversy. Before 1841, antithesis usually emphasized moral rather than policy contrasts. The *Leeds Mercury* published the following set of graphic policy contrasts between the Whigs and the Opposition.

[30] *Cambridge Independent Press,* 12 June 1841; *Globe,* 30 June 1841.
[31] *Cambridge Independent Press,* 12 June 1841.
[32] *Standard,* 25 June 1841.

| EFFECTS OF REMOVING MONOPOLIES | EFFECTS OF UPHOLDING MONOPOLIES |
|---|---|
| 1. Lighter Taxes. | 1. Heavier Taxes. |
| 2. An ample Revenue. | 2. A falling Revenue. |
| 3. Improved condition of the people. | 3. Increased distress. |
| 4. Future reduction of Taxes. | 4. Future addition to Taxes. |
| 5. Extended Foreign Trade. | 5. Diminished Foreign Trade.[33] |

For the *Morning Chronicle,* the most damning charge against the Peelite coalition was that Peel did not *have* a policy. The Conservatives were "identified with no great antagonistic principle or policy; they are only impediments or obstructives in the way of carrying out a policy which they cannot counteract." Their course was merely the "negation" of the "great national good of a freed trade and commerce."[34] The *Globe* said that party unity was comparatively easy among Conservatives, owing to the limited range of subjects they discussed. "Their election addresses often touch on at most two or three topics, wrapping up the rest in vague cloudy assurances of Conservative principles."[35]

Deliberative slogans came to play an important role in British politics. The Whig-Radical coalition rallied around the cry "No Monopoly!" and "Free Trade!" Deliberative slogans replaced emblematic slogans of the early nineteenth century such as "Church and King!" "No Tories," and "No Popery!" The *Leeds Mercury* linked candidates' names with deliberative slogans. "MOR-PETH & MILTON" were associated with "Cheaper Sugar, Better Timber, Cheaper Bread, Fuller Employment, and Freer Commerce." Their opponents in the West Riding, on the other hand, "WOR-TLEY & DENISON," were connected to "Fresh Taxes, The present Monopolies, High Import Duties, The Corn Law, and Diminished Trade."[36] The ultra-Conservative *Standard* said that the "favorite rallying-cry" of the Peelite Government was "*No Monopoly!*" The *Standard* provided ultra-Conservative definitions for Radical and Peelite reform slogans.

---

[33] *Leeds Mercury,* 26 June 1841.
[34] London *Morning Chronicle,* 14 June 1841.
[35] *Globe,* 9 July 1841.
[36] *Leeds Mercury,* 19 June 1841.

What extent of meaning is really attachable to this vague and vulgar rant, cannot be a matter of uncertainty. When accurately analysed, it presents us with the following results:—"No agricultural protection"—down with landlords and farmers. "No sectarian preferences"—down with Bishops and the Church. "No machinery patents"—down with the rights of genius. "No medical corporations"—down with exclusive diplomas. "No privileged lawyers"—down with accredited practitioners. "No magisterial superiority"—down with mayors and justices. "No aristocratic distinctions"—down with peerage and throne.[37]

Addressing deliberative questions, hortatory electioneering discovered new ways to stir public interest. Newspapers sold election supplements to inform electors about issues and political events. A *Leeds Mercury* supplement described the 1841 contest as "one of the most exciting weeks which the town of Leeds has witnessed for many years back." Party flags flew from private houses and public buildings, many with slogans printed on them. The *Mercury* described the slogans on the orange Liberal flags: "All for each," "Freedom to all," "Each for all," "Trade and Industry," "Hume and Aldam, [Liberal candidates for Leeds] the poor man's friends," "National greatness is never achieved so long as commerce is fettered—Free Trade," "Let Monopoly Perish and the People Flourish," "On to Victory," "The People's Cause," "North Ward Reformers," and "Cursed is the man who taketh a bribe, and may he know the want of bread." The *Mercury* itself displayed an elaborate flag with the slogans "Free Trade—Plenty and Prosperity" and "Let us all be one people—Down with Monopoly." In almost every street, "numerous flags were hoisted in front of shops, private houses and inns, and Liberal Orange far outnumbered those of Conservative Blue. Among the former, one of humble size contained the following noble sentiment, 'Not men but principles.' "[38]

The *Mercury* also described the Conservative blue flags in Leeds. These flags bore such slogans as "V. R. [*Victoria Regina*]—Beckett and Jocelyn [Conservative candidates for Leeds]—National ruin

---

[37] *Standard*, 26 June 1841.
[38] *Leeds Mercury*, 3 July 1841.

must follow, when the legislature promotes the interest of one class at the expense of others," "Pro Rege, Lege and Grege" over a representation of the crown, the Bible, and the scepter, "A refuge not a prison for the poor," "Defeat the defamer of the fair," "The Queen, the Nobles and the People," "Vote without fear or favour," "Britons be true," "Performance and not professions," "Open the borough," and several with symbolic embellishments, such as one that had "V. R." lettered above a crown with the slogan "and a better ministry." Another symbolic ensign displayed the slogan "Church and State" flown on a pole headed by a battle-axe.[39] The parties' slogans combined older generic expressions and newer specific language on policy. The symbols, on the other hand—the crown, the Bible, the scepter, and even the battle-axe—borrowed the mythic iconography of church and state.

Compared to the 1841 election, the 1847 election was a rather muted contest. Peel's sponsorship of repeal of the Corn Laws and the Irish Coercion Bill hampered the Conservative attack on the Government. Repeal of the Corn Laws not only resulted in the split of the Conservatives but also meant that the Liberals lost their most effective issue. The Liberal *Morning Chronicle* called the election a struggle for "civil and religious liberty." This slogan reminded Nonconformist electors of Tory appeals to "bigotry." "Would a Dissenter give a lift to a candidate who abhors the first principles of religious liberty, and whose sole political stock in trade is a holy horror of 'Jews and Papists?' No honest Nonconformist could reconcile his civic and social responsibilities by supporting a 'No Popery' zealot and 'High Church exclusionist.' "[40]

One *Standard* editorial combined two prevalent Tory themes. The appeal paid homage to the Bolingbrokian vision of a unitary "Country" interest arising to combat corruption and faction: "There will be but one party having any principle of permanent cohesion, namely 'the Country party'—or, as it may be described by other words, 'the Protestant and Protectionist party.' " It also

---

[39] Ibid.

[40] London *Morning Chronicle,* 29 July 1847. McCord says that after 1846 fear of "a reimposition of protection kept the Liberals more or less united, but it was impossible to conceal the deep-rooted divisions of the party." See *Anti-Corn Law League,* p. 212.

castigated the "motley rabble of Romanists, Infidels, Peelites, Free-traders, Chartists, and Repealers, who designate themselves by the common name of 'Liberals.' "[41]

The name-calling and vituperation reappeared in the 1852 election, when divisions between the parties were along free-trade and religious lines. The election was fought by means of three different rhetorical strategies. For the Liberals and their allies, the election was a referendum on free trade and the past performance of the Liberal governing coalition. Peelites stressed the benefits of free trade and discussed little else. The Derbyites had little incentive to bring up the issue of protection after the obvious success of Corn Law repeal. These ultra-Conservatives found it expedient to raise the religious and cultural issues that defined for Tories what it meant to be English. The *Standard* proclaimed "the really religious nature" of the 1852 election: "Christian Protestantism" opposed "infidelity and Romanism." Referring to Baron Rothschild, a Liberal candidate for the City, it said, "The religious war has begun characteristically in the great fortress of *Jew* infidelity, the City of London, the *Dove Cote* of stock jobbers, loan mongers, usurers, and 'old clothes' men."[42]

Religious education figured as an important issue in 1852 for both Liberals and Conservatives. The Liberal *Bristol Gazette* inquired whether "those clergymen entertaining evangelical principles," and "the Dissenters generally," would "support a Government which would hand over the religious teaching to the uncontrolled management of Tractarians and Popish Bishops and Parsons?" The *Gazette* drew a series of antithetical comparisons between Liberal candidates and their Conservative opponents.

> The *former* are for progression, the *latter* for stagnation. The *former* are for extending the privileges of the people, the *latter* are for contracting them. The *former* are for throwing open wide the gates of the Constitution, the *latter* are for shutting them. The *former* are for Civil and Religious Liberty, the *latter* are against it. The *former* are for unlimited freedom of Trade and Commerce, the *latter* are for "modifying, mitigating, reversing it." The *former* gave us cheap

[41] *Standard,* 9 August 1847.
[42] Ibid., 7 July 1852.

Sugar, the *latter* are for taking it from us. The *former* took off the timber duties, the *latter* are for reimposing them. The *former* abrogated the shipowners' monopoly, the *latter* seek to restore it.[43]

The Conservative candidate for Bristol responded in the same issue of the *Gazette,* announcing his determination to uphold "the Protestant Institutions of the Empire, and to guard the religion of this Protestant country."[44] The *Globe* blamed the ultra-Conservatives for the resurgence of religious issues over more important trade policies. The Tories "have played the mutes to Protection; they have played the resurrection-men to Protestantism."[45] But Liberal newspapers were also very guilty of injecting religious issues into the 1852 election.[46]

The newspapers in London were close enough to Westminster to feel the changes in nuance articulated by party leaders. At the same time, London constituted a testing ground for shifts in public opinion. After more than a decade of controversy on free trade, *The Times* declared the issue was dead in the 1852 election. It called upon its readers to "let the triumph of free trade be loud, clear and decisive, so that the question may be set at rest forever."[47]

The victory of the Liberals and Peelites in 1852 set the stage for the repeal of the "taxes on knowledge." Final assault on the taxes began the next year under the Aberdeen government. The new chancellor, William Gladstone, announced that he would "be delighted to see the day when the duty on newspapers might be reduced," but he doubted whether that day had yet arrived in 1853. Benjamin Disraeli, the shadow chancellor, agreed that the advertisement duty should be eliminated. Thomas Milner-Gibson moved for its repeal on April 14, 1853.[48]

---

[43] *Bristol Gazette,* 8 July 1852.

[44] Ibid.

[45] London, *Globe,* 7 July 1852.

[46] See, for example, the salience of the religious issue in the *Bristol Gazette,* 8 July 1852, described above.

[47] *The Times,* 5 July 1852.

[48] H. R. Fox Bourne, *English Newspapers: Chapters in the History of Journalism* (London, 1887), 2:216; George Macaulay Trevelyan, *The Life of John Bright* (London, 1913) pp. 212–14.

On July 1, 1853, Gladstone restructured his budget to favor a complete elimination of the advertisement duty rather than an abatement of the tax on supplements. On July 20, Gladstone noted in his diary that the Government "made a holocaust of the Advt. Duty." In May 1854, Milner-Gibson introduced another motion, so cautiously worded that there was no division. The laws "in reference to the provincial press are ill defined and unequally enforced"; the resolution called for the subject to receive "the early attention of Parliament." The stamp duty expired on June 15, 1855, without much fanfare. After "years of attention to the subject," John Bright was convinced that "never was so large a measure involved in a small measure, so to speak," the case "for making the press free."[49]

By the late 1850s, no fewer than 120 MPs supported the abolition of the paper duty. Gladstone put forward a bill in 1860 which failed to pass the House of Lords. Gladstone incorporated the measure into the budget and the paper duty died on October 1, 1860.[50]

Ironically, the end of the stamp duties marked the end of direct American influence on British political rhetoric. Even before the repeal of the Corn Laws, the influence of the unstamped press had begun to wane. At the same time, however, the hortatory rhetoric preserved by Cobbett and Hetherington carried over into the stamped press during the Anti-Corn Law agitation. The middle class imbibed the emphatic slogans and stark contrasts that had adorned the pages of the unstamped press in earlier decades. But the major parties devised their own style of hortatory electioneering.

With the end of the taxes on knowledge, the press established greater independence from political parties. An editor no longer conceived of his newspaper as an "organ" of a political party but something closer, in Stephen Koss's words, to an "appendage." Favored journals continued to be subsidized in this period, but

---

[49] Gladstone, *Diaries*, 4:543; Koss, *Political Press*, 1:66, 68; Bourne, *English Newspapers*, 2:218–19; *Hansard Parliamentary Debates*, 3d ser., vol. 138, (March 19, 1855), pp. 810–11.

[50] James Grant, *The Newspaper Press: Its Origin, Progress, and Present Position* (London, 1871), 2:317–20; Koss, *Political Press*, 1:69.

circulation and advertising provided more revenue than subsidies. In the 1850s, the relationship between party and press was more one of manipulation than of coercion.[51]

In the 1850s, with the number of electors still very limited, both parties employed hortatory language, not mobilizing support for new policies as in the Corn Law controversy, but reinforcing earlier voting habits based on religious and regional cleavages. At a time when the parliamentary parties showed great instability, individual members maintained their majorities by appealing to old prejudices in a new form. The great division of British politics and society, between Anglo-Saxons and Celts, Anglicans and non-Anglicans, offered Liberals, Peelites, and Conservatives predictable support.

At the end of the 1850s, in both Britain and the United States, old party values had broken down. In Britain, the parliamentary parties likewise disintegrated but the old party values sustained individual members' majorities in election contests. The parliamentary parties dissolved in coalition and reemerged a new form. Conservative cries of "Protection" and "Protestantism" and Liberal-Peelite shouts of "Free Trade" and "Civil and Religious Liberty" reinforced old values in a new vehement style. The result was the preservation of consistency in popular politics and the sanctioning of mass prejudice.

Nathaniel Hawthorne made a perceptive comparison in 1858 of the different emphasis the English and Americans placed on parliamentary discourse. The English scheme of government requires its Cabinet members "should be orators, and the readiest and most fluent orators that can be found."

And it is only tradition and old custom, founded on an obsolete state of things, that assigns any value to parliamentary oratory. The world has done with it, except as an intellectual pastime. The speeches have no effect till they are converted into newspaper paragraphs; and they had better be composed as such, in the first

---

[51] Koss, *Political Press*, 1:411.

place, and oratory reserved for churches, courts of law and public dinner tables.[52]

The end of the taxes on knowledge formalized the end of the period of limited freedom and a new political role for the press in Britain. Political orators henceforth directed their speeches to the same audience American politicians addressed: newspaper readers. Whether appealing to old prejudices or formulating new policies, political revivalists in the 1860s reinvigorated their language to reach a larger audience.

[52] Nathaniel Hawthorne, writing from Florence, July 1858, "Notes on Travel," in *The Complete Writings of Nathaniel Hawthorne* (Boston, 1888), 22:160. Quoted in part by Schlesinger, *Age of Jackson,* pp. 51–52n; also partly quoted in Jamieson and Birdsell, *Presidential Debates,* p. 69.

# CHAPTER SIX

# The Rhetorical Civil War
# in the Northern Press:
# New York, 1860–1868

By their own assumptions, or by quasi-popular consent, leading
and influential journals like our own are in some sort regarded
as watchmen on the walls, to look for approach of danger toward
what their readers hold dear. They have had thrust upon them
the duty, not always pleasant, of acting as conservators of the
public good, often at the expense of their private interests. Men
look to them not only for facts, but for opinions. They do not
often create, but they shape and give direction to public
sentiment. They are the narrators of facts, the exponents of policy,
the enemies of wrong.

*Chicago Daily Tribune*

T he uncertainties facing the United States in the election
of 1860 and in the two elections thereafter made the
political values of the antebellum years less compelling.
Moral exhortation did play a prominent role in the election of
1860; Abraham Lincoln's Cooper Union speech is a fine example.[1]
Exhortation works best, however, in a period of moral certainty.
Already in 1860, the imminent peril of the Union weakened
appeals to the older political values. Familiarity seemed inappropri-
ate. In a time of crisis editors and politicians returned to formality:

[1] Lincoln, *Complete Works*, 5:293–328.

they relied upon voters' existing political attachments and appealed to their sense of responsibility. Exhortation gave way to instruction. Civil War rhetoric often used events as a dramatic backdrop for warning partisans of the consequences of failing to vote.

Editors during the Civil War often allowed events to speak for themselves. Newspapers in this troubled and anxious period were the augurs of the Union: battles served as political portents. By ordering and interpreting wartime events—as "narrators of facts"—journalists wielded a powerful persuasive weapon. At the same time, journalists concentrated less on politics. Electioneering had a lower priority in the Union and in much of the Confederacy political contests had a muted tone. The war transformed the political rhetoric of the republic and brought at last a kind of hollow uniformity to both sides after the conflict. In the election of 1860 and during the war years, the Union and Confederacy spoke to different concerns and confronted different necessities. Even among northern newspapers, the wartime need for uniformity subdued some of the previous rhetorical excesses of Republicans and Democrats.

An exception to this generalization occurred in New York, where important newspapers served a very wide array of political sympathies from Radical Republicans to Conservative Democrats. New York was not the only city that witnessed fierce rhetorical exchanges during the 1860s, but it was a cauldron of clashing politics, war aims, and journalistic competition. New York thus seems a particularly appropriate arena in which to examine Civil War political rhetoric away from the immediate intrusion of the war itself.

Journalists' concentration on their role as narrators began well before the onset of war. Nevertheless, the Civil War drove home to northern editors the importance of news events in stimulating circulaton. The outbreak of hostilities created a demand for accurate information about the war. Instantaneous communications facilitated the transmission of war reports. The belligerents spoke the same language, and both sides in the conflict permitted the press a wide latitude. Publishers determined to make this conflict as vivid as possible for the reader at home.

War correspondents reported firsthand from the battle front. Between 1861 and 1865, James Gordon Bennett of the *New York Herald* paid out between $500,000 and $750,000 for war news. New methods of lithography permitted the publication of maps and vivid illustrations, which brought war to the home front as never before.[2] Headlines "packaged" the newsworthy event and put an interpretive gloss on it. Journalists interpreted the news within the framework of so-called objective reporting; editorials, in the *Chicago Tribune*'s words, did not create public opinion but shaped it and gave it direction.[3]

Not merely by according primacy to events did the Civil War profoundly affect politics. The war produced a new mechanism of mass mobilization. After Fort Sumter, editors North and South fixed as never before on the metaphors of war. The imagery of war had always been a part of political rhetoric. Fascination with the military had already intruded on the ritual aspects of American political culture: antebellum parties had adopted military formations, uniforms, and nomenclature.[4] Editorials before 1860 often drew analogies between political and military "victories," and between the victorious generals on the field of war and their subsequent "triumphs" in political "campaigns." Editors during the Civil War, however, stepped up the vehemence of their attacks. They stirred voters' hatred for their partisan "enemies." Newspapers frequently admonished voters not to lose at the ballot box the victories won on the battlefield.

[2] Bennett's priorities were summarized by one of his correspondents: "To obtain the most accurate information by personal observation, and forward it with utmost dispatch, regardless of expense, labor or danger." D. P. Conyngham, *Sherman's March through the South* (New York, 1865), p. 6. Bennett spent a record $1,275 on telegraphic dispatches in one week in August 1860. See Douglas Fermer, *James Gordon Bennett and the "New York Herald": A Study of Editorial Opinion in the Civil War Era, 1854–1867* (New York, 1986), p. 140; J. Cutler Andrews, *The North Reports the Civil War* (Pittsburgh, Pa., 1955), p. 641; J. Cutler Andrews, *The South Reports the Civil War* (Princeton, 1970), p. 516; Frederic Hudson, *Journalism in the United States from 1690 to 1872* (New York, 1873), pp. 483, 717; James L. Crouthamel, "James Gordon Bennett and Sensationalism," pp. 294–316.

[3] Schudson, *Discovering the News*, pp. 4–5.

[4] Jean H. Baker, *Affairs of Party: The Political Culture of Northern Democrats in the Mid-Nineteenth Century* (Ithaca, N.Y., 1983), pp. 261–316.

Editors were waging a rhetorical civil war in the headlines and on the editorial pages of northern newspapers, especially the New York papers. Greeley's *New-York Tribune* sympathized with the Radical wing of the Republican party. Henry J. Raymond's *New York Times* supported conservative Republicanism. The *New York World*, begun in 1860 by Alexander Cummings, started out as a religious daily. The *World* sustained heavy losses and merged with the *Courier and Inquirer*. Under the editorship of Manton Marble, the *World* became a principal voice of the Conservative wing of the Democratic party. James Gordon Bennett's *New York Herald* took a position against Lincoln in 1860 and against both Lincoln and McClellan in 1864. In 1868 the *Herald* supported the candidate Bennett had favored in 1864: Ulysses S. Grant.[5]

In 1860 journals of all persuasions announced the impending collapse of the old order. Newspapers urged preparation for the most critical election the United States had ever faced. The *New-York Tribune* called upon its readers to scrutinize every possible fraudulent voter. "Republicans! no challengers dare to do their duty unless well backed by you. Be ready, then, to stand up for fair play wherever your services may be needed." The *New York Herald* urged its readers to quell the pernicious influence of the Republicans and their threat to the Union. "Your time for deliberation is passed," the *Herald* observed. Conservatives "of all parties, creeds and classes" should devote election day "to the rescue of the Union and the constitution." The *New York Times* appealed to conservatives to vote for the Republicans. "The attitude of the Republican Party is eminently national and conservative,—and its success will do more to suppress the Slavery question than any other result."[6]

The *Herald* perceived the country as poised on the brink of revolutionary disaster, and employed a particularly vivid image to

[5] Fermer, *Bennett and the "New York Herald,"* p. 36, passim. See also Jeter A. Isely, *Horace Greeley and the Republican Party, 1853–1861* (Princeton, 1947); Harlan H. Horner, *Lincoln and Greeley* (Urbana, Ill., 1953); Meyer Berger, *The Story of the "New York Times," 1851–1951* (New York, 1951); Francis Brown, *Raymond of the "Times"*; George T. McJimsey, *Genteel Partisan: Manton Marble, 1834–1917* (Ames, Iowa, 1971).

[6] *New-York Daily Tribune*, 6 November 1860; *New York Herald*, 6 November 1860; *New York Times*, 6 November 1860.

dramatize it. "The Union is rapidly drifting to dissolution, like a canoe above the Falls of Niagara."[7] The ship of state metaphor usually celebrated strong and competent authority. In an editorial from the *Baltimore American,* however, the metaphor conveyed the incompetence of what historians later called the "blundering generation." The passage condemned "those unskillful pilots who have brought the stoutest ship of State that was ever built out of the smoothest and safest channel that ever a vessel floated in, and managed to strike her upon the only rock in the wide ocean."[8] In another editorial, the *American,* a Constitutional Unionist newspaper, declared that if Maryland voters believed "secessionism at the South is no whit less reprehensible than sectionalism at the North, then let them vote for Bell and Everett."[9] The *New York Herald* warned its readers that any "derangement" of political relations with the South would result in consigning "the ranks of our financial, commercial and manufacturing classes to bankruptcy, and the mass of our laboring population to idleness and destitution."[10]

Newspapers of all persuasions looked not only to the future, but also to the past. Historical referents offered a reassuring context in which to order the cataclysmic events of this war. The *New York World* observed a resemblance "between the temper and the tendencies of the Abolitionists in this country and the Jacobins of the French Revolution."[11] Employing the same theme for opposite ends, the *New-York Tribune* likened Southern anti-abolitionism to the worst excesses of Jacobinism. "A Reign of Terror has been created throughout the South," it said.[12] The *New York Herald* resurrected Patrick Henry for an election editorial. Not surprisingly, the Virginia firebrand urged caution on the quick. He informed *Herald* readers that he hoped all anti-Lincoln men would vote early. A group of French Jacobins appeared in this fantasy, shouting

---

[7] *New York Herald,* 30 October 1860.

[8] *Baltimore American,* 2 November 1860.

[9] Ibid., 20 October 1860.

[10] *New York Herald,* 5 November 1860.

[11] *New York World,* 27 October 1864.

[12] *New-York Daily Tribune,* 24 October 1860. The editorial continued, "The manifest intent of the dominant aristocracy of that region is to crush out every vestige of inquiry or free thought with regard to Slavery."

"Hurrah for the guillotine! Down with the government! Property is theft! Elect Lincoln! Dissolve the Union! Smash everything generally!"[13]

Editors occasionally found themselves employing historical figures from an unfamiliar perspective. The previous generation of Democratic newspapers praised Cromwell as a champion of the common man. The *New York Herald* now cast him as a usurping tyrant, analogous to Lincoln. For the Democratic journals in the North, the analogies to Cromwellian "excesses" proved particularly effective in warning their Irish Catholic readers, who nursed their own historical grievances against Cromwell.

> Thousands in Yankeedom of the lineal descendants of the followers of Cromwell have been led to believe that they have a better right to go and take possession of the South and drive out the impious slaveowners, than had their pilgrim ancestors to dispossess the aboriginal inhabitants at the North, on the ground that the land belonged to them.[14]

In "WORKMEN NOT SLAVES," the *New-York Tribune* revived the polemic against "slavery" in its eighteenth-century sense. Greeley condemned Tammany for obliging workingmen to vote Democratic without considering their individual interests and moral sensibilities. Greeley proclaimed workingmen's interests sadly betrayed by the Democratic party. "So it has come to pass in this 'free country,' " said the *Tribune*, that the man who sells his labor even at famine prices "must sell his principles with it, or starve."[15]

Biblical appeals often cropped up in Greeley's electioneering language. "Republicans of New-York! the Philistines are upon you!" said the *New-York Tribune*. "The utter desperation of their cause elsewhere impels them to more vehement exertion here." The *Tribune* warned its rural readers of Lincoln's Fusionist opponents,

---

[13] *New York Herald,* 6 November 1860.

[14] *New York Herald,* 26 October 1860. For a discussion of Cromwell as a positive referent for the North but also as a figure analogous to the Confederacy's "Stonewall" Jackson, see Terry Dopp Aamodt, "Righteous Armies, Holy Cause, Apocalyptic Imagery, and the Civil War" (diss., Boston University, 1986), pp. 105, 165–96.

[15] *New-York Daily Tribune,* 3 November 1860.

whom it likened to the biblical plague of locusts. Fusionist orators were as "thick as locusts, but they cannot seduce nor shake you!"[16]

By the time of the 1864 election, news about the war superseded political news. At the same time, journals sometimes slanted war news to serve partisan interests. Editors often insinuated their political opinions into war reportage. Democratic papers devoted much attention to the poor conduct of the war, to the number of battles lost, and the low morale of the troops. Republican newspapers published news of many a "Great Victory!" and spoke as if the war were on the verge of conclusion. Newspapers speculated about which presidential candidate the Confederates preferred: this was the ultimate negative testimonial. The Republicans claimed the Richmond government preferred McClellan because of the Democrats' "defeatist" platform. The Democrats claimed the Confederates preferred Lincoln because his war aims were unrealistically "revolutionary."

The *New York Herald,* which did not endorse a candidate in 1864, scathingly described this editorial wrangling: "If we may believe the democratic journals," said the *Herald,* Lincoln's reelection would produce "an absolute military despotism established over us; we shall have another draft, a war of extermination against the South for negro emancipation, a doubling of our federal taxes, a collapse of the federal treasury, a grand financial revulsion, universal bankruptcy" and "other horrible misfortunes too numerous to mention." The *Herald* said that if one believed the Republican papers a McClellan victory would mean "the Chicago peace copperheads will rule the roost, there will be 'a cessation of hostilities,' a withdrawal of our fleets and armies from the rebel States, a surrender to Jeff. Davis, a Southern confederacy, two or three other confederacies, a general break up, universal anarchy, and the reign of ruffianism and mob law."[17]

---

[16] *New-York Daily Tribune,* 18 October 1860, alluding to Judg. 16:20 AV; ibid., 1 November 1860, alluding to Exod. 10:12–2 AV. The "Fusionists" were the Douglas Democrats, Breckinridge Democrats, and Constitutional Unionists in New York, who combined their tickets in the presidential election to stop Lincoln.

[17] *New York Herald,* 7 November 1864. James Gordon Bennett supported Grant in 1864, even though he was not a candidate. Bennett believed Lincoln would not stand up to the Republican Radicals and McClellan would not disavow the Copperheads. For a detailed description of Bennett's twists and turns during the

In a more serious contrast, the Democratic *New York World* pro-claimed that "Providence itself" had set the contrast "in letters of fire and blood and tears" between the Republicans' "fatal experi-ment of a reckless and tyrannical fanaticism" and the Democrats' "guarantees of liberty and of law; of respect for established rights, of justice and of true unanimity." "There are but two candidates and one difference: LINCOLN and Anarchy; McCLELLAN and LAW." The *World* claimed Lincoln had more in common with Jefferson Davis and his "revolutionary" excesses than he had with McClellan. The "principle of disloyalty to the Constitution on one side is secession, and on the other Lincolnism; both equally wrong, both equally revolutionary."[18]

The *Tribune* dismissed the Democrats' gloomy prognosis: birds "of evil omen," said the *Tribune*, speaking of the Democratic press, "can never forbear croaking on the eve of an election." Greeley, however, raised the prospect of Democratic conspiracy to sustain Republican vigilance. The Democratic party resorted to frauds and attempted to gain power "by villainies hitherto unknown in any political canvass." The *Tribune* accused the Democrats of the ultimate political sacrilege: stealing the votes of dead Union sol-diers. "The patriot soldier who sleeps by the Chickahominy cannot be made to vote against the cause he died for if it is known that he is dead." Only the "very madness of passion and of desperation" could have moved men "to resort to a scheme so stupendous in its infamy to gain political power."[19] The *New York Times* warned that the greater danger to the Union came not from the battlefield but from the ballot box. The worst the Confederates could do on the battlefield was "to defeat our armies; but if they conquer us at the ballot-box" through the victory of McClellan, "they secure the control" of the government and ultimately the end of liberty.[20]

The Democratic press concentrated much of its editorial fire on Lincoln. Democratic journals depicted Lincoln as incompetent,

---

1864 presidential election year, see Fermer, *Bennett and the "New York Herald,"* pp. 251–78.

[18] *New York World*, 6 November 1864, 3 October 1864, 14 October 1864.

[19] *New-York Daily Tribune*, 1 November 1864, 27 October 1864, 5 November 1864, 28 October 1864.

[20] *New York Times*, 7 November 1864.

a tool of Republican interests or as "America's First Usurper," bent on trampling the rights of any who resisted him. In Marble's *New York World,* Lincoln was both at once. One editorial described Lincoln as a "leering buffoon," a "charlatan among statesmen," and a chameleon. In another *World* editorial, "DESPOTISM IN MARYLAND," Lincoln was a ruthless tyrant who crushed the civil liberties of the Border States. "When the Constitution and laws no longer restrain him; when the security and perpetuity of his own power are his only rule of action; we all hold our liberties by his forbearance." The *New-York Tribune* published its own charges of "despotism." The American republic was "already ripe for the worst of despotisms—the despotism of party destitute of public virtue, led by men unscrupulous and infamous." In another editorial, Greeley raised the threat to liberty from a southern "aristocracy." Southern politicians "had rejected the idea that a people is capable of self-government, and were bent on establishing an aristocracy or monarchy, involving the subjugation and Slavery of the mass of the people, white as well as black." In this goal Southerners "had the sympathy and secret support of the leaders of the Northern Democracy." The *Tribune* called upon the soldier-citizens to be wary of their party enemies. "Boys, look out for grayback guerrillas in blue overcoats! You know their treachery and their venom! Bid them keep their distance and let you alone!"[21]

The militarization of politics reached its apogee after the Civil War. The language of combat intruded in admonitory rhetoric as never before in the 1868 election. Headlines often linked political events directly to the war and sometimes to the Bible.

### OUR TERMS ARE
### UNCONDITIONAL SURRENDER

proclaimed the *New-York Daily Tribune* about the Republican strategy in 1868.[22]

---

[21] *New York World,* 29 October 1864, 20 October 1864, 19 October 1864, 18 October 1864, 4 October 1864, 5 October 1864; *New-York Daily Tribune,* 29 October 1864, 11 October 1864, 4 November 1864.

[22] *New-York Daily Tribune,* 17 October 1868.

### ANOTHER APPOMATTOX

proclaimed the *Baltimore American* after a Republican success in Pennsylvania.

### .   THE DAY OF JUBILEE HAS COME

read a subsequent headline in the Baltimore paper. "Success in the field," said the *Baltimore American,* "is victory over our armed enemies; success at the polls is victory over the traitors in our camp, the foes of our own household."[23]

Political iconography sometimes mimicked the design of headlines. The Democrats took out a full-page advertisement in the *New York Herald,* covering the page with a matrix design. This advertisement appealed to political and religious conservatives alienated from the Republicans' reformist tendencies.

### AMERICA
### MEANS FREEDOM
### IN SPEECH AND RELIGION,
### AND IS THE DOCTRINE ADVOCATED BY
### SEYMOUR AND BLAIR.
### SEYMOUR AND BLAIR.
### SEYMOUR AND BLAIR.

### NO ISMS[24]

Two very different moral hierarchies revealed themselves in the *Baltimore American*'s headline "THE DAY OF JUBILEE HAS COME" and in the *New-York Herald*'s "NO ISMS." For the Radical Republican *American,* observance of the day of jubilee paralleled that of the Hebrews in the Old Testament. The Union, by freeing the slaves, had acted according to God's will.[25] The *Herald*'s antipathy to

---

[23] *Baltimore American,* 6 October 1864.

[24] *New York Herald,* 2 November 1868.

[25] *Baltimore American,* 18 October 1868, alluding to Lev. 25:10 AV, "And ye shall hallow the fiftieth year, and proclaim liberty throughout all the land unto all the inhabitants thereof: it shall be a jubile unto you." *New York Herald,* 2 November 1868. For a discussion of Old Testament themes in northern Civil War rhetoric, see James H. Moorhead, *American Apocalypse: Yankee Protestants and the Civil War, 1860–1869* (New Haven, Conn., 1978).

"isms," on the other hand, reflected the deep distrust James Gordon Bennett had for abolitionism, sabbatarianism, temperance reformers, and other species of "Protestant popes."[26]

Every turn in the election campaign provoked a military analogy. "Pennsylvanians! your political Gettysburg is to be fought to-morrow," said the *New-York Tribune*. Every man worthy to be a son of Pennsylvania should dedicate himself "to the great task remaining before us—to take from the honored dead of the State increased devotion to the cause for which they gave 'the last full measure of devotion!' " Greeley admonished his readers not to let the Democrats win by fraud. Democrats could not defeat Grant "by fair means." A task "proved too mighty successively for Floyd, for Beauregard, for Pemberton, Bragg, and Lee, is entirely beyond their strength."[27]

The *Tribune* closed another appeal with Grant's most publicized slogan in the campaign. The "immediate result and the great relieving idea in Grant's election is embodied in his brief but comprehensive platform, 'Let us have peace.' " Former "Peace" Democrats found this slogan particularly galling. "Radicalism the party of peace! The party rather of bloodshed, the party of cold-blooded, calculating, premeditated murder," said the *World*. "Stand aside, with your bayonets, and let the principles which ruled this country for a half century in glory now restore it to peace."[28]

The *Baltimore American* used another slogan of Grant's: "PUSH THINGS," urging its readers to assure Republican victory. "We therefore say to every friend of General Grant in Maryland, it is your bounden duty to the great cause in which you are engaged to 'push things' with all the strength, energy and perseverance [of which] you are capable." The *New York Times* declared, "GRANT and his soldiers thought only of the work to be done—never of the pain and cost of doing it. Those who would guard the triumphs of the war, and perpetuate the Union saved at so great a cost must to-day cultivate their spirit."[29]

---

[26] *New York Herald*, 16 January 1859, quoted in Fermer, *Bennett and the "New York Herald,"* p. 119.

[27] *New-York Daily Tribune*, 31 October 1868.

[28] Ibid., 19 October 1868; *New York World*, 24 October 1868.

[29] *Baltimore American*, 31 October 1868; *New York Times*, 3 November 1868.

A *World* editorial urged the Democratic soldier-citizens to "CHARGE ALONG THE WHOLE LINE!" "The heads of the tickets incarnate the issues," said the *World*. The *World* went on to contrast what it saw as the antithetical positions these two candidates represented, echoing the hortatory form of contrast prevalent at the time in Britain.

> Needless now to explain the points in contrast. They are as plain as last year's events. SEYMOUR and Union! GRANT and Disunion. SEYMOUR and Security; Grant and a battle of races, already begun in but half expectation of success. SEYMOUR and peace; GRANT and war between the people of a third of the States. SEYMOUR and Economy; GRANT and revenue slavery. SEYMOUR and the equality of the three branches of government; GRANT and Congressional despotism, judicial subserviency, and Presidential cipherhood. SEYMOUR and Prosperity; GRANT and financial ruin. SEYMOUR and concord; GRANT and perpetual division. SEYMOUR and law; GRANT and arbitrary power. SEYMOUR and the equality of States; GRANT and the extinction of Statehood. SEYMOUR and patriotism; GRANT and sectionalism. SEYMOUR and harmony; GRANT and internecine violence. SEYMOUR and honesty; GRANT and Radical roguery. SEYMOUR and the government; GRANT and a despotism. SEYMOUR and republicanism; GRANT and abolitionism.[30]

Editorials attacked the other party's "troops" as well as their "generals." Attacks on partisan "armies" often exploited religious and ethnic antagonisms. One such *Tribune* editorial had the title "PRIVILEGE AND COLOR": "The great majority of our recent immigrants from Europe" ally themselves with "the champions of Privilege and Caste—of Caste based upon Color."[31] The *World* responded directly to the *Tribune*, charging Republicans with infringing the southern whites' freedom. "Privilege and Caste," especially of "Caste based upon Color" were "distinguishing characteristics of the party which makes a Southern negro [ *sic* ] a voter, primarily because he is a negro and can be controlled in the Radical interest." The *World* satirized the *Tribune*'s emphatic typog-

[30] *New York World,* 27 October 1868.
[31] *New-York Daily Tribune,* 15 October 1868.

raphy: "By printing the words Color and Caste with big letters, and adding thereto a bit of bosh about "Impartial Freedom" in startling capitals," some rural Radicals could be persuaded "that Democrats, and not Republicans," were the "enemies of freedom."[32]

In a sense the rhetorical civil war ceased after 1868. Disillusioned with idealistic oratory and and chastened by the horror of warfare, political rhetoric seemed more subdued after the war. In another sense the rhetorical civil war continued for another twenty years. Editors kept the voters perpetually ready for political combat. Editors had used the exploits of Washington, Jackson, Cromwell, and Napoleon before the war; Civil War generals and battles likewise became rhetorical sources. The Civil War had an impact on American political language and culture more profound than all the previous conflicts lodged in collective memory.

The Civil War dislodged the old moral premises of the parties, but the war did not create fresh premises on which to anchor new political convictions. Americans became disillusioned with moral struggles in the Civil War and Reconstruction. For the American electorate in the Civil War, political obligations came to resemble the responsibilities of combat-hardened soldiers. Voters marched to the polls on election day as they had (or had not) marched in battle. Like battle-hardened veterans they fought for ends that were tangible and immediate.

The duties of the citizen-soldiers and the imperative of combat influenced rhetoric a generation after Lee's surrender at Appomattox. The war's effect on American politics had many positive characteristics: competitive elections (outside the South), consistent party identification, and high voter turnout. The nation suffered nevertheless: political rhetoric fed upon bitter animosities. Without providing any means for reconciliation, admonitory rhetoric of the later nineteenth century fed old enmities in the battle ground of the ballot box.[33]

---

[32] *New York World*, 16 October 1868.

[33] Richard Jensen, *The Winning of the Midwest: Social and Political Conflict* (Chicago, 1971), pp. 2, 6; Paul Kleppner, *The Cross of Culture: A Social Analysis of Midwestern Politics, 1850–1900* (New York, 1970), pp. 128–29.

## The Personality Contest Between
## Gladstone and Disraeli, 1855–1880

The casual crowds who gather together resemble in nothing the burgesses assembled in their borough-courts and the shire-motes. Idle lookers-on, hired ruffians, heated partisans, meet to stare at the candidates, to prevent their being heard, and to excite angry passions, personal and political, in preparation for the performance of duties which require a collected mind and a calm judgment.

—London *Daily News*

**B**ritish rhetoric did not suddenly change after the repeal of the taxes on knowledge. With the passage in 1867, however, of the Second Reform Act, the electorate nearly doubled. The parties and the press faced the task of communicating with nearly two million voters.[1] The 1860s expanded the opportunities for political oratory beyond the halls of Westminster and into the lecture halls and mass assembly meetings.

With the lifting of constraints, the British press expanded dramatically. In the dozen years between stamp duty repeal and the

---

[1] The extension of the franchise after the passage of the Second Reform Act changed the character of British politics in a fundamental if subtle fashion. The number of electors before 1867 in England and Wales was 1,056,000. After the extension of the franchise to household suffrage in the boroughs, 938,000 electors were added to the rolls. See Charles Seymour, *Electoral Reform in England and Wales: The Development and Operation of the Parliamentary Franchise, 1832–1885* (New Haven, Conn., 1915), p. 533.

Second Reform Act, the number of daily newspapers doubled, and the circulation of the dailies and the weeklies expanded more than three and a half times.[2] No longer did a single copy of a newspaper circulate among many readers. Editors and publishers adopted new tactics to widen circulation.[3] Editors like the *Daily Telegraph's* Edward Levy looked to the American "penny press" as the appropriate model for their news coverage, advertising strategy, and typographical display.[4]

While the press expanded to reach a new audience, the parties responded to the challenge of an enlarged electorate by organizational consolidation. Party organizations developed in the decade following the Second Reform Act. The Conservative Central Office appeared in 1870 and the National Liberal Federation in 1877. These new organizations made election communications among politicians, editors, and voters consistent and efficient.

Politicians and editors reacted to the challenge of an enlarged audience with rhetorical innovation. Before 1867, newspapers exploited the old divisions over religious and foreign policy. After 1867, while newspapers did not abandon these reliable themes, journalists focused increasingly on personalities, and particularly on "the gladiators," Disraeli and Gladstone. Editorials fused the personalities of party leaders with their policies. This became a

---

[2] A. P. Wadsworth, "Newspaper Circulations, 1800–1954," *Manchester Statistical Society Papers* (1954–1957):34.

[3] Lee and Cranfield have noted the practice of letting out newspapers that seemed to have been quite common in the 1840s. In the public houses and in the coffeehouses, the political dailies and weeklies were rented out at the rate of one penny an hour. See Alan J. Lee, *The Origins of the Popular Press in England, 1855–1914* (London, 1976), p. 64; G. A. Cranfield, *The Press and Society: From Caxton to Northcliffe* (London, 1978), pp. 119, 193–94.

[4] On September 17, 1855, the *Daily Telegraph*, a three-month-old twopenny daily, was taken over by J. M. Levy, who reduced the price by a penny. He announced his intentions for the paper in the editorial for that day: "There is no reason why a daily newspaper, conducted with a high tone, should not be produced at a price which will place it within the means of all classes of the community . . . The working man will feel assured that we consider that he is deserving of having had before him a newspaper compiled with care which places it in the Hamlet and secures its perusal in the Palace." *Daily Telegraph*, 17 September 1855. The *Telegraph* was the first serious political newspaper directed at the lower-middle-class audience. See Virginia Berridge, "Popular Journalism and Working Class Attitudes" (diss., University of London, 1976), p. 271.

favorite way of emphasizing party differences for the newly initiated audience. Newspapers portrayed political debate as a form of edifying entertainment. In this "age of aggression," British rhetoric focused on the "pugilistic" bouts between "Dizzy" and "the People's William."[5] Gladstone and Disraeli presented a very suitable contrast in temperament as well as in their respective approaches to policy. Gladstone was a moralist, Disraeli a pragmatist. Editors used these stereotypes in personifying the parties.

"Human-interest" stories and interviews, both of which were American imports, arrived in British newspapers in the 1870s. The average length of an editorial shrank, reduced from one and a half columns to a single column's length. This is not to say that newspapers ignored the substantive aspect of politics: they continued publishing parliamentary speeches verbatim until the 1890s.[6] The style of journalistic language also changed in these years. In 1856, J. F. Stephen complained that journalists had imbibed the flowery style of the middle class. "They form their style upon the newspapers, and more especially on the penny-a-lining department." By contrast, Frederick Greenwood described journalists' language at the end of the century, as "refreshing": the "unpedantic, nervous, flexible good English of common life."[7]

Despite changes in the press's language, electioneering themes before and after the Second Reform Act had some consistency. Parties still exploited the great religious fault lines within British society.[8] The Liberals carried over from the early 1850s their cry of "Civil and Religious Liberty." The Conservatives proclaimed

[5] Gay, *Cultivation of Hatred*, pp. 274–87; for a discussion of Disraeli and Gladstone as the "pugilists," see H. J. Hanham, *Elections and Party Management: Politics in the Time of Disraeli and Gladstone* (London, 1959), p. 201.

[6] T. R. Nevett, *Advertising in Britain: A History* (London, 1982), pp. 121–22.

[7] Alan Lee, *Popular Press*, pp. 129–30. The "penny-a-lining department" referred to those paid one penny for each line they wrote.

[8] Feuchtwanger has described the influences on political debate in the 1850s and early 1860s. In the period of fluctuating party alignments between 1852 and 1867, a period which has been called the era of good feelings in British party politics, religious issues were frequently predominant. Church and state, the influence of Catholicism, the Ritualist movement, Modernism, Church Schools—matters such as these were repeatedly in the forefront of public controversy. E. J. Feuchtwanger, *Disraeli, Democracy, and the Tory Party: Conservative Leadership and Organization after the Second Reform Bill* (Oxford, 1968), p. 99.

their devotion to "Church and King." Before and after the extension of the franchise, the Liberals organized their appeals to the voters around the principle of "Liberty." The Conservatives framed their appeals around the principle of "One Nation." Consistent themes organized around durable values provided a stable basis for party identification.

The Liberals' cry of "Civil and Religious Liberty" arrayed the English Nonconformists and the "Celtic Fringe"—Scottish United Presbyterians and Free Presbyterians, Welsh Nonconformists and Irish Catholics—against the Church of England. Strains were already beginning to show in the Liberal coalition, however. Many Liberal Anglicans felt hesitant about the disestablishment of the Irish Church. Catholics wavered on Palmerston's foreign policy and Gladstone's educational policy. Nonconformists dissipated their political energies on a wide range of issues, most of which Parliament ignored. The Liberals had to prevent their adherents from flinging themselves enthusiastically in opposite directions or in many different directions at once.[9]

In the 1850s, Nonconformist Liberalism spawned single-issue associations known as "One-Pledge" groups, which formed around issues of concern like sabbatarianism, nonsectarianism, and "Protestant Defence." "Anti-ism" reappeared in the One-Pledge issues of the 1850s. "Anti-Poor Law" and "Anti-State Church" movements hoped to achieve the same success as the Anti-Corn Law League and the Anti-Slavery Society. Anti-Puseyism, for example, opposed the ritualism the Oxford Movement introduced into the Church of England. Anti-ism, whether it was Anti-Puseyism, Anti-Popery, Anti-Poor Law, or Anti-State Church (or as Palmerston discovered, anti-foreignism) helped sustain a sense of consistent political identity for Liberal voters.

According to the *Cambridge Independent Press,* groups such as the Liberation Society, the National Anti-Poor Law League, the Religious Liberty Society, the Lord's Day Observance Society, the Aborigines Protection Society, the Anti-State Church Society, the Protestant Defence Society, and The Central Currency Committee, had all issued circulars to the electors. The Cambridge journal

[9] Parry, *Democracy and Religion,* pp. 78, 80, 261–67.

claimed "these enthusiasts" inflicted injury on the cause of reform. Such pledges would insure an overwhelming majority of "Tory Members admitted into Parliament by One-Pledge Liberals."[10]

Before the Second Reform Act, for both the Conservative and the Liberal press, the contrasts arising out of the abortive attempts at reform took on a personal dimension. According to the Conservative *Standard*, the "question to be decided" in the 1859 general election was a choice between Conservative Lord Derby and Radical John Bright.[11] The Liberal *Daily Telegraph* made Disraeli the issue in 1859. The one-time Radical was "now a Minister of State, but formerly an advocate of assassination; recently a champion of law and order, but in earlier years an admirer of PONTIUS PILATE of late a foe of democracy, but once a partisan of the Ballot." Disraeli had been "consistently and consecutively a Parliamentary actor."[12]

Liberals stressed the theme of "Liberty" in the election of 1865. The *Cambridge Independent Press* contrasted Liberal "friends of civil and religious liberty" with "the bigotry and intolerance of the Tories."[13] The *Globe* attacked the Conservative's preoccupation with church issues. However conscientiously "a public man may adhere to his own religious communions; he must adopt some other political mission at the present day."[14]

Until the passage of the Second Reform Act by the Conservatives in 1867, the Liberals asserted an exclusive claim to the allegiance of reformers. The Liberals perceived themselves as the party of the future. The Liberal *Daily News* proclaimed the Conservatives the party of the past; the Liberal had a future as well as a past.[15] John Stuart Mill described Liberalism as looking to the future and Conservatism as oriented to the past. In an address to Westminster electors, Mill observed that "a Liberal is he who looks forward for

[10] *Cambridge Independent Press*, 4 April 1857.
[11] London *Standard*, 30 April 1859.
[12] London *Daily Telegraph*, 4 May 1859. See Parry, *Democracy and Religion*, p. 139.
[13] *Cambridge Independent Press*, 1 July 1865.
[14] London, *The Globe*, 10 July 1865.
[15] London *Daily News*, 8 July 1865. The *Daily Telegraph* framed one editorial with an eye to the future, using the deliberative question: "What have Liberalism and Toryism done respectively, and what, respectively, will Liberalism and Toryism do?" *Daily Telegraph*, 10 July 1865.

his principles of government, a Tory looks backward." For the Conservatives, the "real model of government lies somewhere beyond us in the region of the past, from which we are departing further and further."[16] Mill quoted Gladstone's maxim: "Liberalism is trust in the people, limited by prudence; and Toryism distrust of the people, limited by fear."[17]

Fearful or not, the Conservatives opened a new political era with their extension of the franchise in 1867. The change in the conduct of general elections after the Second Reform Act provoked comment from many newspapers in the election of 1868. "The modern nomination," said the *Daily News*, "has no affinity with the old procedure." Parliamentary elections were "scarcely recognizable for what they were a quarter of a century ago in England." "The banners, the ribbons, the cockades, the bands of music, are all gone."[18] The profusion of party names in the 1868 election provoked comment by the *Daily Telegraph*. Classical pseudonyms no longer adorned the letters to the editor. Candidates adopted functional descriptions of themselves and their programs for the benefit of the new voters.

What on earth have the remarkable men who have started up to assure us, in oratory or in print, that they are the only possible "popular," "Constitutional," "working man's," "resident," "independent," or "tried" candidates been doing with themselves all these years? How is it that we never heard of five out of six of them before? Why have they hidden their light for so long under a bushel? We have heard of MENENIUS AGRIPPA; we know all about DEMOS; the name of LUCIUS JUNIUS BRUTUS is familiar to us, and CATO the Censor has admirably represented his constituents in many Parliaments; but

[16] *Daily Telegraph,* 7 July 1865.

[17] Gladstone's observation was an example of *isocolon* (a scheme in which two or more phrases are similar in structure and in length). "The Liberal," said Mill, "*looks forward* for his principle of government, believing that we have not yet attained, that degree of perfection which human institutions can reach and will reach. The Tory looks backward, hankering after fading feudalisms and 'yesterday six weeks' and is always privately convinced that nothing but 'reaction' can save the State. What can be truer—what can better explain the crab-like movements of Conservatism, or more proudly justify and define 'Advanced Liberalism?' " *Daily Telegraph,* 7 July 1865.

[18] London *Daily News,* 16 November 1868.

we confess that, when TOMPKINS tells us that he has been the friend of the people all along, we are staggered; that when SIMPKINS recites his long list of claims to our political confidence and gratitude, we are amazed; and that, with the hardest trying, we fail to remember the particular occasion on which HOPKINS "stood in the breach of our venerable Constitution so wantonly assailed."[19]

The *Daily Telegraph* described a new inverted social hierarchy that prevailed in British electioneering. During the contest "everything assumes an abnormal, paradoxical, and eminently uncomfortable aspect," said the *Telegraph*. "Distinctions of rank and social position are inverted. Haughty patricians descend to fawn and cringe to petty shopkeepers. Servants bully their employers. Journeymen butchers think themselves entitled to cross-examine the heir to a dukedom."[20]

During the 1868 election, the parties sought to establish clear, opposite identities for themselves in appealing to the enlarged electorate. To the Radical *Morning Star* the difference between the Liberals and the Conservatives was clear. The choice was "not merely between one popular leader and another" but "between two opposing theories of Government, two rival and irreconcilable policies."[21]

*The Times* evenhandedly contrasted the parties over the previous decade. While the Conservatives had been very effective in promoting good policies, the Liberals clearly possessed the advantage in the matter of principles. "If one party had the true creed, the other might show the true practice." *The Times* described it as "the old controversy between faith and works, politically expressed." Faith "has never yet been beaten by works. There is a sturdy Calvin-

---

[19] *Daily Telegraph*, 17 November 1868. The name "Constitutionalist," provoked an outburst by the *Manchester Guardian*. "Rarely, if ever, does any good thing appear in this world but there springs up some paltry counterfeit, exaggerating its shortcomings, caricaturing its virtues, burlesquing and disgracing its generosity and getting accepted by a great many innocent persons as the genuine article. A striking instance of this mischievous kind of imposture is exhibited by the parade which is just now being made by the people calling themselves 'Constitutionalists.' " *Manchester Guardian*, 11 October 1868.

[20] *Daily Telegraph*, 17 November 1868.

[21] *Morning Star*, 17 November 1868.

ism in the political creed of Englishmen which does demand sound doctrine as well as proper conduct." Public servants should have good character. When their motives "sprang from interest rather than principle there is always the chance of backsliding. The cloven foot will peep out now and then."[22]

The Conservative *Standard,* on the other hand, portrayed the contest in the same stark moral terms as the Radical *Morning Star:* the election of 1868 would decide "some of the gravest issues that ever were submitted to the constituencies of England." That Liberals even suggested disestablishment of the Irish Church should cause alarm. Recalling "the religious faith, sympathies, prejudices of ten or twelve generations of Englishmen, the lofty notions of public honesty, of political morality, of national honour, which have characterised the Parliaments and the people of this country, since the Reformation," it declared "no English or Scotch constituency" would return a Liberal candidate "to outrage the religion of centuries."[23]

Not all editorials concentrated on religion. In the contest to win over the newly enfranchised voters in 1868, editors often portrayed the two party leaders as combatants. The *Scotsman* referred to Gladstone's "staggering blows" against his opponents. It described Disraeli as "a clever general," who stayed away from the front initially while "his lieutenant," Lord Stanley, made "a smart *reconnaissance* preparatory to the battle of this week." The *Daily News* referred to Disraeli as "a political soldier of fortune."[24] At the Alhambra Music-hall at Bootle, the audience serenaded the Liberal party leader with the borrowed tune of an American Civil War marching song: "When Gladstone's marching home."[25]

Liberals invoked not just the American Civil War but the English Civil War.[26] Historical references to the latter conflict had as much

[22] *The Times,* 17 November 1868.

[23] *Standard,* 16 November 1868.

[24] *Scotsman,* 14 November 1868, 16 November 1868; *Daily News,* 16 November 1868.

[25] *Leeds Mercury,* 16 November 1868; in the same issue *Leeds Mercury* published a Liberal campaign song sung to the same American Civil War marching song, starting with the words "When Baines is sent to Parliament / Hurrah, Hurrah . . ." Baines was the son of the *Mercury*'s proprietor.

[26] Hill, "Norman Yoke," pp. 60–61.

significance for an English audience as references to the War between the States. The *Bee-Hive,* a workingmen's newspaper, asked its readers if anyone could doubt "how Milton would vote, were he alive in England next week, or Cromwell, or almost any other of our forefathers, who were devoted to freedom and progress, and whose memories we are proud of?"[27]

The *Daily News* used a historical simile from the eighteenth century as a negative referent. The journal observed that Disraeli had once professed to be a radical patriot "after the fashion of JOHN WILKES"; now he was "a 'King's Friend,' of the type of Lord BUTE." Each was an example of "opposite degeneracy of political character." Disraeli had shown "that vices hitherto deemed incompatible can be united."[28]

The emphasis on leaders' personalities could only succeed if voters associated the leaders with party principles, said the *Leeds Mercury.* "Each party instinctively feels that it is useless trying to conjure with a name, unless that name stands associated with a distinct policy." Disraeli's policy was "a mere negation—the policy of keeping in office as long as he can—and his name has therefore, been hardly mentioned by his friends." Gladstone's policies, on the other hand, were "positive, progressive, pacifying and his followers are too ardent in their admiration of its character to forget the name of its author."[29] The *Scotsman* declared that Tory policy was an oxymoron: "Briefly described, it is a declaration of 'no policy.' " "What are they going to do in the future? The Oracle is dumb."[30]

The Conservatives learned from their own defeat in the 1868 election. In the six years before the next general election, the

---

[27] The London *Bee-Hive* claimed it could not "conceive Milton as voting against Mr. Gladstone and for the unscrupulous politician whom fate has ironically made Premier of England for the time being." *Bee-Hive,* 14 November 1868. For a more detailed examination of the *Bee-Hive* and its role as the journal of the working class, see Stephen Coltham, "The *Bee-Hive* Newspaper: Its Origin and Early Struggles," in Briggs and Saville, eds., *Essays in Labour History,* pp. 174–204; see also Stephen Coltham, "George Potter and the *Bee-Hive* Newspaper," (diss., Oxford University, 1956).

[28] *Daily News,* 16 November 1868.

[29] *Leeds Mercury,* 21 November 1868.

[30] *Scotsman,* 16 November 1868.

Conservatives developed a highly centralized organization and better press communication. They identified themselves with policies that appealed to working-class voters. The Liberals meanwhile lost their advantage in the intervening years: Gladstone's moral and personal appeal could not in and of itself keep the party together. Liberal editors in 1874 focused the greatest attention on abolition of the income tax. "Economy," the *Daily News* said, was "the watchword" of the Liberals, and "Liberal union" was "the principle which is to be put in opposition to Conservative reaction."[31]

The association of personality and policy was very noticeable, as this editorial from the *Leeds Mercury* attests. "MR. GLADSTONE'S name is now identified with the abolition of the Income-Tax," said the Leeds paper, "far more closely than it would have been if MR. DISRAELI had known when to 'seize occasion by the hand.' " The Conservative leader had "distinctly pronounced against the great financial reforms proposed by his rival, and has at the same time admitted that he has no policy of his own to propound."[32] The *Mercury* said the country would decide between a Liberal government "with a reduced expenditure, remitted taxation, and a continuance of sound measures of reform" or a Conservative government, "with a profligate increase of the expenditure, additional to the taxes and the debt, and—in place of home legislation—a 'vigorous' foreign policy."[33]

The Liberals again charged Disraeli with having "no policy" but this time with far less success. Still, the *Standard* showed some defensiveness in rebutting the charge. "Those persons who are so fond of asking if the Conservative party has 'a policy' must have found, we think, by this time a tolerably comprehensive answer." Moreover, said the *Standard,* alluding to the traditional concerns of Tory electors, Disraeli had "referred us to the organic institutions of the country to say whether the defence of these alone

---

[31] *Daily News,* 29 January 1874. This was the only issue on which Liberals claimed an advantage, and the Conservatives did their best to embrace abolition as well.

[32] *Leeds Mercury,* 3 February 1874.

[33] Ibid.

against the numerous antagonists which threaten them is not a policy by itself."[34]

Disraeli ignored the taunts of "no policy" and went on the offensive. He accused Gladstone of a lack of specificity. Rather than attacking the Liberals' domestic legislation, where they had the advantage, Disraeli attacked Liberal tax policy using a traditional Conservative slogan from imperial policy.[35] Disraeli condemned the waiver of navigation rights in the Straits of Malacca and accused Gladstone of "plundering and blundering" there. Gladstone retorted that Disraeli's persistent raising of the issue showed he was "foundering and floundering." The *Standard* declared that "a joke of any sort is so rare a gift from Mr. GLADSTONE that we confess ourselves thankful for the momentary friskiness which led him to the rather elephantine attempt."[36]

The verbal sparring between the parliamentary leaders lent presence to gladiatorial imagery. Using the gladiatorial metaphor to describe the contest between Gladstone and Disraeli, the *Leeds Mercury* noted that Disraeli had "rushed into the arena unarmed and unarmoured." The result was "a great rhetorical and logical triumph for the PRIME MINISTER." The *Mercury* thought Gladstone's "happiest hit" was his sardonic response to Disraeli's Straits of Malacca speech.[37] A *Daily Telegraph* editorial described the debate between Conservatives and Liberals as though it were a naval battle.

The naval action in "the Straits of Malacca" opened imposingly on Saturday last with broadsides from three first-rate line-of-battle ships. On the same day there were some scattered engagements, in which the enemy had the best of it; but these were mere preliminary fights, and the real business begins with the three notable men-of-war of

[34] *Standard,* 6 February 1874.

[35] H. C. G. Matthew had said that Disraeli "created for the new electorate the myth of the imperial party with its 'patriotic' underpinnings of Queen, Church and Empire." See his introduction to Gladstone, *Diaries,* 9:xxxv. For the importance of the Empire to newly-enfranchised Conservatives, see Robert McKenzie and Allan Silver, *Angels in Marble: Working Class Conservatives in Urban England* (Chicago, 1968), p. 3–73. For an example of Disraeli's attack on Liberal tax policy, see the *Daily News,* 27 January 1874.

[36] *Standard,* 30 January 1874.

[37] *Leeds Mercury,* 3 February 1874.

which we speak. Every gun fired on both sides will be marked along each line of battle, and if we give the first place to Mr. DISRAELI'S, it is more because we wish the action to be chivalrous than because much damage was done by his oratorical artillery.[38]

The now-Conservative *Globe* gave a disparaging account of Gladstone's campaigning, observing that "the great orator was quite in his old 'form' of 1868," when he "went storming through the county morning, noon and night, to the amusement of his adversaries and the alarm of his friends, who wondered whether it would be possible for such a whirlwind of rhetoric ever to subside again, or for such a volcano of declamation to cool to the normal temperature of a parliamentary assembly."[39] The *Standard* contended that although Gladstone "had the first word and struck the first blow," the "Conservative champion has responded gamely to the challenge, and that in the first round he has not disappointed the hopes of his backers."[40]

In the aftermath of the Liberal defeat in 1874, the press puzzled over Gladstone's decline in popularity. The *Mercury* struggled to explain this development. "A few years ago he was the most popular as well as the most powerful man in England." Gladstone was "the most brilliant and able of living statesmen, the possessor of intellectual powers far surpassing those with which his successful rival is endowed." Perhaps, mused the *Mercury*, unrelieved distinction eventually becomes monotonous: like Athenians, Englishmen eventually tired of "calling ARISTEDES the Just."[41]

The *Edinburgh Courant* blamed unfulfilled promises for the Liberals' defeat. Gladstone obtained a majority in 1868 "on the faith of promises." The time had come to consider whether he had fulfilled his engagements. "Has he restored Ireland to loyalty? Had he administered the affairs of the Empire wisely and creditably? Has his foreign policy been worthy of a great nation like ours? Has his domestic legislation tended to advance the general welfare

[38] *Daily Telegraph*, 2 February 1874.
[39] *Globe*, 29 January 1874.
[40] *Standard*, 2 February 1874.
[41] *Leeds Mercury*, 12 February 1874.

of the community?"[42] *The Times* concurred with the view that the Liberals had promised too much. *"Repulsion rather than attraction has been the muse of power during the past few days."* If the Conservatives were unknown, *The Times* declared that Gladstone and the Liberals were too well known. "They have stood too long in the fierce glare of publicity."

> In these days of relentless journalism, a Minister cannot be judged merely by his public acts, retaining a kind of personal privacy, while his political self is attacked or defended. A literary *carte de visite* has to be presented to a certain class of readers, and they expect to be told not only what [he] said, but how he looked when he said it, how he took the answer of the other side, and how he looked when he replied to it. . . . This kind of gossip is unfortunate, and we never remember so much personality in conversations as within the last three or four years.[43]

Secure after the Conservative triumph in 1874, Disraeli retired two years later to the House of Lords. Despite all his efforts to put himself above the fray, the Conservative leader now faced the same "fierce glare of publicity" that had vanquished his great rival.

Gladstone, meanwhile, retired from the Liberal party leadership in 1874 to write about religious issues. He did not remain in retirement for long, however. In November 1874 he wrote to his successor, the Earl of Granville, "Nothing will rally the party but a cause: or such portentous blundering as is almost beyond hope or fear."[44] After the Turkish atrocities against the Bulgarians in 1876, Gladstone found a cause; in 1879, after five years of Conservative rule, Gladstone perceived sufficient blundering to answer his hopes and fears. According to R. T. Shannon, Gladstone became a

[42] *Edinburgh Courant,* 5 February 1874.

[43] *The Times,* 7 February 1874. According to Koss, after cutting loose from the Liberals, "the *Telegraph*—to use its own vocabulary—became 'imperial.' The newspaper referred to the interests of the 'Empire at large' and it spoke of the 'duty' to further 'the support of the Imperial Government.' " In January, 1878, the paper claimed to have supported this line since the summer of 1876 "without heeding party ties or any dictates except those of sincere patriotism." Koss, *Political Press,* 1:203.

[44] Letter to Granville, November 25, 1874, in W. E. Gladstone, *Political Correspondence of Mr. Gladstone and Lord Granville,* ed. Agatha Ramm (London, 1952), 2:461.

"leader of the masses" with the Bulgarian agitation. "He did not know the masses, or care very much what they wanted," Shannon says. On a moral issue "which excited his imagination, he found he could employ mass enthusiasm in a righteous cause."[45] Gladstone rebuilt his popularity with astonishing success, beginning with the Bulgarian agitation, and consolidated his gains with the Midlothian campaign.[46]

The Midlothian campaign of 1879 was a speaking tour, not an election campaign; Gladstone nevertheless seized the attention of the nation as no other politician had attempted to do. In a speech at Glasgow, Gladstone revived the Whiggish charge of Tories abetting repression abroad: "To call Disraeli's foreign policy 'Conservative,' " said Gladstone, was "a pure mockery and an abuse of terms." The possessors of authority had inverted and degraded the "principles of free government."[47] In a speech at Motherwell Station, Gladstone attacked Conservative domestic policy by a scheme of repetition (anaphora). Statesmen must be guided by "the great principles" of justice, economy, and reform. "In my firm and sad belief, those principles of justice, those principles of economy, those principles of reform, have been either neglected or gravely compromised, and even trodden under foot."[48]

Gladstone's tour was a personal triumph but he had to wait until 1880 for vindication at the polls. In the 1880 general election, *The Times* observed that "the time has now gone by" when speeches "can have any material effect beyond the immediate range of the audiences to which they are addressed."[49] *The Times* was wrong.

---

[45] R. T. Shannon, *Gladstone and the Bulgarian Agitation, 1876* (London, 1963), p. 12.

[46] As H. C. G. Matthew has observed, "Having retired once and turned away from the party battle, future intervention had to be explained, to himself and to the public, in terms of unusual crises and special causes." See Matthew's introduction to Gladstone, *Diaries*, 9:xxiv. Two years before Midlothian, the American novelist Henry James met Gladstone at a dinner party. He wrote his brother William that Gladstone's "apparent self-surrender to what he is talking of, [is] without a flaw." Letter to William James, March 29, 1877, in Henry James, *The Letters of Henry James*, ed. Percy Lubbock (New York, 1920), 1:53. See also Gladstone, *Diaries*, 9:207.

[47] Speech at Glasgow, December 5, 1879. Gladstone, *Midlothian Speeches*, p. 210.

[48] Speech at Motherwell Station, December 6, 1879. Ibid. p. 213.

[49] *The Times*, 31 March 1880.

Stephen Koss observed that, "Gladstone proved it possible to stir the country without stirring the press; and Disraeli, after stirring the press, was rejected by the country." In his otherwise masterful study, Koss may have misstated the case.[50] Gladstone did use the press to stir the country; and Disraeli never stirred the press effectively. Gladstone took advantage of verbatim transcription as no politician had done before. Editorials in the provincial journals and the London press did not have to praise Gladstone's Midlothian campaign as long as transcripts of his speeches filtered down to the provincial towns and were read aloud to the people, as Lloyd George's uncle did in Llanystumdwy.[51]

When poll results came in from the 1880 general election, *The Times* observed that "the time for verbal fence" was over. *The Times* seemed puzzled at Gladstone's decisive victory and perplexed by his style of campaigning. "If we cannot accept Mr. GLADSTONE's view that the crisis is one of the greatest in our recent history," said *The Times,* "yet we cannot but acknowledge that the moment when the country reviews its past policy and determines its future conduct is, and must always be, one of great import and consequence."[52] Disraeli was the loser and Gladstone the victor in the 1880 election because Gladstone understood how to campaign *through* the press rather than *with* it.[53]

*The Times* was correct in observing that "the crisis" of 1879–80 was not overwhelming, but Gladstone had created a crisis atmosphere among the electors in his Midlothian speeches. "If there is one single elector who has not by this time determined how he means to vote and for what reasons, it is clearly beyond the power of human speech and political debate to help him to a decision,"

[50] In fact, Koss quoted Lloyd George, who recalled traveling "fourteen miles to Portmadoc and back to get a London newspaper with a full report of one of Mr. Gladstone's speeches." Koss, *Political Press,* 1:215.

[51] Frank Owen, *Tempestuous Journey: Lloyd George, His Life and Times* (London, 1954), p. 32.

[52] *The Times,* 31 March 1880.

[53] H. C. G. Matthew says Gladstone discovered "the central feature of modern political communication: the use of one medium to gain access to another" (in this case, the use of a political meeting to gain access to the national debating society made possible by the popular press). See Matthew's introduction to Gladstone, *Diaries,* 9:lix.

said *The Times.* Through the power of human speech and political debate, Gladstone roused wavering voters "by the very dregs of electioneering rhetoric."[54] Whatever the style of electioneering, *The Times* conceded that in the election of 1880, "the speeches of acknowledged leaders must be regarded as addressed, not to their individual audience, but to the whole electoral body of the country."[55]

Organizationally, the Conservatives achieved greater success than their Liberal rivals, partly as a result of the greater funds at their disposal and better managerial talent. In their relations with the press, the Conservatives won over most of the important Liberal journals between 1855 and 1880. The Liberals, on the other hand, possessed the decisive advantage in rhetorical innovation and they held this advantage thanks to Gladstone.[56] The Liberal party leader thus conveyed his message to a national audience despite a wholesale defection of formerly Liberal journals. The shift in the relationship between Gladstone and the press proved advantageous for both. Gladstone received relatively unbiased coverage from Conservative newspapers in "news" stories and these papers exploited public interest in Midlothian to widen their circulation.[57]

Gladstone, by exploiting public enthusiasm over Midlothian, generated more press and public attention than the Conservative Central Press Agency could. This resourceful speaker had mastered many different styles of public appeal since his youthful days as a

[54] *The Times,* 31 March 1880.

[55] *Ibid.*

[56] Gladstone, according to Matthew, "became the supreme exponent of the rhetorical alternative." As Robert Blake has observed, "The Conservative tradition was against 'stump oratory' until Lord Randolph Churchill put an end to such false modesty." See Matthew's introduction to Gladstone, *Diaries,* 9:lvii; Robert Blake, *Disraeli* (London, 1966), p. 701.

[57] H. C. G. Matthew, in his introduction to volume 9 of *The Gladstone Diaries,* describes this phenomenon insightfully; see esp. Gladstone, *Diaries,* 9:lx-lxi. Matthew notes that Gladstone, in one of his first journalistic essays, wrote a piece "On Eloquence," including "Advertising . . . Eloquence." See W. E. Gladstone, "On Eloquence," *Eton Miscellany* 2 (1827): 110, quoted in Gladstone, *Diaries,* 9:lxi. See also H. G. C. Matthew, "Rhetoric and Politics in Great Britain, 1860–1950," in *Politics and Social Change in Modern Britain: Essays Presented to A. F. Thompson,* ed. Philip J. Waller (New York, 1987) pp. 34–58.

staunch Conservative.[58] None was as original as his Midlothian departure. The Conservatives were not slow to catch on to the reasons for Gladstone's success. The editors grasped the changed situation even more quickly. A new era in the relations of party and press had arrived. As Lincoln had used his debates with Douglas, Gladstone used the Midlothian tour: as a dramatic setting to build a national audience. Gladstone kindled a national debate on policy, not confined to Westminster but extending to newspaper readers in all three kingdoms.

[58] Boyd Hilton has described Gladstone's justification for changes in his convictions. See Hilton, *Age of Atonement,* p. 354. Gladstone remained profoundly conservative in his view of the people's role in politics. See W. E. Gladstone, "Postscriptum on the County Franchise," in *Gleanings of Past Years,* 1843–1878 (London, 1879), 1:201, quoted in Matthew's introduction to Gladstone, *Diaries,* 9:lxv. Gladstone prevailed among the intellectuals as a result of the Bulgarian agitation. This helped him in 1880; by 1886, however, they were mostly against him on Home Rule. See Shannon, *Bulgarian Agitation,* especially pp. 147–238; Parry, *Democracy and Religion,* pp. 429–52.

# CHAPTER EIGHT

# The Loss of Public Principles and Public Interest: Gilded Age Rhetoric, 1872–1896

> From camp to camp, through the foul womb of night,
> The hum of either army stilly sounds,
> That the fix'd sentinels almost receive
> The secret whispers of each other's watch.
> Fire answers fire, and through their paly flames
> Each battle sees the other's umber'd face.
>
> —Shakespeare, *Henry V*

Writing in 1870, Walt Whitman described in *Democratic Vistas* the transformation of the mores and the language of the Union after the Civil War. "Genuine belief seems to have left us," Whitman observed. "The underlying principles of the States are not honestly believ'd in, (for all this hectic glow, and these melodramatic screamings)."[1] "Genuine belief" proved difficult enough to sustain in a time of probity and stability. The Gilded Age was neither. Earlier normative moral values of a predominantly rural, predominantly Protestant society seemed less secure in an age of immigration and urbanization.

Parties faced the daunting task of motivating their adherents without recourse to lofty principles or intimate familiarity. In an

---

[1] Walt Whitman, *Democratic Vistas*, in *Specimen Days, Democratic Vistas, and Other Prose*, ed. Louise Pound (Garden City, N.Y., 1935), p. 269.

age of rampant individualism they sought to motivate the voters by praising party allegiance for its own sake. Where antebellum rhetoric emphasized political values such as liberty and equality, Gilded Age editorials stressed duty, loyalty, courage, spirit, and resolve.[2]

The Gilded Age celebrated two kinds of virtues: those of the soldier and those of the entrepreneur. The virtues of the latter were celebrated at length in speeches, sermons, and lecture halls throughout the nation. Rugged individualism was not conducive to political mobilization, however. For that, politicians and editors relied upon what we might call the *collaborative imperative:* their rallying cry was for the army, the team, the party, the race, or the nation.

Editorials praised voters for their courage and determination; they urged electors to "stand by their colors." The party press encouraged voters to exercise traits of self-control: discipline, vigilance, and hard labor. Loyalty was the preeminent virtue, reiterated repeatedly—to party, to family, to religious faith, to the Union. Steadfast allegiance to these institutions fixed the voter in an array of reassuring identities.[3]

In the Gilded Age the press experienced its own crisis of identity. In the immediate aftermath of the Civil War, most of the press proclaimed a militant partisanship that sustained their readers' political loyalties. Over the course of the next three decades, however, the press became increasingly independent of party leadership and organizations. In 1881, approximately five percent of the newspapers in New York City proclaimed themselves as "independent." Ten years later, perhaps twenty-five percent of northern American dailies and weeklies—including many of the largest metropolitan journals—used that term to describe themselves."[4]

---

[2] Mark W. Summers, *The Plundering Generation: Corruption and the Crisis of the Union, 1849–1861* (New York, 1987), passim, makes the point that moral decay was observed and lamented a dozen years before the Civil War.

[3] Robert Wiebe, *The Search for Order, 1877–1920* (New York, 1967), pp. 1–75.

[4] The first figure is my estimate, derived from the *American Newspaper Annual, 1881* (Philadelphia, 1881) published by N. W. Ayer & Son. For 1891, I rely on McGerr's reckoning from *American Newspaper Annual, 1891* (Philadelphia, 1891) also published by *N. W. Ayer & Son.* See McGerr, *Decline of Popular Politics,* p. 120.

The Petersburg, Virginia, *Index-Appeal* summarized the incentives for declaring political independence on the editorial page. In a newspaper advertisement appearing in 1891, the newspaper declared it was "Wholly Independent in Politics." The next line read, "And has a Larger Circulation, City and Country, than any other paper published in Southside Virginia." Independent newspapers appealed to readers of all parties; that meant larger circulation and more advertising revenues.[5]

The other seventy-five percent of the newspapers, however, remained tied to political parties and many used militant partisan language in editorials and in some "news" stories as well. The *New York Times,* still militantly partisan in 1872, expressed a typical election-eve sentiment in this editorial: "What the country wants is not merely a defeat of Democracy in 'the last ditch,' but such a dispersion of their forces as took place in LEE'S after Appomattox." Editors described election "battles" as "nearly won"; editors urged the voters to "watch and fight" or to "work with untiring vigilance" to insure "the day is ours."[6]

In the Gilded Age, parties organized themselves on a national basis. By creating a presidential campaign publicity office, parties could organize political communications around a series of central themes. Communications offices focused on issues in the late nineteenth century, culminating in the "educational" campaigns of 1876, 1888, and 1892.[7] Editors also fixed on subsidiary themes that appealed to the widest readership. Military themes appeared prominently; conspiracy, corruption, and morality also figured as prevalent topics. Over the course of two decades these recurrent themes evolved in response to a changing political context.

The imagery of battle lent politics a presence long after the war ended.[8] Gilded Age rhetoric in the 1870s and 1880s explicitly linked the duties of the voter with those of the soldier. "The efficiency of an army," said the *New York World,* depends "on the spirit, discipline, and fidelity of its soldiers." Moderation "is not

---

[5] *American Newspaper Directory* (New York, 1891), published by George P. Rowell and Co., p. 2119. See also McGeer, *Decline of Popular Politics,* pp. 113–22.

[6] *New York Times,* 4 November 1872.

[7] McGerr, *Decline of Popular Politics,* pp. 69–106.

[8] Jensen, *Winning of the Midwest,* pp. 11, 14.

to be expected when soldiers make an assault on a strongly entrenched enemy, and rush with fierce courage into an imminent deadly breach." If the "tide of battle" went against the Democrats, said the *World*, it was "manly and soldier-like to retreat in good order, with lines unbroken and disciplined step."[9] "Democrats!" said the *Indianapolis Daily Sentinel* in 1880, "you can not afford a moment's waiting or rest."[10] The *Chicago Daily Tribune* in 1888 said the Republican party had "come to the front of the battle, ready and eager for the contest with its old time enemy." Republicans had the duty "to watch and fight, to work with untiring vigilance."[11]

Allusions to duty were hardly new in Anglo-American politics. At the very beginning of the nineteenth century, editors appealed to the voters' sense of duty. A typical example was this address to the voters published in 1802 in the *Boston Gazette:* "You are called upon to rally round the standard of your Country's honor, and to discharge a most sacred duty:—a duty, not the less sacred, because it is common."[12]

The eighteenth-century notion of duty often connected it to filial obligations. Joseph Addison spoke in 1710 of the duties of a son to his parent; other duties followed from that primal obligation: "THE Obedience of Children to their Parents is the Basis of all government, and [is] set forth as the Measure of that Obedience which we owe to those whom Providence hath placed over us."[13] In Addison's *Cato* (1715), on learning of the death of his son Marcus in defense of Roman liberty, Cato says, "Thanks to the Gods! my Boy has done his Duty."[14] Royall Tyler's *The Contrast* (1787) also speaks of filial duty: when he learns of her unhappy engagement to another, Manly says to Maria: "We are both

[9] *New York World*, 17 October 1872, 4 November 1872, 10 October 1872.

[10] *Indianapolis Daily Sentinel*, 23 October 1880.

[11] *Chicago Daily Tribune*, 6 November 1888.

[12] *Boston Gazette, Commercial and Political*, 3 November 1800. The address continues, "It is in vain that you have toiled for freedom, if you do not elect *good men to bear the Ark of your political Salvation.*" See 1 Kings 2:26, "I will not at this time put thee to death, because thou barest the ark of the Lord God before David my father."

[13] Joseph Addison, *The Spectator*, No. 189 (6 October 1710): 80.

[14] Joseph Addison, *Cato, A Tragedy*, 4.4.79, 7th ed. (London, 1713), p. 65.

unhappy; but it is your duty to obey your parent,—mine to obey my honour."[15]

Duty in the eighteenth century was personal, familial, and sacred. To be sure, that sense of duty persisted. Daniel Webster had a similar sense of his duties in his speech supporting the Compromise of 1850: "The ends I aim at shall be my country's, my God's and Truth's. I was born an American. I will live an American. I shall die an American; and I intend to perform my duties incumbent upon me in that character to the end of my career."[16] Francis Wayland spoke of the duties of citizens in *The Elements of Moral Science,* first published in 1835: "It is manifestly the duty of every member of society to choose such agents as, in his opinion, will truly and faithfully discharge those duties to which they are appointed." Any citizen who would act "for the sake of party prejudice" would act "to sap the very foundations of society."[17] By 1880, however, in *Culture and Anarchy,* Matthew Arnold identified this sense of duty with the archaic values of the aristocratic "barbarians": "With Mr. Tennyson they celebrate 'the great broad-shouldered genial Englishman,' with his 'sense of duty.' "[18]

Duty in the latter nineteenth century connoted something slightly different, especially in America. Peter Gay has observed that a Darwinian "call to duty was the dominant refrain of imperialistic rhetoric throughout these decades."[19] Epitomizing this "dominant refrain" was Josiah Strong, the Social Darwinist, Anglo-Saxon supremacist, and evangelizing Christian. To Strong, the Anglo-Saxons had contributed two enduring ideas to world civilization, a love of liberty and "pure *spiritual* Christianity." The time would soon arrive when the world would enter a new stage of history: "*the final competition of races, for which the Anglo-Saxon is being schooled.*" According to Strong, "God has laid upon Christian nations the work of evangelizing the heathen world. If this duty were accepted

---

[15] Royall Tyler, *The Contrast, A Comedy in Five Acts,* 4.2.86–87 (1787; Philadelphia 1790) p. 65.

[16] Daniel Webster, *The Papers of Daniel Webster: Speeches and Formal Writings,* ed. Charles M. Wiltse and Alan R. Berolzheimer (Hanover, N.H., 1988,) 2:577.

[17] Francis Wayland, *The Elements of Moral Science* (London, 1868), p. 305.

[18] Arnold, *Culture and Anarchy,* pp. 150–51.

[19] Gay, *Cultivation of Hatred,* p. 85.

by all Christians, the burden would rest lightly upon each; but great multitudes in the church are shirking all responsibility."[20]

Duty in Strong's sense was national as much as personal. It proceeded from the general to the specific; not the other way around, as it had for Wayland. Duty for Strong was not familial but racial: it originated not as it did for Addison, with a son's duty to his father, but with one race's destiny to assume responsibility for civilizing the world. Duty was not only irrevocable because it was "sacred," but also because it was "scientific," defined by the immutable laws of biology. Duty described a *collaborative imperative* in an age celebrating unchecked individualism. And nowhere did this collaborative imperative and the reminder of duty occur more often than in repeated military analogies.

Editors exploited military imagery beyond the immediate experience of the American Civil War. Editorials made allusions to other wars. The *Baltimore Sun* in 1872 revived an analogy between Radical Republicans and Puritan Roundheads. "The worst form of despotism with which our liberties have been threatened has been a parliamentary despotism," said the *Sun*. Reconstruction under the Radicals "recalled the history of the famous Long Parliament of Charles the First's time."[21]

In 1872, the *New York World* likened the Republicans to the Saxons, who "spent the eve of the battle of Senlac [the Norman name for the battle of Hastings] in feasting and drinking," while the Normans, like the Democrats, "with the mighty future of ENGLAND hidden in their camp, lay watchful and stern upon their arms."[22] In an editorial appearing in 1876, the *New York World*, quoting the Chorus from Shakespeare's *Henry V* at the battle of Agincourt, proclaimed that the "armies have taken up their position, the lines are dressed for to-morrow's fight and dimly through the mists of preference and prejudice each battle sees the other's umbered face."[23]

[20] Josiah Strong, *Our Country: Its Possible Future and Its Present Crisis*, 2d ed. (New York, 1891), pp. 213–4, 226.

[21] *Baltimore Sun*, 4 November 1872.

[22] *New York World*, 11 October 1872. This was an inversion of the Norman Yoke; the Normans and Saxons had their usual roles as heroes and villains reversed.

[23] *New York World*, 6 November 1876; quoting *Henry V*, 4. Chor. 9.

Another virtue the Gilded Age celebrated was loyalty. One of the most damning charges against a public figure was disloyalty. Samuel Tilden was allegedly disloyal to the Union; Grover Cleveland was disloyal to the mother of his illegitimate child. James G. Blaine was disloyal to his Catholic grandmother. Henry Ward Beecher was disloyal to his wife and to the Republican party. Republican editorials perennially chastised the South for disloyalty to the Union. The best-known alliterative phrase in American political rhetoric, "rum, Romanism and rebellion," preceded Samuel Burchard's pledge of allegiance to candidate Blaine: "We are loyal to the party. We are loyal to you."

The *Philadelphia Inquirer* said that the overriding issue in 1876 was "whether the Rebel Democracy [i.e., Democrats] are to be victorious over the loyal Republicans at the polls, after they were beaten by loyal Republicans in the field." The *New York Times* raised a distinction in 1876 between "loyal" and "disloyal" Democrats. The *Baltimore Sun* accused the Republicans of acting "disloyally by defrauding the federal government" with specious war claims. The *New-York Tribune* in 1880 said, "Republican triumph means loyalty, justice to all, a free vote and a fair count." "Arraigned for disloyalty, the Democratic party could hardly have done more to make the charge conclusive," said the same newspaper in 1888.[24]

What made loyalty such an attractive virtue in the Gilded Age? Perhaps the philosopher of loyalty, Josiah Royce, provided the best answer in a rhetorical question.

> Where, in our distracted modern world, in this time when cause wars with cause, and when all old moral standards are remorselessly criticised and doubted, are we to find such a cause—a cause, all-embracing, definite, rationally compelling, supreme, certain, and fit to centralize life? What cause is there that would justify for us the martyrs' devotion?[25]

[24] *Philadelphia Inquirer*, 30 October 1876; *New York Times* quoted in *Baltimore Sun*, 2 November 1876; *Baltimore Sun* quote in same issue; *New-York Daily Tribune*, 1 November 1880; 3 November 1888.

[25] Josiah Royce, *The Philosophy of Loyalty* (New York, 1908), pp. 47–48. Royce began working on this subject since the publication of *The Religious Aspect of Philosophy* in 1885. For a treatment of loyalty in Royce's work, see John E. Smith, "Royce's Spirituality: The Integration of Philosophical Reflection and Religious

In 1889, John Dewey described the problems besetting American democracy. Dewey argued that democracy defined merely as the aggregation of individual interests worked to defeat the larger interest of society. Dewey suggested that "democracy and the one, the ultimate, ethical ideal of humanity" were synonymous. "Democracy," said Dewey, "not only does have, but must have, a common will; for it is this common will which makes it an organism."[26]

For philosophers like Dewey and Royce as well as polemicists like Strong, the Gilded Age lacked a "common will" and a force to mobilize it. Philosophers and polemicists alike appealed to altruism, aggression, competition, and allegiance: all of these offered possibilities for a collaborative imperative. Editors and partisans seized on the same opportunities as their more learned contemporaries, with varying success.

One means of motivating the voters was by resorting to Tocqueville's "box with a false bottom": promoting old themes to serve new values. Gilded Age rhetoric gutted these old themes and stuffed them with new meanings. Conspiracy, and corruption became, again, two of the more familiar themes in American politics. Reincarnated in admonitory form, they reiterated old fears and served to warn voters of the failures of collaboration.

Old republican rhetoric laid much emphasis on "conspiracy." In the 1870s, however, editors invoked "conspiracy" mostly to promote vigilance against ballot fraud. An editorial entitled "The Republican Conspiracy," appeared in the *Louisville Courier-Journal* in 1876. "From the way in which the Republican managers boldly talk," said the *Courier-Journal*, they seemed inclined "to inaugurate HAYES in opposition to the voice of the people at the polls."[27] "Conspiracies" alleging election frauds figured importantly in the 1884 campaign. "The rump of the Grand Old Party is again to subvert the will of the people and to make elections a farce," said

Insight," introduction to *Josiah Royce: Selected Writings*, ed. John E. Smith and William Kluback (New York, 1988), pp. 4–24.

[26] John Dewey, *The Ethics of Democracy*, in *John Dewey: The Early Works, 1882–1898*, vol. 1, *1882–1888* (Carbondale, Ill., 1969), pp. 248, 232. See also James T. Kloppenberg, *Uncertain Victory: Social Democracy and Progressivism in European and American Thought, 1870–1920* (New York, 1986), p. 97.

[27] *Louisville Courier-Journal*, 6 November 1876.

the *New York World.* "Forewarned is forearmed. Let the citizens of the threatened States take means to thwart the conspiracy and to bring those concerned in it to grief."[28] The *New-York Tribune* in the same year urged readers "to weigh the consequences of supporting an immoral candidate and a corrupt party, united to-day in a conspiracy for plunder and spoils."[29]

The most prevalent cry of conspiracy raised in the late 1880s drew upon the notion of conspiracy as a form of economic collusion. "The 'Trust' idea of limiting production to raise prices is spreading fast," said Joseph Pulitzer's *New York World* in 1888. "The farmers have precisely the same right to enter into a conspiracy of this kind against society that the sugar-refiners or oil-mill owners have." In 1892 the *New York World* attacked both political and economic conspiracies. The "Democratic party is engaged in a contest for the people against a conspiracy of politicians without patriotism and plutocrats without pity."[30]

The word "combinations" connoted both conspiracy and another word with some resonance from the Jacksonian age: monopoly. Editors associated combinations with political fraud on the one hand and economic concentration on the other. "Here in Georgia," said the Atlanta *Constitution* in 1876, "we have congressmen to elect against a powerful and corrupt combination, that does not stop to consider means." James G. Blaine, in a speech at Binghamton, New York in 1884, raised the specter of combinations and conspiracy to good effect. He made a connection between "combinations" and the "disloyalty" of the South. The South, once "arrayed in war" against the Union, now attempted, "by a great combination" to seize the government of the United States. Returning the accusation, the *Louisville Courier-Journal* charged that Blaine had gathered around him "criminals and political freebooters." "Rule or ruin is the motto of this combination." "Republican orators," said the *Baltimore Sun* in 1888, "pose as the people's friends while their hands are in the people's pock-

---

[28] *New York World,* 27 October 1884.

[29] *New-York Daily Tribune,* 1 November 1884.

[30] *New York World,* 8 October 1888, 24 October 1892. See also the *New Orleans Times Democrat,* 8 November 1892; Atlanta, *The Constitution,* 6 November 1892.

ets, abstracting therefrom the sustenance of monopolies, trusts and other like odious combinations." "The money combinations to corrupt the ballot are on the Democratic side," said the *New-York Daily Tribune* in 1892.[31]

The most frequent charge in the Gilded Age vocabulary was corruption. Editors gradually redefined this word to fit the transformed values of the nineteenth century. Corruption had a long connection with Anglo-American political rhetoric, beginning early in the eighteenth century and continuing through the antebellum era.[32] Even in the Gilded Age, corruption still retained some eighteenth-century connotations of decay from a state of political equilibrium. Beginning in the Jacksonian era, however, a different connotation of corruption appeared in electioneering rhetoric. Corruption became increasingly synonymous with thievery rather than with decay. The twin perils of "theft and corruption" replaced the dangers of "corruption and tyranny." Corruption in this sense meant lack of personal probity, dishonesty, improper personal conduct, rather than a more general abuse of political power. It often connoted abuse of economic power as much as political power.[33]

The *Boston Post*, as late as 1872, employed the early republican meaning of corruption. "Corruption," according to the *Post*, was "flagrant abuse of power, the insolent encroachment of the Executive on the other branches of the Government [and] the absorption of authority by the Administration." In 1876 the *New Orleans Picayune* used the word in its newer sense, indicating "thievery" rather than "tyranny." The *Picayune* said the Grant administration had "incurred the reproach of civilized nations on account of the dishonesty and corruption of Republican officials. A nation cannot

---

[31] *Constitution*, 5 November 1876; James G. Blaine, speech made at Binghamton, New York, on October 23, 1884, quoted in *Louisville Courier-Journal*, 2 November 1884, with reply; *Baltimore Sun*, 2 November 1888; *New-York Daily Tribune*, 5 November 1892.

[32] Gordon Wood writes that "the exploitation of public office for private ends—that is, corruption—was of course not new to American politics; it had been common in the colonial governments." *Radicalism*, p. 320.

[33] Mark Summers has written an exhaustive analysis of corruption in antebellum America. Summers' work indicates that the economic connotations of "corruption" were already common before the Civil War. See Summers, *Plundering Generation*.

maintain confidence and respect abroad or at home, while the men who conduct its affairs convert public office into a private perquisite."[34]

The *Chicago Tribune* in 1876 summed up the allegations Republicans leveled against urban Democrats. The northern Democratic campaign was "inspired and dominated by Tammany Hall," in 1876; "plunder, theft, corruption, and the spoils-system have always been the policy of Tammany. The *New-York Tribune* said Tilden's "life-long association with the worst politicians of a rotten party in the most corrupt city in the Union cannot be forgotten when he promises reform." A vote against Blaine, said the *Louisville Courier-Journal* in 1884, was a vote "against hypocrisy, against corporate corruption, against the sale of public influence." The Atlanta *Constitution* charged Republican "desperadoes" were "accumulating a corruption fund."[35]

If newspapers of both parties derided their opponents for corruption, partisan newspapers often celebrated their own candidates as champions of "morality." Morality assumed an antithetical relationship to corruption. Questions of probity gradually assumed overriding salience in political campaigns: no one any longer took a candidate's honesty for granted. Morality connoted more than just honesty. Editorials contrasted morality with a multitude of sins, public and private, from fraud and dishonesty to fornication.

In 1872, the *Boston Post* referred to public morality: "If intellect, public morality, experience, accomplishments, integrity and wisdom are desirable at all in the formation and preservation of a party, it can safely be said of Grantism that its existence is but a fleeting fraud and fiction." In 1876 the same newspaper referred to the low moral tone of the Grant presidency, not in individual conduct but in public practice: it spoke of "the grossly loose morals,

[34] *Boston Post*, 2 November 1872; *New Orleans Daily Picayune*, 6 November 1876. See also Atlanta *Constitution*, 5 November 1876; *Boston Post*, 4 November 1876. For eighteenth-century connotations of corruption, see Bailyn, *Ideological Origins*, pp. 22–93. Jeremy Bentham gives a standard eighteenth-century definition of corruption in his *Handbook*, p. 149.

[35] *Chicago Daily Tribune*, 5 November 1876; *New-York Daily Tribune*, 2 November 1876; *Louisville Courier-Journal*, 2 November 1884; Atlanta *Constitution*, 29 October 1884.

both of legislation and administration," which presented a picture "without a parallel in this country."[36]

Private as well as public morality appeared as an important editorial subject in the presidential campaign of 1880. The *New Orleans Times* commented in 1880 that "the private characters and public records of the candidates have been dissected and suspected with a thoroughness that leaves nothing more to be said about them." The *New York World* said the "personal integrity, firmness and solid moral qualities" of presidential candidates had been "a leading question" with leaders of both parties.[37]

In the 1884 election, the public and private conduct of the two presidential candidates, Grover Cleveland and James G. Blaine, played a particularly important role in campaign rhetoric. Partly because both candidates were vulnerable on this subject, the contest degenerated into *ad personam* attacks on a scale unprecedented since the early 1800s. If rhetoric in Britain used the personalities of Disraeli and Gladstone to incarnate the parties' policies, rhetoric in the United States used the personalities of Blaine and Cleveland to incarnate the parties' vices.

The Democratic *Louisville Courier-Journal* warned a victory for Blaine would "make the standard of morality which prevails among the criminal classes the standard of uprightness in political life." In an editorial entitled "FOR MORALITY ONLY," the *New-York Tribune* declared that the "conscience and common-sense of the American people revolt against the idea" of Cleveland's election. There was "scarcely a religious newspaper in the country to-day that dares to urge its readers to vote for him. From a thousand pulpits in the land rises the cry, 'Unclean! Unclean!' " A *Chicago Tribune* editorial referred to Cleveland as a "confessed libertine." "If confession is good for the soul," said the *Chicago Tribune*, "there is great promise for the purification of the soul of Grover Cleveland."[38]

Reverend Henry Ward Beecher excused the Democratic nominee's past by declaring, "If every man in New York State who has

---

[36] *Boston Post*, 4 November 1872, 25 October 1876.

[37] *New Orleans Times*, November 2, 1880; *New York World*, 25 October 1880.

[38] *Louisville Courier-Journal*, 2 November 1884; *New-York Daily Tribune*, 2 November 1884; *Chicago Daily Tribune*, 29 October 1884.

broken the seventh commandment should vote for Cleveland he would be elected by a 200,000 majority." The *Chicago Tribune* could not resist drawing its readers' attention to the parallel between Cleveland's moral failings and those of Beecher himself, who had been listed as co-respondent in the Tilton adultery case ten years earlier."[39]

Business interests and their political preferences figured prominently in the 1884 campaign. Editorials often appealed to "honest" businessmen as the moral arbiters of late nineteenth century American politics; at the same time they attacked "speculators" and "monopolists" as the instigators and abettors of corruption. For both Democratic and Republican journals, the distinction between honest businessmen and speculators or monopolists appeared many times during the campaign. Particularly for the Democratic press, the distinction between honest businessmen and the "Money Kings" supporting Blaine was an important one.

According to the Atlanta *Constitution,* the "movement of business men" to the Democrats was "the most remarkable feature of the campaign." "The real business men," said the *Constitution,* thought "less perhaps of themselves than of their children and their country." They were "going over to Cleveland and honest government in droves."[40] The *New-York Tribune* proclaimed the businessmen would decide the state election. "The conservative men of this great city see that this choice must be made by them," said Whitelaw Reid's editorial. Businessmen made "the wise and almost the inevitable decision that public welfare" required "Republican success."[41]

The Democratic press referred to Blaine's 1884 dinner at Delmonico's with industrialists and financiers as a feast with the "Money Kings," likening it to Belshazaar's feast in the Book of Daniel. According to the *New York World,* money was "the principal dish to be served up at the BLAINE banquet at Delmonico's" The banquet "is to be a Feast of Finance, a Dinner of Dollars." Did the people know the men at the "Corruption Feast" who thus conspired "to defraud them of their rights?" Did they see "the millionaire

---

[39] *Chicago Daily Tribune,* 29 October 1884.

[40] Atlanta *Constitution,* 28 October 1884.

[41] *New-York Daily Tribune,* 30 October 1884.

monopolists and speculators as pure patriots willing to give their money to serve their country? . . . Or do they know them for selfish, grasping, unscrupulous men who have corrupted Legislatures and Courts in the past, and who give their money to help BLAINE because they know, if elected, BLAINE will help them?"[42]

In "BLAINE AND THE MONEY KINGS," the *Boston Post* asserted that Blaine was the "willing tool of the money kings of Wall-street, and that his election depends upon the size of their contributions to his corruption fund." Blaine was the honored guest of "the very men who debauch the ballot, corrupt the judiciary and purchase legislatures." They are "selfish, grasping, unscrupulous monopolists," said the *Post*.[43]

In the 1888 campaign, the press began to search for new ways to persuade the voters to turn out at the polls. Many of the independent newspapers appealed to voters in the purely deliberative "educational" campaign. Deliberative questions had been addressed before to a mass audience. In 1876, 1888, and 1892, however, the national party organizations boldly attempted to put the issues before the voters without many of the usual rhetorical embellishments. In an 1888 editorial the "independent" *New York Times* declared, "Now that the canvass is over, while the result has not yet been declared, is an appropriate time for the country to congratulate itself on having had, for the first time in the history of young, or of middle aged voters, an educational campaign."[44]

The *Times* may have been premature in its congratulations. The country had benefited from presidential contests waged over deliberative questions in 1876, 1888, and 1892. The voters found more electioneering manifestoes on tariff policy and civil service reform than ever before. That did not impel the average voter to the polls. "Tariff treatises are for the college room, not for the open field of a great popular controversy," said the *New York Sun*.

---

[42] *New York World*, 29 October 1884, 31 October 1884, referring to Walt McDougall's cartoon in the *World* titled "The Royal Feast of Belshazzar Blaine and the Money Kings," and alluding to Dan. 5:1–4 AV. See my discussion of McDougall's cartoon in Chapter 10.

[43] *Boston Post*, 1 November 1884.

[44] *New York Times*, 6 November 1888.

"The people must feel they are battling for the political champion-ship."[45]

Pure deliberation did not prove as effective as the educational campaigners had hoped. In 1892 voter turnout declined for the first time in twenty years. On the day after the 1892 election, the *New York Times* hailed Cleveland's victory. "The campaign on the Democratic side has been one of candid and able discussion. There have been no claptrap, no appeals to purblind prejudice, no paltering in a double sense with the questions of the day."[46]

Yet even the *New York Times* recognized that deliberation alone, lacking inspiration, did not motivate voters. On election eve the paper had engaged in a different style of campaigning. If Mr. Cleveland were elected, said the *Times,* it would be "a victory like that which was won in 1860 over the sordid and corrupting influ-ence of the slave power." Images of the Civil War seemed more effective in getting out the vote than pure deliberation, even among the *New York Times's* readership.[47]

The voters greeted the educational campaigns with apathy and confusion. The party press may have helped boost voter interest by continuing to publish admonitory editorials in the educational campaigns. Even the partisan press complained, however, of the fragmentation of the common interest. The parties failed in their high-minded attempt to provide a purely deliberative campaign for the American voters. The deliberative campaigns lacked a moral message that connected to earlier partisan themes. Without a gifted orator, a Lincoln or a Gladstone, to convey the message, the deliberative educational campaign offered the voters only policy prescriptions. The educational campaign did not manufacture public interest in public principles.

Hortatory rhetoric had not disappeared in Gilded Age politics. Those on the margins of politics, such as labor reformers, single

---

[45] *New York Sun,* 7 September 1892, partially quoted in McGerr, *Decline of Popular Politics,* p. 102. Turnout in 1892 was 74.7 percent of the eligible voters. See U. S. Department of Commerce, Bureau of the Census, *Historical Statistics of the United States, Colonial Times to the Present,* 2 vols. (1975; White Plains, N.Y., 1989), 1:1072. See also McGerr's discussion of the educational campaign and low turnout, *Decline of Popular Politics,* pp. 102–4.

[46] *New York Times,* 9 November 1892.

[47] Ibid., 8 November 1892.

taxers, and populists still employed inspirational language for their audiences. One orator in the late nineteenth century restored a moral vision to the center of American politics. William Jennings Bryan joined the language of battle and Bible and reinvigorated electioneering. He had much in common with Jacksonian and antebellum orators. Bryan also borrowed from admonitory rhetoric: he reminded partisans of their political responsibilities and warned them of the consequences of failing to do their duty.

In the 1896 campaign Bryan described a choice for the voters "between Man and Mammon, between democracy and plutocracy." Voters should view all questions "from a moral standpoint and arraign evil at the bar of public conscience." Bryan spoke about a distinction between corporate and natural man that echoed the language of Genesis. God gave man a soul and "warned him that in the next world he would be held accountable for the deeds done in the flesh; but when man created the corporation he could not endow that corporation with a soul, so that if it escapes punishment here it need not fear the hereafter."[48]

In his speech at the Chicago Democratic convention in 1896, Bryan revived the old republican theme of "independence," likening the struggle for bimetallism to the struggle of the Founders for self-determination. "Our ancestors," said Bryan, "had the courage to declare their political independence of every other nation. . . . Shall we, their descendants," he asked, "declare that we are less independent than our forefathers?"[49]

Bryan linked the struggle for bimetallism to the Democratic value of "equal rights." In the most famous passage from the speech, he likened the sufferings of "toilers everywhere" to the dominant image in Christian iconography.

Having behind us the producing masses of this nation and the world, supported by the commercial interests, the laboring interests, and

[48] William Jennings Bryan, *The Commoner Condensed*, 7 vols. (Chicago, 1907), 5:1–2; William Jennings Bryan, "Commerce," a speech delivered at Chicago on October 7, 1908, in *Speeches of William Jennings Bryan*, 2 vols. (New York, 1911), 2:409–10.

[49] William Jennings Bryan, *The First Battle: A Story of the Campaign of 1896* (Chicago, 1896), p. 206.

the toilers everywhere, we will answer their demand for a gold standard by saying to them: You shall not press down upon the brow of labor this crown of thorns, you shall not crucify mankind upon a cross of gold.[50]

Among Fundamentalists, accustomed to intermingling scriptural and political subjects, Bryan generated an overwhelmingly enthusiastic response. To mainstream Protestants, Bryan's electioneering constituted a profanation of Christian sensibility. Catholics believed Bryan exploited sacred iconography to serve sectarian political ends. Jews may have heard anti-Semitic overtones in the references to bankers and crucifixion.[51]

Bryan grew up believing that the Bible was "not only the Word of God but the fountain of Wisdom."[52] Bryan and other fundamentalists saw no impropriety in drawing upon "the fountain of Wisdom," for political as well as religious inspiration. Lincoln and Lovejoy had sprinkled their orations with allusions to the scriptures. Bryan, on the other hand, drew upon the central components of biblical narrative, from such sources as Genesis, the book of Kings and the Gospels to convey his political analogies. He combined religious homiletics and secular exhortation in a way that would have seemed blasphemous to a pious American audience a century earlier. Bryan employed the ultimate symbol of

[50] Ibid.

[51] Rev. Charles S. Parkhurst of New York's Madison Square Presbyterian Church remarked that "mutual confidence does not exist today and attempts are being made, deliberate and hot blooded, to destroy what little of it remains. I dare, in God's pulpit, to brand such attempts as accursed and treasonable." Dr. Robert S. McArthur of the Calvary Baptist Church on New York's West Fifty-Seventh Street said of the "Cross of Gold" speech, "Really the author of that composition must be a very commonplace sort of a citizen." The Catholic bishop of St. Paul, Minn., James Ireland, suggested that Bryan's candidacy was "the great test of universal suffrage and popular sovereignty." Ibid., pp. 471–72. According to Richard Hofstadter, anti-Semitism in the American silver movement "did not go beyond a kind of rhetorical vulgarity, since no programmatic steps were urged against Jews as such." See "Free Silver and the Mind of 'Coin' Harvey," in *Paranoid Style*, p. 300. Hofstadter also observed that "the Greenback-Populist tradition activated" modern American anti-Semitism. See "The Folklore of Populism," in *The Age of Reform: From Bryan to F.D.R.* (New York, 1956), pp. 80–81.

[52] William Jennings Bryan and Mary Baird Bryan, *The Memoirs of William Jennings Bryan* (Philadelphia, 1925), pp. 43–44.

Christian iconography, the cross, to carry a secular political message.

James Bryce observed that stump speeches in America had the same primary importance that parliamentary oratory had in Britain. Congressional oratory "never gained that hold on the ideas and habits of the people which parliamentary debate held in England." "Stimulation," said Bryce, "not instruction or conviction, is the aim which the stump orator sets before himself."[53] Bryan had shown that stump *preaching* could create a new form of morally grounded political appeal. Bryan could stimulate his audience and instruct them in their political and moral duty. He did not succeed, however, in mobilizing Dewey's "common will." By disregarding the sensibilities of nonfundamentalist Democrats, Bryan condemned himself, his party and his style of rhetoric to a lengthy sojourn in the political wilderness.

At the end of the nineteenth century, American political rhetoric had not found an effective form of communicating with a mass electorate. Hortatory rhetoric inspired voters on principle but it also polarized them; it had brought the nation into civil war. Admonitory rhetoric instructed voters in their duties but did not inspire them; it made for sordid campaigns with charges and counter charges and it further debased the already lowered tone of politics. Pure deliberative rhetoric educated the voters on policy but it alienated them from politics. Politicians and editors seemed at the end of the century to have run out of solutions for simultaneously informing and persuading a mass electorate. Editors gradually decided they would inform and persuade their readership of other things besides politics.

[53] James Bryce, *The American Commonwealth* (Chicago, 1891), pp. 674, 671.

# CHAPTER NINE

# Fire and Strength, Sword and Fire:
# British Rhetorical Battles, 1880–1900

Well it is that no child is born of thee.
The children born of thee are sword and fire,
Red ruin, and the breaking up of laws,
The craft of kindred and the godless hosts
Of heathen swarming o'er the Northern Sea
                —Tennyson, *Idylls of the King,* *"Guinevere"*

I n the late nineteenth century a significant portion of the American press severed ties with political parties and became "independent." American politicians faced the problem of campaigning through a neutral press and they experimented with pure deliberation. British politicians faced a different problem in the late nineteenth century. In Britain, the press remained partisan but the numerical balance shifted in favor of the Conservatives. Between the Second Reform Act in 1867 and the Midlothian Campaign of 1879, many Liberal newspapers shifted their allegiance to the Conservatives. When Home Rule split the Liberals in 1886, many more cast their lot with the Liberal Unionists. The Conservatives had an overwhelming advantage among the metropolitan dailies by 1886. Liberal journals constituted a shrinking minority even among provincial dailies.

The Liberals faced the difficult challenge of communicating to the voters through an increasingly hostile press. Thanks to Gladstone's rhetorical abilities, the Liberals succeeded in mobilizing the voters *through* the press rather than *with* the press. In the United States, hortatory rhetoric declined in the late nineteenth century, whereas in Britain it persisted: the Liberals won elections through moral exhortation despite their lack of press support.

Before Midlothian, public opinion was "discovered" in Parliament. After Midlothian, Gladstone shifted the process of discovery via the press to the nation at large. He put his moral vision at the center of the general election campaigns. "Mr. GLADSTONE towers above the motley array," said the *Daily Telegraph* in 1880, "a whole party in himself." "Mr. GLADSTONE's electioneering campaign may be said to have begun at King's Cross, but so long as his energy and endurance last it is impossible to say where it may end," said *The Times* in the same year. Gladstone "has touched the imagination of the people," said *The Times* in 1885.[1] The *Leeds Mercury* observed in 1886, "The supremacy of the PRIME MINISTER, not merely in argument, but in moral force, stands out with striking distinctness." "GLADSTONE's chief mission," said the *Mercury* was to "touch and awaken those better and truer sentiments in the hearts of men which underlie the shibboleths of party and the cant of politics."[2]

Gladstone's oratory in the general election of 1880 displayed what Matthew Arnold called "fire and strength." Quoting Tennyson, Gladstone addressed the Conservative Chancellor, Sir Stafford Northcote, thus: "The children born of thee are sword and fire, red ruin and the breaking up of laws." The *Pall Mall Gazette* remarked that the Liberals possessed "a righteous blood-thirst, like that we find celebrated in certain passages of the Old Testament."[3]

While the Liberals faced the challenge of communicating through a hostile medium, the Conservatives faced their own communications problems. They had increasing support among the editors and proprietors but they lacked anyone with Gladstone's

[1] *Daily Telegraph*, 30 March 1880; *The Times*, 31 March 1880, 24 November 1885. *The Times* the following year denounced Gladstone's practice of placing "momentous" issues before the electors directly. This innovation closely resembled "that instrument of tyranny invented for the enslavement of Frenchmen and called by the French name of *plébiscite*." *The Times*, 1 July 1886.

[2] *Leeds Mercury*, 29 June 1886.

[3] Arnold, *Culture and Anarchy*, p. 152; Gladstone is quoted in the *Daily Telegraph*, 30 March 1880. Gladstone words are from Tennyson's *Idylls of the King*, "Guinevere," lines 422–23. *Pall Mall Gazette*, 30 March 1880.

ability to inspire and mobilize their supporters. The Conservatives
often found themselves responding to Liberal rhetoric and repudi-
ating Liberal initiatives. The *Pall Mall Gazette* observed in 1885,
"It is a veritable game of political hunt-the-slipper. The Liberal no
sooner invents a cry than the Conservative endeavours to trump
it."[4] Some Conservatives were quite effective at trumping the Liberals. The most effective—and often most intemperate—responses
to Gladstone's speeches came from Lord Randolph Churchill.
One report in the *Pall Mall Gazette* suggests Churchill's abilities
when he delivered a speech before the 1886 Tory Caucus.

> Lord Randolph told his audience that the Empire was in danger,
> that Mr. Gladstone was a liar and a madman; that the Irish problem
> was insoluble; that if the English withdrew from Ireland the Anglo-
> Saxon Protestant and the Roman Catholic Celt would fall and destroy
> each other.[5]

In the United States, military imagery, organization, ritual and
discipline had been important components of the political culture
well before the Civil War. Battle imagery appeared surprisingly
often in British electioneering appeals as well. In the late nineteenth century the British became infatuated with the idea of
politics as combat. British political language portrayed political
conflict in the rich figurative language of battle.[6]

*The Times* portrayed the 1880 election not as gladiatorial combat
but as the clash of armies. "The great battle for which all parties
have been diligently girding themselves for the last three days
has now begun in earnest," it said. "Yesterday a few undefended
positions were secured, some by one side, and some by the other;
but between to-day and the end of the week the real struggle will
be fought out, and the substantial victory will fall to one side or
the other." The Conservative *Globe* likewise saw no reason for "a

---

[4] *Pall Mall Gazette,* 23 November 1885.

[5] Ibid., 28 June 1886. See also R. F. Foster, *Lord Randolph Churchill: A Political
Life* (Oxford, 1981), p. 412.

[6] Perhaps historians should consider both British and American infatuation
with the language of combat in politics as part of a larger phenomenon, having
nearly as much to do with the dominant ethic of aggressiveness and competitive-
ness as with the immediate experience of imperialism or the Civil War.

despondent view of the general battle field." The Conservatives would see "that the struggle is of an exceptionally fierce and close sort." They should "acquit themselves like men on behalf of the great principles in whose truth they believe." It was the "paramount duty of Conservatives," said the *Globe,* "to show by their zeal and determination that the spirit which gave them power in 1874 burns as fiercely as ever."[7]

The editorials suggested that voters should submit to their superiors. The time had come, the Conservative *Globe* declared, "for each individual elector to exert himself as strenuously as if the issue of victory or defeat depended on his vote and influence." "We are now on the eve of the actual battle," said the *Standard.* "It is for the people now to decide under which banner they will fight, and which master they will serve."[8] The Liberal *Daily Chronicle* declared, "We are right in the heat and press of the great electoral battle which is to decide not only the fortunes of parties, but, in a certain sense, that of England as well. In a few days 'the dumb debate of the ballot-box' will settle the chief controversy of the hour." All members of the Liberal party "should be up and doing"; they should "meet the event, as LONGFELLOW has it, 'with a heart for any fate.' "[9]

British editorials on occasion explicitly borrowed the imagery of the American Civil War. The Liberals opposed to Irish Home Rule adopted the name "Unionists," self-consciously identifying themselves with Abraham Lincoln and the cause of the American North. The Liberal Unionists associated themselves with Lincoln: as Lincoln had resisted southern secessionism, so the Unionists in Britain would resist Irish nationalism.

Their opponents within the Liberal party, the supporters of Irish Home Rule, had a very different view of the Unionists. Home Rule supporters linked the Unionists themselves with Confederate secessionism, since the Unionists threatened to withdraw from the Liberal party. "The Liberal party is engaged in a civil war," said

---

[7] *The Times,* 31 March 1880; London, *Globe,* 1 April 1880.

[8] *Globe,* 24 November 1885; London *Standard,* 19 November 1885.

[9] London *Daily Chronicle,* 20 November 1885, quoting Henry Wadsworth Longfellow's "A Psalm of Life," line 34.

the *Liverpool Daily Post* in 1886, likening the party split to "the great Secession struggle": "Let us hope that when the Liberal civil war is over Liberals will be brothers again, and while it lasts there will be no bitterness or hatred."[10]

The British had additional reasons for the increased linkage of battle and ballot box in the 1880s. The Ballot Act in 1872 established the secret ballot for British electors. "The ballot," said the *Leeds Mercury*, had "wrought a revolution in the old system, and we have to wait until the poll is declared before we can, as a rule, anticipate the results of the battle."[11] The Corrupt Practices Act of 1883 made traditional forms of bribery and influence illegal. The British elector, secure from intimidation or bribery, could exercise the franchise in secret.[12]

The Third Reform Act extended the franchise in 1884. The Liberal *Leeds Mercury* in 1885 offered an unusually positive view of the new political order after the Third Reform Act, even invoking Abraham Lincoln.

> We are standing on the watershed of two epochs. Behind us lies the toilsome road by which many a pause and struggle, emerged from the dark days of political slavery; before us lies the future in which the nation will be master in its own house, in which the reign of privilege will cease, and in which, in the memorable words of LINCOLN, "government of the people, by the people and for the people," will be established throughout the land.[13]

Other Liberal newspapers expressed a less confident view of politics in the aftermath of the Third Reform Act. When "the throne of Demos is surrounded by a new and abject race of flatterers, who make his caprice their law—it is not surprising that every one should be very much in a fog as to where we are going, or what is going to be settled at the polls," said the *Pall Mall Gazette.* The *Manchester Guardian* in 1885 said that "in place of an orderly

---

[10] *Liverpool Daily Post*, 30 June 1886.

[11] *Leeds Mercury*, 30 March 1880.

[12] Cornelius O'Leary, *Elimination of Corrupt Practices in British Elections* (Oxford, 1962), passim.

[13] *Leeds Mercury*, 23 November 1885.

and intelligible struggle in which every point is noted and every change is understood," the election had become "a confused medley—a Babel of voices in which each champion seeks only to claim the attention of his limited audience while the larger movements of a contest on a great scale are wanting."[14]

The Liberals in 1885 centered their campaign around Gladstone, despite his intention to make the general election a referendum on further concessions of governmental authority to Ireland. Sir William Harcourt expressed the party's view in addressing a London gathering. "The Liberal party has a leader such as no party in any age or in any country has ever known," he said. "We shall fight for the old cause and for the old man." The Liberals would go forth, appealing "to the millions whom Mr. Gladstone has enfranchised, we shall go forth 'conquering and to conquer.' "[15]

In 1885 the Conservatives warned of the fundamental threat posed by the Liberals to church, state, and empire. To the *Standard*, the issue in the 1885 general election was the survival of English institutions. If the Liberals triumphed, "the England we have known—the England of history, the England built up by our ancestors with such infinite wisdom, valour, and public spirit—will disappear, and a new and very different England will take her place." The election was a struggle between "those who would maintain and those who would mangle and mutilate" the Constitution. If "we are to enter upon an era of Church Disestablishment, revolution of the land laws, reorganisation of local government, and a general overturning of our national Institutions," said the *Standard*, "we shall be simply jumping out of safety into Chaos."[16]

In the June general election of 1886, Gladstone made Ireland again the center of the election. The Liberal Government of the spring of that year had introduced Home Rule and witnessed the departure of Radicals and Whigs alike. Ireland became for Gladstone a kind of holy crusade for the rest of his political life. Speaking in Midlothian, Gladstone called upon his listeners to

[14] *Pall Mall Gazette*, 23 November 1885; *Manchester Guardian*, 27 November 1885.

[15] William Vernon Harcourt, *"Resignation of the Gladstone Government": Speech of the Right Hon. Sir William Vernon Harcourt at the Meeting of the London and Counties Union at St. James's Hall, June 16, 1885* (London, 1885).

[16] *Standard*, 19 November 1885.

reflect on Home Rule, "in the name of Almighty God, each one of you in the sanctuary of his chamber, in the sanctuary of his heart and of his soul."[17]

Ireland's conflicts in religion, representation, and its assimilation, or lack thereof, into the British political culture helped reaffirm traditional Conservative values. The Conservatives used the Irish question in reaffirming their appeals for "Unity" and in warning of threats to the established church, the Acts of Union, and the security of the empire. Conservatives responded to Gladstone in 1886 by asserting the importance of the empire. "To-morrow practically begins the great battle which is to decide whether Englishmen are to retain control of the Empire," said *The Times* in 1886, or whether they would be persuaded by Gladstone to "strike their flag at the demand of a mere handful of arrogant enemies marshalled by the lost leader of English Liberalism."[18] The *Standard* referred to the 1886 general election as one of "the most momentous Electoral Battles in which the English people have ever been engaged." The *Standard* inquired whether the nation would "divorce itself from this history of its past and the continuity of its future, and in a fit of bewilderment and fear abandon the obligations of duty and prove insensible to the whispers of honour." "The English Parliament has come to some momentous decisions big with the fate of nations," said *The Times*, but none had been "more critical, when looked at in the light of its near and remote consequences," than Home Rule. *The Times* said the "subversion of the whole constitution of these islands is an enterprise which at the lowest calls for some little deliberation."[19]

The Unionist *Daily Chronicle* invoked the specter of the French Revolution to condemn Gladstone's temporizing with the Irish Nationalists. "It is, alas! the fixed delusion of the Girondist that he can control the Jacobin, and that when he has sown the wind the harvesting of the whirlwind will give him no trouble." Home Rule would have two results, said the *Chronicle*. "The first result is

<hr>

[17] William Ewart Gladstone, *The Speeches and Public Addresses of the Right Hon. W. E. Gladstone*, ed. A. W. Hutton and H. J. Cohen, 10 vols. (London, 1892–94), 9:150.

[18] *The Times*, 1 July 1886.

[19] *Standard*, 1 July 1886; *The Times*, 1 July 1886.

separation. The second is the torture of Protestant minorities all over Ireland." The *Manchester Guardian* argued for Home Rule on the grounds of expediency. "It is certain that Home Rule extended at long last, after a continuous struggle, would not be the same thing and would not be received in the same spirit as Home Rule given ungrudgingly and frankly now. It is a great issue, and we only hope that Manchester may rise to the occasion."[20]

Gladstone in the 1892 campaign again took up the cause of Home Rule and made it the central issue of the election. In a Newcastle address the year before, Gladstone explained to his listeners why a Liberal victory was essential. "Six millions of you, by your votes, determine the course which the Imperial policy is to follow, and with that power you must accept the duties and responsibilities which belong to it. If Ireland is oppressed hereafter it will be oppressed by you, by the people of this country."[21]

During Gladstone's general election tour of Scotland in 1892, Gladstone was due to make an important speech at the Theatre Royal in Glasgow. In the hours just before, John Morley found him poring over a volume of Horace. "I've just thought of something," he said to Morley. "Castor and Pollux will finish my speech at Glasgow."[22] Gladstone declared that Liberal policy in Ireland would bring about brotherhood: "We whose political wisdom is for so many purposes recognized by the nations of civilised Europe and America have at length found the means of meeting this oldest and worst of all our difficulties, and of substituting for disorder, for misery, for contention, the actual arrival and the yet riper promise of a reign of peace."[23]

The press had a mixed reaction to this speech. The Liberal *Daily News* hailed the Theatre Royal speech as the most remarkable Gladstone had delivered for a long time. It deserved, said the *Daily News* "to be ranked with an immortal passage in the greatest speech of DEMOSTHENES, and with the closing sentences of BURKE'S noble oration at Bristol."[24] The *Standard* had a different view: "There is

---

[20] *Daily Chronicle,* 2 July 1886; *Manchester Guardian,* 2 July 1886.
[21] Gladstone, *Speeches,* 10:395.
[22] John Morley, *The Life of William Ewart Gladstone,* 3 vols. (London, 1903), 3:492.
[23] Speech at Theatre Royal, Glasgow, July 2, 1892, quoted in ibid., p. 492.
[24] London *Daily News,* 2 July 1892.

nothing in the speech which MR. GLADSTONE delivered at Glasgow on Saturday to convert a single voter to his view of the Irish Question." The *Standard* described "the great battle between the champions of the Unity and the advocates of the Disruption of the Three Kingdoms."[25]

Gladstone's speech at Glasgow may not have been sublime, but the response was ridiculous. Rather than concentrating on the merits of Gladstone's Home Rule proposals, editorials focused on how to combat the influence of the Irish Catholic clergy. The *Standard* warned that Gladstone seemed oblivious to the influence of the Roman Catholic clergy on "the 'illiterate voter' and of the scandalous manner in which the priests have acted as personating agents in the polling booths."[26] The *Manchester Guardian* took an equally absurd position on Home Rule and clerical influence, arguing that Home Rule "will seriously weaken and in the long run destroy the present great influence of the Irish Catholic clergy." The *Guardian* again argued from expediency, saying that "if there were no prospect of Home Rule a similar battle would have to be fought by the next British Government, and so on *ad infinitum*."[27] "Nothing more grotesquely at variance with plain and palpable facts could be imagined than the suggestion that this election has not been fought on Home Rule, or not fought at close quarters," said the *Pall Mall Gazette*. The Anglican Archdeacon of London declared that he found in the general election of 1892 "much to make a philosopher laugh and a Christian weep."[28]

Home Rule, religious disestablishment, temperance, and unity stood out in 1895 as the prominent themes of the general election. The Liberals waged this campaign without Gladstone's oratorical direction. According to the *Morning Post*, the choice between the parties amounted to a decision in favor of a Government "pledged to maintain in all parts of the Kingdom law and order and public liberty," or for a Government "pledged to advance Home Rule, to abolish the House of Lords, to disestablish two Churches, to

---

[25] *Standard*, 2 July 1892, 4 July 1892.
[26] Ibid., 4 July 1892.
[27] *Manchester Guardian*, 4 July 1892.
[28] *Pall Mall Gazette*, 4 July 1892.

ruin the publicans, and to disfranchise the House of Commons for engaging in a programme of social reform." The *Daily Telegraph* expressed hope that Londoners would not be "willing and anxious to place England once more under the Irish heel, and to hand over its most vital interests to be bought and sold in the electioneering market." The Liberals would create "a weak, a divided and a discredited Realm in place of the strong, united, and respected State which our fathers bequeathed to us."[29]

"We are, indeed, fighting with our backs against the wall," said the *Globe* in 1895, "and our success in this supreme struggle depends upon the effort of every member of the party." England was standing "at the parting of the ways, and it is for those of her sons who are conscious of their duty to their mother country, and the splendour of their own birthright, to show her the path which she should follow."[30] *The Times* refused to believe "the people of Great Britain will place their trust in those who have trafficked with what MR. BRIGHT truly called 'a rebel party' for the disruption of the United Kingdom."[31]

The Liberal papers warned their readers to beware of Conservative "obstructionism." The *Daily News* said the issue in the election of 1895 was the "obstructionism" of the House of Lords. "The House of Lords is becoming more and more the question of the day. . . . Every Liberal election address, every Liberal speech throughout the country, testifies: 'there is the enemy.' "[32]

With Gladstone's death in 1898, rhetorical polarization subsided. Gladstone's moralistic appeals antagonized the Conservatives and helped split his own party in the years between 1879 and 1895. The Liberal party faced daunting challenges after Gladstone's death: the continued hostility of the press and internal party divisions. Without a new message, and a skillful messenger, the Liberal party might face permanent minority status.

Liberal rhetoric required a new voice to articulate a new theme; one Liberal politician showed the ability to inspire the Liberal

[29] *Morning Post*, 13 July 1895; *Daily Telegraph*, 12 July 1895, 9 July 1895.
[30] *Globe*, 13 July 1895.
[31] *The Times*, 13 July 1895.
[32] *Daily News*, 11 July 1895.

electors. In some ways, David Lloyd George's rhetoric resembled Gladstone's. Like Gladstone, he linked his partisan moral appeals to apocalyptic imagery. Like William Jennings Bryan, Lloyd George alluded directly to the scriptures. Raised a Baptist, he understood the importance of biblical reference as a moral authority. In a speech in 1902, Lloyd George described the scriptures as "the voice of the best friend" children had.[33] Lloyd George used biblical examples to illustrate the popularity of Nonconformism in Wales. "If you recollect, it was Elisha who cleansed Naaman's leprosy but it was Gehazi who secured the emoluments. It is Nonconformity that cleansed the moral leprosy which had afflicted Wales under the quack doctoring of the Established Church, but it is the Gehazi of the Establishment that is enjoying the emoluments!" On another occasion he declared, "A Holy War has been proclaimed against Man's inhumanity to Man, and the people of Europe are thronging to the crusade." The "Dark Continent of Wrong is being explored, and there is a missionary spirit abroad for its reclamation to the Realm of Right." Lloyd George often used recurrent historical themes in his speeches as well. Lloyd George praised tenants' resistance against landlords. The landlords, he said, "woke the spirit of the mountains, the genius of freedom that fought the might of the Normans for two centuries."[34] If Gladstone built his exhortation on his own religious sensibility, Lloyd George exploited religious sensibility for his secular vision of social justice. Lloyd George's rhetoric proved very effective in mobilizing resentment; it turned those resentments into Liberal votes.

Lloyd George did not have a monopoly on hortatory rhetoric at the turn of the century, however. The Liberals lost some of their best speechmakers to the Unionists in 1886. Like Lloyd George, Joseph Chamberlain was a Nonconformist. Although he was a Unitarian, he used his religious background as Lloyd George

---

[33] Lloyd George, "Speech at Lincoln," December 12, 1902, quoted in Herbert Du Parcq, *Life of David Lloyd George* (London, 1912), 2:411–12. For the scriptures as a source of authority, see Ernst Cassirer, "Judaism and the Modern Political Myths," in his *Symbol, Myth, and Culture: Essays and Lectures of Ernst Cassirer, 1935–1945*, ed. Donald Philip Verene (New Haven, 1979), p. 237.

[34] Quoted in Owen, *Tempestuous Journey*, pp. 59, 54, 23. Lloyd George was referring to 2 Kings 5: 9–14, 20–27 AV.

and Bryan did, to inject moral authority into his appeals. After his break with the Liberals, Chamberlain used his considerable rhetorical abilities in warning against the perils of Home Rule. As the century turned, Chamberlain focused his attention on the empire. Chamberlain extolled empire by praising the Conservative value of unity.

> The new conception of Empire is of a voluntary organisation based on community of interests and community of sacrifices, to which all should bring their contribution to the common good. It is this new spirit, I believe, which we have need to infuse into our colonies. Our kinsfolk may be educated to this great ideal, but the gospel must be preached from colonial pulpits. It is not enough to lecture our children in addresses from home. Missionaries of Empire must spread the faith by personal intercession.[35]

Conservatives continued to appeal to "Unity" as Liberals appealed broadly to "Liberty." The transcendent values to which British parties appealed endured till the end of the century. At the end of the nineteenth century the parties and the press had succeeded in creating a participatory political system. Rhetoric mobilized the voters; rhetoric reinforced their partisan identities. Voters identified with their parties, understood their differences on policy, and turned out consistently to vote in general elections. The British political system had survived the challenge of democratization without revolution or civil conflict. Political campaigning at the end of the century polarized the nation to such an extent that dissolution became inevitable. Britain, already facing deep division lapsed into a different form of electioneering in the "khaki" election of 1900. "Fire and strength" as Matthew Arnold observed, offered fleeting influence over the "Barbarians," "Philistines," and "Populace" that constituted the British upper, middle, and lower classes respectively.

> Candidates for political influence and leadership, who thus caress the self-love of those whose suffrages they desire, know quite well

---

[35] Speech at Guildhall, London, May 20, 1903. Quoted in Joseph Chamberlain, *Imperial Union and Tariff Reform: Speeches Delivered from May 14 to November 4, 1903* (London, 1903).

they are not saying the truth as reason sees it, but that they are using a sort of conventional language, or what we call clap-trap, which is essential to the working of representative institutions.[36]

In a sense the Boer War marked the rhetorical victory of claptrap in all the parties. Under Gladstone the Liberals had won all the previous rhetorical battles; in 1900 their rhetorical advantage disappeared and the Conservatives won this political war. The mandate claimed by the Conservatives in 1900 was short-lived and not entirely convincing. The popular vote margin was 1.8 million for the Conservatives to 1.6 million for the Liberals; both major parties lost seats.[37] Nevertheless the Conservative and Unionist press proclaimed the election a victory for unity. According to Northcliffe's *Daily Mail*, the Liberal party had "fallen into disrepute for two reasons—firstly, because it has failed to interpret the sentiment of the nation, and has imagined that an appeal to purely selfish interests would capture the electorate and give it power; and secondly, because it has failed as a whole to show in the hours of a great national crisis that its heart was for England and the Empire."[38] The empire provided a context for restoring the traditionally Conservative value of unity to a place of prominence, not only with the Tories and their Unionist allies but with the Liberals themselves. The Boer War provided an appropriate contextual setting in which to promote the new call for unity, supported by all parties. In "The Foundation of Unity," the Unionist *Daily Mail* called for unity and efficiency; "for a strong, united Government, for a permanent settlement in South Africa, and for the thorough re-organisation of our Army and defences . . . upon a business-like and efficient footing."[39] In "The Issue Before the Country," the *Daily Mail* said the election should prove a mandate for the future, "a demonstration to South Africa and the world that the

[36] Arnold, *Culture and Anarchy*, p. 152.
[37] F. W. S. Craig, *British Parliamentary Results, 1885–1918* (London, 1974), pp. 576, 578.
[38] London *Daily Mail*, 18 September 1900.
[39] Ibid., 19 September 1900. On the subject of business-like efficiency, see Geoffrey Russell Searle, *The Quest for National Efficiency: A Study in British Politics and Political Thought, 1899–1914* (Berkeley, 1971).

British people is not the weak creature of emotional reactions."
The Boers "must be made to see that the nation is united and
determined on the settlement."[40] The *Daily Telegraph* said the
Unionists "represented the feeling of the country, expressing its
determination and its hopes."[41] The *Daily Express* fastened its Liberal Unionist colors to its masthead and proclaimed itself in favor
of the new universalism.

### OUR POLICY.

Independent—Imperialist

Recognising the fact—hitherto apparently unknown in
newspaper circles—that there is something to be said on both
sides of most questions.

Advocating strenuously Home Reforms when
South Africa is settled.[42]

The problem for the Liberals of rebuilding a majority coalition
seemed far more serious than the Conservative victory in the
"khaki" election. For too long the Liberals had labored to preserve
a dwindling coalition under Gladstone's steadily expanding calls
for "liberty." The Liberal leader Lord Rosebery said that the object
of Liberalism should be to return to the positions of the party
before 1885. The best that could be said about "the khaki issue"
was that it "prevented the Liberals from regaining ground already
lost," said the *Daily News*.[43]

Some Liberals objected to their opponents' attempts to identify
Conservatism and Unionism with patriotism in the war. Sir Edward
Grey denounced the "gigantic imposture" of claiming patriotism
for one party. The *Westminster Gazette* denounced the electioneering tactics of Joseph Chamberlain in particular. "There never
was a cheaper kind of electioneering than this, and since it comes
from 'Imperialists' who are always talking to us about continuity

[40] *Daily Mail,* 21 September 1900.
[41] *Daily Telegraph,* 18 September 1900.
[42] London *Daily Express,* 21 September 1900.
[43] *Daily News,* 5 October 1900.

in external politics it is doubly bad. So far as the one issue is concerned it is the silliest kind of sham-fighting."[44]

Many Liberal newspapers enthusiastically embraced imperialism, claiming credit for the Liberals in creating the empire. Herbert Asquith reminded the voters that the "Empire was largely created by Liberal enterprise, and has been consolidated by Liberal policy, while the largest and most progressive nation in the world was lost to our Empire by Tory obstinacy." The *Daily News* gave credit to the Liberals for creating the Empire. "The Colonies are the creation of Liberalism." The Liberal party would not "be ousted from its proud position in relation to these Colonies in order to recognise the Tory party as the foster-parent."[45]

The new nationalism promoted social reconciliation. British Liberals and Conservatives alike called for increased cooperation between capital and labor. The *Daily Telegraph* observed the opportunity for social harmony after the 1895 general election. "Capital, so far from being the worst enemy of Labour, is in reality its best and truest friend." The voters had affirmed their belief "that labour is dependent for its very existence on Capital." If "no other moral were elicited by the General Election," said the *Telegraph,* this lesson had "almost incalculable advantage and importance."[46]

At the end of the nineteenth century, both in Britain and the United States, there was an increasing divergence of interest between publishers and party organizations. Newspapers in both countries became more independent of parties and increasingly intent on appealing to a universal market. As the newspapers became more independent they began to consider their primary role as conveying commercial information rather than political news or opinion. The political soldier had been transformed, as far as the press was concerned, into the economic consumer. In both Britain and the United States, there was a profound change in the marketing of newspapers for mass consumption and their content showed the influence of this change. The "Northcliffe

[44] *Westminster Gazette,* 27 September 1900.

[45] Asquith quoted in the *Daily News,* 17 September 1900, with comments from same issue.

[46] *Daily Telegraph,* 22 July 1895.

Revolution" underway in Britain and the "yellow journalism" of William Randolph Hearst and Joseph Pulitzer in America decisively affected electioneering rhetoric. Although these operations differed in marketing techniques and organizational approach, their electioneering style was similar.

Their new "universalist" rhetoric paradoxically stimulated a new exclusionism. One means of eliciting harmony among the general readership was to issue affirmative expressions of national superiority. At the end of the century, this tactic succeeded because of popular interest in the imperial quest for territory. Not surprisingly, Northcliffe led the cheering section for shouldering the special burdens incumbent on Anglo-Saxons. Election rhetoric in Britain and the United States reconverged around a set of reassuring themes. Electioneering language and visual images at the beginning of the twentieth century appealed to the widest audience possible, but political rhetoric had forfeited by this very effort at universal appeal the ability to mobilize a mass audience on controversial policy questions.

Rhetoric had temporarily exhausted itself as an instrument of mass mobilization at the turn of the century. Pure deliberation as practiced by the American Progressives and the British Fabians never generated mass enthusiasm. The hortatory rhetoric of Gladstone, Lloyd George, and especially Bryan turned away nearly as many voters as it converted. At the turn of the century, parties in both countries suffered an identity crisis. Rhetorical politics restored itself in the early twentieth century, with Theodore Roosevelt's election in 1904 and the Liberals' victory in 1906. Even strongly partisan newspapers shifted their attention inexorably towards a different form of persuasion, to the reader as consumer rather than as voter. For the readers of Northcliffe, Hearst, and Pulitzer, politics no longer furnished the primary source of their readers' interest or entertainment. Readers found themselves attracted by other "features" in the newspaper and the old form of electioneering enthusiasm declined.

The rhetoric of the yellow press had its effect in other ways as well. Partisans and press imprisoned themselves in their own distortions. "Everywhere," said J. A. Hobson, "the less reputable organs of the press are rightly regarded as disturbers of the public peace, living upon strong sensations; unwilling and often unable, to check the accuracy of the wild rumours they promulgate."[47] Rhetoric failed to provide a means of broader identification beyond the mere bonds of nationality. Release for this mobilized hostility came in the next decade; the result was a popular outburst of unprecedented ferocity. Events after 1914 dictated a curious reconciliation of rhetoric and reality.

[47] J. A. Hobson, *The War in South Africa: Its Causes and Effects* (London, 1900), p. 206.

# The Appeal to the Eye:
# Visual Communications in the
# United States and Britain, 1880–1900

For one person who is impressed by a speech, ten are convinced
by a cartoon. Even the best election speech is diffuse, and your
ordinary elector finds it as difficult to detect the points as to find
a needle in a bundle of hay. But a political cartoon is all point
and no padding.

—*Pall Mall Gazette*

At the end of the eighteenth century editors mimicked the
emphasis and rhythms of oral speech on the printed page.
A new form of communication emerged that helped to
expand a receptive audience for political rhetoric in newspapers.
At the end of the nineteenth century another important form of
communication emerged using visual forms of expression. It
helped to sustain a receptive audience.

Beginning in the 1880s, photochemical reproduction allowed
the publication of line drawings in daily newspapers. This meant
that cartoonists such as Thomas Nast, whose work had previously
appeared in *Harper's Weekly*, could now be published daily and
syndicated to a national audience. Cartoons and other graphic
illustrations began to assume an increasingly important role in
political persuasion.[1] With the retreat from familiar to formal ver-

[1] Morton Keller, *The Art and Politics of Thomas Nast* (New York, 1968), p. 327.

bal discourse, audiences could not as easily discover the moral import of much Gilded Age rhetoric. In an age seeking a "collaborative imperative," American cartoons were a vehicle providing moral focus and direction in the face of complexity and ambiguity.

If the illustrator often expresses the world as it is, the cartoonist creates a vision of what might be. Cartoonists are often moral saboteurs. Not coincidentally, cartoonists in the Renaissance, in Regency England, and in Cold War Eastern Europe were among the most creative—and subversive—of artists.

Judged from the late twentieth century, visual persuasion had nothing like the influence it would later enjoy through photography, cinema, and television. Unlike oral tradition, visual communication was a relatively new means of persuasion; like speech, however, it had a pronounced impact on the mass audience. Its very newness seemed to lend it greater persuasive power. Moreover, cartoons traditionally made use of what Rhys Isaac calls the "Speaking books" of "oral performance": especially the Bible and Shakespeare. Finally, visual persuasion was not subject to the same rules of relation, proof, and refutation governing print and oral argument.[2]

Cartoons enjoyed an important role in politics long before photochemical reproduction. Cartoonists of the late nineteenth century drew on a repertoire of visual satire extending back nearly two centuries. Three great traditions of caricature and graphic satire inspired Nast and his contemporaries. The first of these was the broadside, which flourished on both sides of the Atlantic, particularly in the eighteenth century. Broadsides (and two-sided broadsheets) often appeared in conjunction with newspapers, as extra sheets describing and illustrating calamities, executions, public events, crimes, and proclamations. They were often illustrated with woodcuts, either commissioned for the occasion or using an appropriate block already available. Broadsides declined in

---

[2] According to Isaac, " 'Speaking books' is a suitable term to convey the function of the highly important bodies of written words, such as the Bible and the common law reports. . . . The sacred texts had originated in oral peformance settings, and their constant recitation in churches and lawcourts ensured their exalted authority in the word-of-mouth culture of the common people." *Transformation of Virginia*, p. 123. Kathleen Hall Jamieson, *Eloquence*, makes the point that visual communications lack a logic and a grammar for argument, pp. 11–13, 59–61, 66.

importance, however, as newspapers exploited the typographical and visual devices of oral culture.[3] Broadsides in Britain endured until the elimination of the taxes on knowledge; thereafter they suffered the same decline as in the United States. Papers like *The Illustrated London News* catered to the broadsides' audience, offering a mixture of crime, sporting events, and public festivities.[4]

The second tradition which influenced cartoonists was English caricature, from William Hogarth in the 1730s through James Gillray and Thomas Rowlandson in the age of the French Revolution and the Napoleonic conflict. Gillray and Rowlandson brought the same scathing ridicule to graphic forms of satire that the *Anti-Jacobin* and the *Port-Folio* brought to verbal satire. Gillray drew caricatures for the *Anti-Jacobin,* including a visual contrast of William Pitt and Charles James Fox, entitled "Two Pair of Portraits" derived from John Horne Tooke's pamphlet of the same title (see Figure 1).[5]

In the 1840s, British caricature simplified its mockery, in the drawings of *Punch's* Richard Doyle and John Leech. *Punch* began publishing in 1841, in the midst of the Anti-Corn Law agitation, and it spawned a host of imitators, including the short-lived American magazine *Yankee Doodle* (1846–47). By mid-century *Punch* dominated British caricature and continued to do so for most of the century.[6]

The third important influence on cartoonists was French caricature. Some of the most important innovations in visual satire occurred in France after 1830. After the July Revolution, political satire in visual and verbal form appeared in *La Caricature, Charivari,*

[3] See Baumgardner's introduction to her *American Broadsides;* Mason I. Lowance and Georgia B. Baumgardner, eds., *Massachusetts Broadsides of the American Revolution* (Amherst, Mass., 1976); Ola Elizabeth Winslow, *American Broadside Verse; From Imprints of the Seventeenth and Eighteenth Centuries* (New Haven, 1930).

[4] Thomas Gretton, *Murders and Moralities: English Catchpenny Prints, 1800–1860* (London, 1980).

[5] Keller, *Art and Politics of Nast,* pp. 4–5; M. Dorothy George, *English Political Caricature, 1793–1832: A Study of Opinion and Propaganda* (Oxford, 1959); M. Dorothy George, *Hogarth to Cruikshank: Social Change in Graphic Satire* (New York, 1967); Cornelis Veth, *Comic Art in England* (London, 1930); Michael Wynn Jones, *The Cartoon History of Britain* (London, 1971). *Anti-Jacobin Review and Monthly Magazine,* October 1798; John Horne Tooke, *Two Pair of Portraits, Presented to All the Unbiassed Electors of Great Britain* (London, 1788).

[6] Jones, *Cartoon History of Britain,* pp. 154–55.

*Pair of Portraits;—presented to all the unbiafsed Electors of Great Britain, by John Horne Tooke.*

1 James Gillray's "Two Pair of Portraits" makes use of the familiar scene in *Hamlet* to compare Pitt and Fox. The caricature first appeared in the *Anti-Jacobin's* review of John Horne Tooke's pamphlet, October 1798.

and *Journal pour Rire,* and later in *La Lanterne.* Grandville, Cham, Garvarni, Philipon, Gustave Doré, and Honoré Daumier were important lithographers who contributed to French caricature.[7]

The word caricature is derived from the name of Annibile Carraci, who allegedly said of his craft, "A good caricature, like every work of art, is more true to life than reality itself." In the mid-

[7] Keller, *Art and Politics of Nast,* pp. 5–6. On Daumier, see Oliver W. Larkin, *Daumier: Man of His Time* (New York, 1966); Howard P. Vincent, *Daumier and His World* (Evanston, Ill., 1968); Jacques Lassaigne, *Daumier,* trans. Eveline Byam Shaw (New York, 1938); George Besson, *Daumier* (Paris, 1959); Eduard Fuchs, *Der Maler*

nineteenth century, however, the cartoon was beginning to assume a form different from simple caricature. Caricature gains its power by exaggeration of physical features.[8] In that sense caricature is the visual equivalent of hyperbole. Symbolism, the other visual form used with some success before the end of the nineteenth century, is the visual analogue of metonymy. Symbols achieve their success by creating a connection between an abstraction (e.g., king) and an adjunct or attribute (e.g., crown).

Cartoons, as they developed in the middle of the nineteenth century, were neither caricature nor symbolism, although they borrowed from both. Cartoons as a form of social commentary are didactic in nature and allegorical by necessity. Gillray, Rowlandson, and George Cruikshank drew visually complicated arrangements of prominent figures. Cartoons in the Regency period emphasized the verbal over the visual. Cartoonists penned elaborate dialogues into the available space in balloons. The French graphic satirists dispensed with these elaborate dialogues and used visual symbols instead. These symbols, such as cornucopias, olive branches, swords, and shields, had very clear associations and made the drawings easily comprehensible.

British and American cartoonists gradually adopted the simpler French style. Nowhere does this simplification appear more clearly than in the pages of *Punch*. To the twentieth century eye, Richard Doyle's cartoons in the 1840s appear much simpler and thus much clearer than those of his contemporary, John Leech. Doyle, who was the son of cartoonist John Doyle (known as "H.B.") echoed the line and shading of the French.

Perhaps the most popular of the mid-Victorian cartoonists was John Tenniel, who was the principal cartoonist for *Punch* from 1864 to 1901. Tenniel was a skillful draftsman, although his lines were often obscured in the process of wood engraving. Like the French, and the younger Doyle, Tenniel made his drawings comprehensible by symbols and allegories. Doyle and Tenniel often

---

*Daumier* (Munich, 1930).

[8] E. H. Gombrich observed that "the cartoonist can *mythologize the world by physiognomizing it.*" See Gombrich, "The Cartoonist's Armory," *South Atlantic Quarterly* 62 (Spring 1963): 219.

depicted the leading political figures in theatrical costume, frequently in Shakespearean or classical roles. Doyle cast Lord John Russell as Macbeth in 1847; Tenniel drew Gladstone as Pegasus in 1865, Disraeli as Hamlet in 1868, and a newly emancipated American slave as Caliban in 1863.[9]

The reliance on familiar themes was not new; cartoonists had always found it necessary to depend on recognizable contexts. Doyle and Tenniel and their successors emphasized the visual over the verbal; this meant they were more reliant on familiar themes. Tenniel's visual innovations were not matched by sharp-edged satire, however. By the middle of the century *Punch* had become institutionalized: in the words of one historian it "refrained from raising the hackles of its viewers."[10]

*Punch*'s long dominance of British caricature had no parallel in the United States. The short-lived *Yankee Doodle* was a pale imitation with far less influence.[11] Humor magazines only began to achieve success after the Civil War, with the appearance of *Puck* in 1876, *Judge* in 1881 and *Life* in 1889. American cartoons were far from abundant. From 1787 to 1829, only seventy-nine caricatures found their way into print. Britain produced more cartoons on the American Revolution than the Americans did.[12] Before the Civil War American technology lagged behind the British in visual mass reproduction. Wood engravings and lithographs were used sparingly and often reused. In 1834 the *Boston Post*, for example, reprinted a wood engraving, "The Good Ship Massachusetts," which had had been used in 1817 by the *Boston Commercial Gazette* (see Figure 2).[13]

[9] "The Electioneering Cauldron," *Punch* 13 (10 July 1847): 5; "Pegasus Unharnessed," *Punch* 49 (29 July 1865): 37; "Rival Stars," *Punch* 54 (14 March 1868): 115; "Scene from the American 'Tempest,' " *Punch* 44 (24 January 1863): 35.

[10] William Feaver, *Masters of Caricature: From Hogarth and Gillray to Scarfe and Levine*, ed. Ann Gould (London, 1981), pp. 71, 82–83. See also Jones, *Cartoon History of Britain*, p. 119; Ralph E. Shikes, *The Indignant Eye: The Artist as Social Critic in Prints and Drawings from the Fifteenth Century to Picasso* (Boston, 1969), p. 95; Syd Hoff, *Editorial and Political Cartooning* (New York, 1976), p. 67.

[11] Compare Doyle's "Electioneering Cauldron" with Read Del's "Pushing the Subject Home," which also parodies Macbeth, *Yankee Doodle* 2 (1847): 115.

[12] Leonard, *Power of the Press*, p. 98.

[13] *Boston Post*, 8 November 1834; *Boston Commercial Gazette*, 3 April 1817.

2 The wood engraving of "The Good Ship Massachusetts" appeared on the front page of the *Boston Commercial Gazette,* 3 April 1817. It was reused in an election issue of the *Boston Post,* on November 8, 1834. Courtesy, American Antiquarian Society.

American cartoonists had nevertheless played a small but vital role in American politics since Paul Revere's engraving of the Boston Massacre. Elkanah Tisdale's "Gerry-mander" cartoon appeared in the *Boston Gazette* in 1812 and contributed a word to the Anglo-American political lexicon. In the Jacksonian era, cartoonists depicted Old Hickory taking his cane to the "Hydra of Corruption," the Bank of the United States; opposition cartoonists cast Jackson as King Andrew I. Edward W. Clay produced a lithograph entitled "The Times," that blamed Andrew Jackson for the Panic of 1837.[14]

Perhaps because visual symbols and icons assumed such importance in Jeffersonian and Jacksonian politics and advertising, pictures and especially portraiture did not. Photographs could not be feasibly reproduced in newspapers until the halftone process was perfected near the end of the century. In the midst of the Civil War the face of Ulysses Grant was virtually unknown. There was no widely available picture of the Democratic nominee for vice president in 1872, B. Gratz Brown. Thomas Nast drew him as a name card, a visual cipher.[15]

Before the Civil War, editors harbored a prejudice against excessive illustrations in serious journals. Words, not pictures, persuaded. In Britain lavish illustrations were the province of the Sunday press, such as *The Illustrated London News*. The "Sundays" offered lurid crime stories, public spectacles and sporting events, hardly the stuff of serious journalism. The Civil War transformed the role of illustration in the American press. Maps, sketches of camp life, and full-scale drawings of battlefield scenes became a common sight in the American newspaper.[16]

The impact of so much visual information appearing in a brief period of time must have been profound.[17] Newspapers did not provide the same wealth of visual information once the Civil War was over, however, because lithography proved too expensive for ordinary subject matter. Magazines like *Harper's Weekly* and *Frank Leslie's Weekly* made extensive use of lithographs in the 1860s, and the visual medium had an important persuasive effect on the magazine audience. While British cartoonists in mid-century

[14] For Paul Revere's Boston Massacre (1770), see "Monumental Inscriptions," in Baumgardner, *American Broadsides;* for the "Gerrymander" Cartoon, see the Boston *Gazette,* 12 March 1812; for the "Hydra of Corruption" (1832), see the Broadside Collection, New-York Historical Society; for "King Andrew I" (1832), see the Broadside Collection, New-York Historical Society; for Edward W. Clay's "The Times" (1837), see the Broadside Collection, Library of Congress.

[15] Leonard, *Power of the Press,* p. 100.

[16] See Chapter 6, n. 2 herein.

[17] Thomas Leonard has observed of Gilded Age visual thinking, "Perhaps the most difficult thing to grasp is the attraction of abundant illustration in a culture starved for pictures." *Power of the Press,* pp. 98–99.

aspired to draw caricatures for *Punch* or *Vanity Fair*, American cartoonists began to appear in *Harper's* and *Leslie's*, where they had a more direct impact. The most influential of these serious cartoonists was Thomas Nast.

Nast was influenced in his linear technique by Tenniel and he borrowed the dramatic effects of Doré (whom he idolized) and Daumier.[18] Although he was not as good a draftsman as Tenniel, Nast combined simplicity with moral clarity. Unlike Daumier, Nast rarely drew visually funny cartoons; under his influence cartoonists moved away from visual hyperbole towards moral didacticism. As visual moral allegories, Nast's cartoons had a close kinship with drama: cartoons are a graphic rendering, no matter how fantastic, of human action and its moral consequences. Nast, who was a superb stage designer, created cartoons that formed a dramatic moral tableau.

As a cartoonist for *Harper's*, Nast was responsible for such important contributions to visual symbolism as the Republican elephant, the Democratic donkey, the Tammany tiger, Uncle Sam, and Santa Claus.[19] By combining caricature and symbolism in an allegorical setting, Nast made it possible for the cartoon to become radically simplified and still impart a clear moral message.[20]

In the Gilded Age, Nast's didacticism struck a chord in his audience precisely because it lent moral conviction to complex political issues. Thomas Nast and his contemporaries offered a moral directive easily discernible to an audience vexed by the complexities of politics. Like many cartoonists, Thomas Nast was an outsider. Like many outsiders, Nast could more clearly perceive the norms of his adopted society. And like many another outsider, the German-born Nast mobilized his audience by defining "the

[18] Feaver, *Masters of Caricature*, p. 93.

[19] Albert B. Paine, "The Origin of American Cartoon Symbols," *Harper's Weekly* 52 (19 September 1908): 11–12.

[20] In 1872, the *New York Times* expressed its gratitude for the role Nast had played in rallying support against Tammany in the November elections: "Of *Harper's Weekly*, its proprietors and editors, and Mr. THOMAS NAST, we have repeatedly spoken. Their services have been inestimable. *Harper's* has been the only paper on our side in this City." *New York Times*, 5 November 1872.

other."[21] Nast had an idiosyncratic view of "otherness": his drawings of African and Asian Americans refrain from the crude mockery typical of his time. In defining a normative view for his brand of Republican Anglo-Saxon Protestantism, however, he chose an ethnic enemy. That enemy was the Irishman, the most reliable supporter of the northern Democrats. Tenniel and others had drawn crude images of simian Irishmen before, but no other cartoonist equaled the fury and ferocity of Nast.[22] Nast drew other characters without pity: Boss Tweed, Jefferson Davis, Horace Greeley, to name a few. He drew the Irish without humanity. Without ever articulating the message implied in his cartoons, Nast seemed to hold Irish immigrants uniquely accountable for urban squalor, corruption, and sectarian conflict.

State aid to sectarian schools was an issue Nast addressed in several cartoons in *Harper's Weekly*. In Nast's cartoon "The American River Ganges," for example, Catholic bishops, caricatured as crocodiles, are swimming onto the American shore. American children stand undefended against the tide, while Boss Tweed and apelike Irish politicians busily deposit more children on the beach, where the ecclesiastical crocodiles will devour them (see Figure 3). One older child stands guard, with a copy of the Bible in his breast. Behind the children lies a ruin of a "U.S. Public School." In the background, Nast drew Tammany Hall to resemble St. Peter's; it flies the flags of Ireland and the papacy. There is no dialogue but the message is unmistakable.[23]

Nast had created a folkloric enemy—of subhuman immigrants and a papist conspiracy—for Gilded Age Republicanism as surely as Jacksonian Democrats had done with "the Monster Bank." This time, however, the enemy was visual, not verbal. And conjuring up the enemy in monstrous form, verbal or visual, reinforces the collaborative imperative. As press historian Thomas Leonard

---

[21] For one very suggestive analysis of how defining otherness reinforces social norms, see John P. Demos, *Entertaining Satan: Witchcraft and the Culture of Early New England* (New York, 1982), pp. 277–78, 300–309.

[22] L. Perry Curtis, Jr., *Apes and Angels: The Irishman in Victorian Caricature* (Washington D.C., 1971), pp. 26, 29, 35, 58–59, 96.

[23] *Harper's Weekly*, 30 September 1871.

THE AMERICAN RIVER GANGES.

THE PRIESTS AND THE CHILDREN.—[See Page 913.]

3 Thomas Nast's "The American River Ganges" appeared in *Harper's Weekly,* 30 September 1871.

observes, "Illustrators must dredge up images of a monstrous enemy so citizens will not act as if they face real giants."[24]

Nothing better reveals the power of Nast's drawings than a comparison with his British contemporary, Matt Morgan. Frank Leslie recruited Morgan to draw cartoons for his weekly in competition with Nast in *Harper's.* According to Albert Paine, Morgan was "more academic than Nast, he lacked conviction and insight and worst of all, humor."[25] Morgan, like Nast, used familiar themes and symbols but he used them clumsily. In one Morgan cartoon, "Weighed in the Balance and Found Wanting," Horace Greeley

[24] Leonard, *Power of the Press,* p. 116.
[25] Albert B. Paine, *Th. Nast: His Period and His Pictures* (New York, 1904), p. 227.

tips a scale against Grant and all his cronies. The cartoon takes its inspiration from the Book of Daniel. It was a traditional theme for cartoonists: in 1809 Thomas Rowlandson caricatured George III in a cartoon entitled *"The Hand-Writing on the Wall"*; the theme would later inspire Walt McDougall in 1884 (see Figure 8). In many ways Morgan's cartoon has more in common with the cluttered caricatures of Rowlandson than with McDougall. Morgan lacked the sense of dramatic staging that Nast, and later McDougall, possessed. Morgan's cartoon relies on its caption to make its point; the visual design is confused by many subsidiary points that distract the viewer. Morgan's cartoons lack humor for the same reason they seem to lack conviction: they do not convey a clear message (see Figure 4).[26]

Nast achieved clarity through familiarity. To be comprehensible, caricatures and symbols must be recognizable. In his political and electioneering drawings, Thomas Nast created simple tableaus: he exploited Shakespeare, Bunyan, classical mythology, and neoclassical painting. Cartoonists had used these sources many times before, but never with Nast's gift for dramatic staging. Nast could convey a sense of character through physiognomy: his drawings are visually comprehensible because he inscribed the motivations of all his characters on their faces.

The inspiration for many of Nast's drawings came from the École des Beaux Arts. At this time the École was still strongly imbued with neoclassical moral didacticism. Readers of *Harper's Weekly* would have recognized these neoclassical paintings from chromolithographs, which made copies of the original works familiar to middle-class families. In "The Tammany Tiger Loose," Nast's symbol of Tammany Hall ravages the feminine form of the American republic in a Roman arena, with Boss Tweed and his henchmen looking on. Nast modeled the cartoon on the painting by the French Academician Jean-Léon Gérôme entitled *Ave Caesar imperator, morituri te salutant.* In the picture by Gérôme and in Nast's cartoon, the foreground is the arena of the Circus Maximus, littered with corpses; both works display the same panoramic back-

---

[26] *Leslie's Illustrated Weekly,* 10 October 1872. See George, *English Political Caricature,* p. 120.

4 Matt Morgan's "Weighed in the Balance and Found Wanting" appeared in *Leslie's Illustrated Weekly*, October 10, 1872.

ground. For the figures of Caesar and his attendants, Nast substituted Tweed and his supporters.[27]

Gérôme inspired an earlier cartoon of Nast's, "The Political Death of the Bogus Caesar" (see Figure 5), published a few months after Andrew Johnson's impeachment. Nast's drawing is almost identical to Gérôme's painting *The Death of Caesar*, completed in 1867 (see Figure 6). Nast substituted the features of Andrew Johnson, as Caesar, and of Radical Republicans on Johnson's impeachment committee: Thaddeus Stevens as Cassius and Benjamin Butler as Brutus. The caption beneath Nast's cartoon is a quotation from Shakespeare's *Julius Caesar*, "Liberty! Freedom! Tyranny is dead! / Run hence, proclaim, cry it about the streets. / Some to the common pulpits, and cry out / LIBERTY, FREEDOM, AND ENFRANCHISEMENT!".[28]

In another Shakespearean inspiration, entitled "Time Works Wonders," a cartoon published in 1870, Nast drew Jefferson Davis as Iago, looking in at the floor of the Senate, saying, "for that I do suspect the lusty moor hath leap'd into my seat." Hiram Revels, the black Senator from Mississippi, is seated in the background.[29] Nast needed to be derivative in his context in order to be original in his satire.

Nast deserted the Republicans in 1884 at the time of Blaine's nomination. By the time of the 1888 election, his drawings appeared frequently in Democratic newspapers. Despite a new and larger audience, he still relied on classical themes to carry his

[27] For a very informative description of the French influence on American cartoonists see Leonard, *Power of the Press*, pp. 97–105, 125 and Albert Boime, "Thomas Nast and French Art," *American Art Journal* 4 (Spring 1972): 43–65. Tweed's face became quite well known, thanks to Nast's cartoons. Ironically, one of Nast's cartoons thwarted Tweed's attempt to elude justice by escaping to Spain. The Spanish authorities recognized Tweed's face from an American poster using Nast's caricature. Tweed was arrested and deported to the United States. See Charles F. Wingate, "An Episode of Municipal Government," *North American Review* 120 (January 1875); 124. For the story of Tweed's capture, see Denis Tilden Lynch, *"Boss" Tweed: The Story of a Grim Generation* (New York, 1927), pp. 398–400.

[28] The cartoon appeared in *Harper's Weekly*, 13 March 1869. For its French antecedent, see Boime, "Nast and French Art," pp. 53–55; the quotation is from *Julius Caesar*, 3.1. 78–81.

[29] *Harper's Weekly*, 9 April 1870, quoting *Othello*, 2.1. 295–96.

message.[30] In a cartoon entitled "The Modern Perseus," that appeared in the *Louisville Courier-Journal,* Nast drew Cleveland as the mythical hero, rescuing Andromeda and carrying the magic shield of "Reform" (see Figure 7). Behind Cleveland a workingman is fettered to a rock labeled "Monopoly," while at his feet a woman and children weep. A sea monster with the head of Cornelius Vanderbilt stands in the foreground labeled with a dollar sign and the word "Trust."[31]

An 1888 cartoon by Nast in the *Indianapolis Daily Sentinel* portrays Cleveland as Hercules in the lion skin. Cleveland stands on a rock displaying the slogans "The People Are with You!" and "It Is a Question between the Republican Partisans and the Republic."[32] Cleveland appears as the infant Hercules in another cartoon that parodies the infant figure used to advertise Champion Biscuits. Labeled "Our Champion Infant on Real Protection," Cleveland takes the stance of a pugilist, while foreigners, including John Bull, a helmeted Kaiser, a Russian Cossack, and a Chinese mandarin scatter in every direction, intimidated by the Champion's prowess.[33]

Gilded Age newspapers used pictures and the stories that accompanied them to appeal to a larger and less literate audience. Newspapers in the 1880s came to value a capacity for vivid words as well as drawings. The new publisher of the *New York World* played a prominent role in this vivid form of communication. The *World* in 1884 disparaged a Republican polemicist as a "paid stumper," describing his failure as a "partisan word painter." This budding polemicist might "shine as a descriptive stump-speaker," said the *World,* but he could not hope to attain the preeminence of "a word-painter" without "laborious study and continuous effort."

[30] In the 1880s, Nast's cartoons seemed less visually dramatic when they appeared in the newspapers. According to Morton Keller, Nast's earlier work in pencil for block engravings in *Harper's* displayed "a harder, sparser line," while his later pen drawings in the newspapers were "unsparing of deficiencies of technique that had been obscured by the softer medium of block engraving." Keller, *Art and Politics of Nast,* p. 327.

[31] *Louisville Courier-Journal,* 25 October 1888. See McGerr, *Decline of Popular Politics,* pp. 89–91.

[32] *Indianapolis Daily Sentinel,* 5 November 1888.

[33] *Louisville Courier-Journal,* 3 November 1888.

5 Thomas Nast's "The Political Death of the Bogus Caesar," which borrowed heavily from Gérôme, appeared in *Harper's Weekly*, 13 March 1869.

The *World's* new publisher had arrived the year before from St. Louis: his name was Joseph Pulitzer.[34]

Using vivid words and pictures, editors could appeal to principle or prejudice with equal facility by employing the appropriate allegory. In visual communications such appeals were not mutually exclusive. In 1884 the *New York World* caricatured James G. Blaine in a front-page cartoon by Walt McDougall, entitled "Knocked Out in the Second Round." Blaine appeared as a pugilist bested

[34] *New York World*, 19 October 1884. The *World* advised this polemicist to "take a few lessons from the editor of the *New York Sun*," Richard Henry Dana. Dana had earlier described Blaine as "the matured road agent of the Highway of State, proud in the impunity with which he has carried off his booty." Quoted from the *New York Sun*, 10 July 1884.

6 Jean-Léon Gérôme, *The Death of Caesar*, completed in 1867 (Walters Art Gallery, Baltimore).

by a humanized figure of the "Fisher letter."[35] For those who would not or could not read about the Fisher scandal for themselves, the *World* made the evidence clear. By depicting the letter itself as an avenging figure standing triumphant over the prostrate Blaine, the message was unmistakable: truth prevails over Blaine's dissembling.[36]

One of the most famous of all newspaper cartoons in the 1884 campaign was "The Royal Feast of Belshazzar Blaine and the Money Kings" (see Figure 8). Blaine had dined at Delmonico's with a group of powerful financiers and industrialists including John Astor,

[35] The letter, written by Blaine to his business partner Warren Fisher, was designed to extricate Blaine from embarrassment during hearings held by the House of Representatives to investigate charges of Blaine's corruption. For an account of these charges see Edwin P. Hoyt, Jr., *Jumbos and Jackasses: A Popular History of the Political Wars* (Garden City, N.Y., 1960), p. 148.

[36] *New York World*, 4 October 1884.

7 Thomas Nast's "The Modern Perseus" appeared in the *Louisville Courier-Journal,* 25 October 1888; Nast had abandoned the Republican party in 1884 to support Cleveland.

Cornelius Vanderbilt, and Jay Gould. This cartoon drew an analogy from the Book of Daniel, comparing Blaine's meal to the impious feast of the doomed Belshazzar (Dan. 5:1–31). In the background behind the assembled diners, a hand writes on the wall the Hebrew characters " 'MENE, MENE, TEKEL, UPHARSIN.' " God hath numbered thy kingdom and finished it. Thou art weighed in the balance and found wanting" (Dan. 5:27). This was a traditional theme for cartoonists. As noted above, Morgan had used this theme in 1872 and Rowlandson in 1809.[37] McDougall, however, had

[37] *New York World,* 30 October 1884. See George, *English Political Caricature,* p. 120.

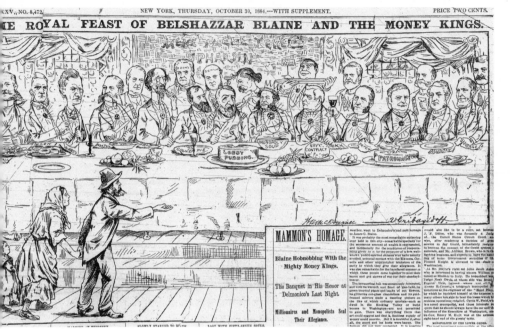

XXV., NO. 8,472.                    NEW YORK, THURSDAY, OCTOBER 30, 1884.—WITH SUPPLEMENT.                    PRICE TWO CENTS.

**THE ROYAL FEAST OF BELSHAZZAR BLAINE AND THE MONEY KINGS.**

MAMMON'S HOMAGE.

Blaine Hobnobbing With the Mighty Money Kings.

The Banquet in His Honor at Delmonico's Last Night.

Millionaires and Monopolists Seal Their Allegiance.

8 Walt McDougall's "The Royal Feast of Belshazzar Blaine and the Money Kings" appeared in the *New York World*, 30 October 1884.

mastered the art of dramatic staging; unlike Morgan and Rowlandson, he made his point visually rather than verbally.[38]

Many McDougall cartoons alluded to Shakespeare. One 1884 cartoon parodied Richard III, portraying Blaine as Gloucester, his campaign manager Stephen Elkins as Buckingham, and Whitelaw Reid as Catesby. Samuel Burchard stands in the foreground, holding a prayer book labeled "Rum, Romanism & Rebellion." In the cartoon, entitled "Shakespeare Recast—The Pious Dodge of the Modern Political Gloster," the future King as the Duke of Gloucester feigns piety.

[38] "Money Kings" was not the most popular term applied to the "captains" of finance and industry. The more familiar name, "Robber Barons," appeared in a cartoon drawn by Ehrhart in *Puck*. In this cartoon corporate magnates exact tribute from farmers and laborers in the same way medieval barons collected tribute from their vassals. To be sure his audience did not miss the historical analogy, Ehrhart provided an insert of the medieval barons receiving tribute. *Puck*, 6 November 1889.

BUCKINGHAM ELKINS TO GLOSTER BLAINE: "The clergymen are here at
hand. Be not you spoke with but by mighty suit. And look you, get
a Prayerbook in your hand and stand between two churchmen, good
my lord, for on that ground I'll make a holy descent."

The cartoon depicts the entrance of a "Delegation of Clergymen
headed by the Rev. Dr. Burchard." "Gloster Blaine" then enters
"between two Bishops, [Jay] Gould and [David Dudley] Field."

DR. BURCHARD:—"See where his Grace stands between two
clergymen."
BUCKINGHAM ELKINS:—"Two props of virtues for a Christian Prince
to stay him from the fall of Vanity. And see! a Book of Prayer in his
hand, true ornament to know a holy man!"

A stage notation indicates that "Here follows Burchard's oration
on 'Rum, Romanism and Rebellion.' " In this cartoon, McDougall
satirized Burchard as a corrupt clergyman, meanwhile providing
an ironic twist by casting Burchard and Blaine to observe the very
rites of "Romanism" Burchard castigated.[39]

McDougall again cast Blaine as Richard III in a drawing entitled
"Blaine's Fateful Vision the Night before his Bosworth Field." This
cartoon reiterated all the scandals that the *World* linked to Blaine
during the sordid campaign of 1884. The caption on the cartoon
was " 'Let me sit heavy on thy soul to-morrow.'—Chorus of Ghosts
of a Hundred Political Crimes, Betrayals and Wrongs."[40] The
intended association of Blaine with Richard III indicates that the
*World* hoped to link Blaine with corruption of office and
unchecked ambition. Blaine's ghosts were not murdered rivals, as
were Richard III's, but personifications of bribery and personal
corruption, the salient vices of the late nineteenth century.

If the businessman was the audience for the Gilded Age editorial,
the workingman was the audience for cartoons and illustrations.
This lesson did not escape the Republican party press in their
wooing of American labor. They began producing more campaign
cartoons in 1892. K. C. Swayze in the *Philadelphia Inquirer* had a

[39] *New York World*, 2 November 1884, alluding to *Richard III*, 3.7. 45–49, 95–99.
[40] *New York World*, 4 November 1884, quoting *Richard III*, 5.3. 118.

CHOOSING HIS GUIDE.
"No, no! Guide Cleveland, I'll keep on solid ground."

9 K. C. Swayze's cartoon, "Choosing His Guide" appeared in the *Philadelphia Inquirer*, 30 October 1892. Like the antithetical juxtapositions of the early part of the nineteenth century, this cartoon offered a stark contrast of Protection and Free Trade for a labor audience.

cartoon that bore the caption "Throwing Dust in His Eyes" showing Cleveland manning a bellows and blinding an "American Workingman," rendering him oblivious of the danger of the "Free Trade Pit" in his path. "John Bull" and "Pauper Labor" lurk behind Cleveland.[41]

Another Swayze cartoon shows a devious Cleveland speaking to a British workingman while a well-dressed man labeled "American

[41] *Philadelphia Inquirer*, 2 October 1892.

Mechanic" stands in the background. A dialogue between Cleveland and the British workingman follows. The British workingman, looking to his affluent American counterpart, asks Cleveland, "Who is that prosperous looking man who just passed—one of the owners of the mills?" Cleveland replies, "A—a—um! I really didn't notice him."[42]

Another *Philadelphia Inquirer* cartoon shows a workingman at a crossroads (see Figure 9). He confronts two guides: Benjamin Harrison sports sensible outdoorsman's clothes, whereas Cleveland wears a pirate's costume. The "Protection Road" leads to a bucolic scene. The "Free Trade Road" leads through a marsh over a ruined causeway made with planks set at odd angles labeled "Low Wages," "Ruined Industries," "Red Dog Money," "Direct Taxation," and "Poverty." In the swamp is a flooded cabin labeled "Wild Cat Bank." The caption reads "Choosing His Guide." The workingman says, "No, no! Guide Cleveland, I'll keep on solid ground."[43]

The Democrats also directed their cartoons at the workingman. A Nast cartoon appeared in 1888 entitled "The Wolf and the Lamb Fable." It showed the wolf as the "U.S. Tax Collector" picking the pocket of the lamb, dressed in workingman's clothes. A cartoon first printed in the *San Francisco Examiner* entitled "The Modern Laocoon" [*sic*] shows a python entwined around a laborer and a middle-class man and woman. The snake bears the labels "Trusts," "Monopoly," and "Corruption."[44]

Even as the audience reading newspapers for political information widened, the educational campaigns in 1888 and 1892 narrowed the appeal of many newspapers. In the educational campaigns, particularly in 1892, cartoons invited the reader to make a choice in policy. "Two Sided Pictures" were back in rhetorical fashion. Once again newspapers cried out to their readers: "Look on this Picture! And on This!"[45] Cartoons rendered policy

[42] *Philadelphia Inquirer*, 16 October 1892.

[43] Ibid., 30 October 1892.

[44] "The Wolf and the Lamb Fable" appeared in the *Indianapolis Daily Sentinel*, 6 October 1888; "The Modern Laocoon" was reprinted in the *New York World*, 31 October 1892.

[45] See, for example, an editorial with that title in the *Louisville Courier-Journal*, 24 October 1888.

choices allegorically. A workingman attempts to decide which guide he will employ for trade policy; a drawing contrasts American Labor's prosperity with British workingmen's adversity.

Cartoonists used personification to make their points. "Trusts," "Free Trade," and "Protectionism" received flesh-and-blood images just as the "Monster Bank" had two generations earlier. In the 1880s Nast had attached the label "Trusts" to specific individuals, such as Cornelius Vanderbilt. In an 1889 *Puck* cartoon, Joseph Keppler caricatured individual "Trusts" as "The Bosses of the Senate." By 1900, in Hearst's *New York Journal*, Frederick Opper portrayed "The Trusts" generically, drawing bloated figures lacking any distinguishing individual features.[46]

Cartoonists developed a new kind of visual persuasion, relying less on traditional forms of moral didacticism in drama, scripture, literature, and painting. The cartoons featured in such yellow newspapers as William Randolph Hearst's *New York Journal*, adapted their messages from the drama of daily life; yellow journalism took its name from the new comic strip "The Yellow Kid," which satirized urban immigrant life. There was some irony in the fact that cartoons had once become a staple of politics by savagely caricaturing immigrants; now immigrants were a staple feature of the comic strips.

American visual persuasion was developing a new form of dramatic context from the vernacular. The American urban worker at the turn of the twentieth century was less likely than earlier generations of urban workingmen to recognize references to Shakespeare, since he was not as likely to speak English as a first language. He was less likely to be familiar with scriptural references, since he was less likely to be an evangelical Protestant.

The Americans had created a popular form of visual persuasion and the British took notice. British editors concluded after the 1886 general election that they ought to publish more political cartoons. In an article entitled "PICTORIAL POLITICS," the Liberal *Pall Mall Gazette* commented on the success Conservatives enjoyed with these appeals.

[46] Compare Keppler's cartoon in *Puck*, 23 January 1889, with Opper's in the *New York Journal*, 21 October 1900.

AMONG the other disadvantages at which we Liberals are labouring in this election is this—the Tories have collared all the cartoons. The weekly picture in the Freeman's Journal is almost the only telling thing on our side in the pictorial press, and that appeals only to Irish eyes, which are already open to the light. We have any quantity of eloquent speakers on the platform, but not a single first rate draughtsman on the press. This is a great loss. . . . Here, for instance, is a specimen of the simplest and least ambitious of such things. To nine electors out of ten a sketch like this will put the nature of the alternatives on Ireland far more clearly than any quantity of the most cogent argument or most eloquent declamation. Candidates and their agents should bear this well in mind. We Liberals are served badly in this way by the press; but that is no reason why

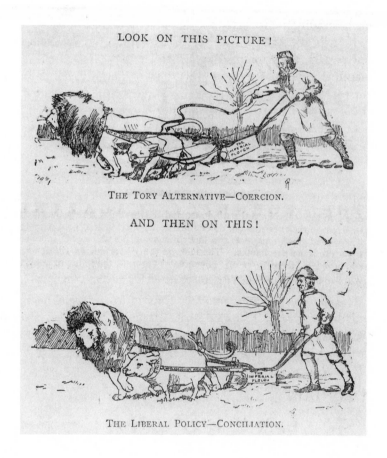

LOOK ON THIS PICTURE!

THE TORY ALTERNATIVE—COERCION.

AND THEN ON THIS!

THE LIBERAL POLICY—CONCILIATION.

we should not avail ourselves of the help of independent political cartoons. Such things did an immense amount of good in 1880, and they might be made to do even more now. In politics, as in general education, we have not learned the full value of the appeal to the eye.[47]

In another example of antithesis, the London *Evening News* placed two pictures, one above the other, entitled "Which Will You Take?" The top picture showed a hansom cab driven by Lord Salisbury, pulled by a steed in fine health wearing blinders, labeled "The Unionist Hansom." The picture beneath displayed an Irish donkey cart, with Lord Rosebery standing behind it, pulled by an animal in the last stages of decrepitude, designated "The Home Rule Car."

British cartoons often used sporting events as allegories. These were almost invariably pursuits of the upper and middle classes; they had been part of British cartoonists' repertoire since the early days of *Punch*. In "The Rickety Radical Crew," depicting a boat race (see Figure 10), the coxswain, Irish Nationalist Timothy Healy, speaks to the stroke, Lord Rosebery. The labeled oars include "Home Rule," "Local Veto," "Disestablishment," "One Man, One Vote," and "Down with Everything." Healy says to Rosebery, "Begorra, your lordship, they'll never take the sthroke you're after setting. . . . The curse of Cromwell seems to be on this crew."[48]

Sporting analogies also appeared in the *Westminster Gazette* in the cartoons of "F.C.G.": Francis Carruthers Gould. The *Daily Mail* described Carruthers Gould as a "cartoonist of pungent wit and striking ability."[49] In one cartoon Lord Rosebery boards the Liberal boat. The implication is that Rosebery will have a firm hand on the tiller of the partisan vessel. Parties, like states, need hierarchy, stability, and leadership, the cartoon implies. In a drawing connected to racing, entitled "Doctoring the Old Horse," Lord Salis-

---

[47] *Pall Mall Gazette*, 29 June 1886.

[48] London *Evening News*, 11 July 1895.

[49] *Daily Mail*, 6 October 1900. The quote appeared in an article titled "FIGHTING 'F.C.G.' " that accompanied examples of Carruthers Gould's best cartoons for the Liberals in the 1900 general election. The *Conservative Daily Mail* lamented, "It is a pity there is no artist worthy of his steel on the other side to meet him parry for parry and thrust for thrust."

# THE RICKETY RADICAL CREW.

The COXSWAIN (Tim Healy) to STROKE : "Begorra, your lordship, they'll never take the sthroke you're after set\ing. I'm thinking we've got mi little chance in the match. The curse of Cromwell seems to be on this crew."

10 "The Rickety Radical Crew" appeared in the London *Evening News*, 11 July 1895.

bury has just given his horse, labeled "Tory Party," a tonic called "Chamberlain Drench" (see Figure 11).⁵⁰

Entertainment also provided subject matter for Carruthers Gould's cartoons. In the cartoon "Juggler Joe and His Vanishing Programme," Chamberlain has a handbill behind him that says that "Joe the Juggler" is expert at "Sleight of Hand!" "Conjuring!" and "Lightning Changes!" The caption reads "JUGGLER: 'I will now proceed, ladies and gentlemen, to roll up this extensive programme into a ball, and the Old Party will swallow it without the slightest difficulty.' OLD PARTY [Salisbury]: 'Look here! I say! I'm not going to swallow all that!' Juggler (*aside*): 'All right my Lord! You sit tight. You've only got to *pretend*. I'll manage all the vanishing business.' "⁵¹

Public school education—a perennial cartoon topic in *Punch*— provided another context for Carruthers Gould's cartoons. In a

⁵⁰ *Westminster Gazette*, 13 July 1895. A drench is a medicinal potion.
⁵¹ Ibid., 9 July 1895.

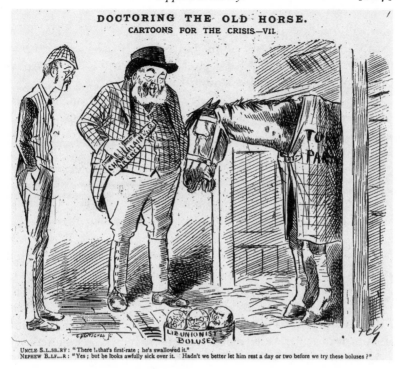

DOCTORING THE OLD HORSE.
CARTOONS FOR THE CRISIS—VII.

UNCLE S..L..SB..RY : "There !.that's first-rate ; he's swallowed it."
NEPHEW B..LF....R : "Yes ; but he looks awfully sick over it.   Hadn't we better let him rest a day or two before we try these boluses ?"

11 Francis Carruthers Gould's "Doctoring the Old Horse" appeared in the *Westminster Gazette*, 13 July 1895. Carruthers Gould's cartoons in the *Westminster Gazette* drew other editors' attention to the importance of cartoons for political campaigns.

drawing again lampooning Salisbury and Chamberlain, Salisbury is a headmaster chastising schoolboy Chamberlain for his earlier pronouncements. Chamberlain explains to Salisbury, "That was in my Radical days. I have since explained that I am proud of being allied with the gentlemen of England and that I am ready to defend the House of Lords against all attacks." Salisbury replies, "Good boy! You shall have a prize."[52] In "Unionist Geography," Salisbury stands before a map of the British Isles. The caption reads, "Professor Salisbury gives a demonstration of the new separatism." Salisbury is saying, "Here gentlemen, is a map of the United Kingdom, brought up to date with Unionist principles.

[52] Ibid., 1 July 1895.

You will kindly cross out Scotland, and Wales, and all Ireland except Ulster. They don't count. England we leave in, in virtue of the Southern part of it, which gives us a majority. This, you perceive, is the way to make a United Kingdom."[53]

Visual communication, like verbal communication, came to serve a new purpose in the twentieth century. As newspapers had subordinated the coverage of opinion to the coverage of events, yellow journalism subordinated the transmission of events to the provision of entertainment, and cartoons and illustrations served that purpose. To William Randolph Hearst, the policy of his *Evening Journal* was "to engage brains as well as to get the news, for the public is even more fond of entertainment than it is of information." According to Melville Stone of the *Chicago Daily News*, the newspaper had three functions: "to inform, to interpret and to entertain." In Britain a corresponding emphasis on entertainment prevailed. *Pearson's Weekly* declared a similar purpose in 1891: "To Interest, To Elevate, To Amuse." In an age in which editors sought to maximize the numbers of their readers, cartoons and illustrations provided more amusement for a larger audience.[54]

The journals of Hearst and Pulitzer in America and Northcliffe and Pearson in Britain relied to an unprecedented extent on visual images, and especially on pictorial images. Technology had developed to such an extent at the turn of the twentieth century that illustrations, engravings, cartoons, sports material, detailed maps, and other graphic visual images routinely appeared interspersed in the columns of text. Commercial advertising also shifted its orientation from typographical devices to pictorial images. The printed word no longer took precedence automatically over cartoons and illustrations.[55]

[53] Ibid., 6 July 1895.

[54] Hearst's policy was stated in the *New York Evening Journal*, 8 November 1896; see also Schudson, *Discovering the News*, p. 99. Thirty years before *Pearson's Weekly* declared its policy, the motto of James Henderson's *Weekly Budget* had been similar, but somewhat more didactic: "To inform, to instruct, to amuse." See Alan Lee, *Popular Press*, p. 130.

[55] The massive demonstration of outrage after the *Evening Journal* published a drawing of a Spanish official imprisoning a déshabillé young Cuban woman testifies to the power of the image. The picture was printed in the *New York Evening Journal*, 24 August 1897; reactions appear in ibid., 26 August 1897.

Cartoons in the yellow journals concentrated on personal mannerisms and foibles of politicians. Cartoons also stressed racial "characteristics." The yellow press's celebration of "unity" required *ad odium* negative references. The word that came to denote such references was originally a printing term: stereotypes. Yellow journals took racial caricature a step beyond Nast's simian Irishmen: they ridiculed Spaniards and Boers not by means of individuated caricature, but by generic mockery of a national "type."[56] Boers slouched and Spaniards leered in illustrations of the battlefronts in South Africa and Cuba. Generic mockery did not always bother even to specify type. Frederick Opper ridiculed European kings not individually, as Nast had done, but as undifferentiated foreigners. Opper drew domestic adversaries as stone-age Neanderthals and black minstrels.

Nast, McDougall, Swayze, and other Gilded Age cartoonists had hoped to inspire their readers. In a time when verbal persuasion seemed to offer little moral incentive for cohesion, these cartoonists created dramatic persuasive gestures borrowing recurrent themes and creating new ones. At the beginning of the twentieth century, visual communications reverted to praise and blame, panegyric and invective, all conveyed in a familiar tone, all created in the name of amusement. Visual hyperbole no longer served the inspirational purpose of late-nineteenth-century political caricaturists. Drawings in the yellow journals poked fun at foreigners and opposing politicians often simply for the sake of entertaining their readers. Cartoonists had once cast political figures as classical heroes and Shakespearean villains; now they were stock figures in a minstrel show.

Political cartoonists did not abandon their attempts at inspiration. The cartoons of David Low in the Second World War, for example, had a hortatory purpose. But rhetorical inspiration moved into new media in the twentieth century. Rhetorical mobili-

---

[56] The *Oxford English Dictionary*, 2d ed., gives as its first definition of "stereotype": "The method or process of printing in which a solid plate . . . cast from a papier-maché . . . mould . . . is used for printing from instead of the form itself." Gerald F. Linderman, *The Mirror of War: American Society and the Spanish-American War* (Ann Arbor, Mich., 1974), pp. 114–47.

zation works most successfully by exploiting new forms of mass communication. Over a century of mass communication, from 1790 to 1900, politicians learned an important lesson: it is easier to find a new means of saying something than to find something new to say.

# Misunderstanding
# and Its Remedies

At parliamentary elections, even when there is an up-to-date register, it often happens that less than half of the electorate use their votes. Things like these are symptoms of the intellectual gulf between the rulers and the ruled. But the same gulf lies always between the intelligentsia and the common man. Journalists, as we can see by their election forecasts, never know what the public is thinking.

—George Orwell, *Propaganda and Demotic Speech*

T he nineteenth century had not eliminated the gulf between the rulers and the ruled in Britain or America. Despite the attempt to create a new language for a mass audience the gulf had only narrowed somewhat. For the persuasive process to succeed, as rhetorical theorists from Aristotle to Kenneth Burke have pointed out, the audience must see the world as the speaker sees it. That empathic connection is, in the best of circumstances, far from perfect. I. A. Richards's definition of rhetoric as "the study of misunderstanding and its remedies" seems more appropriate at the end of this study of electioneering rhetoric than it did at the beginning.[1] From the late eighteenth century to the early twentieth century, orators, party organizers, and journalists sought to fortify the tenuous empathy between author and audience. Sometimes

[1] Richards, *Philosophy of Rhetoric*, p. 3.

the empathy seemingly established was a false one; often the identification process became confused; in many cases neither author nor audience actually understood the basis of empathy between them. Electioneering persuasion often related only indirectly, and sometimes only incidentally, to policy determination. In the words of Marvin Meyers, "political rhetoric responds to, though rarely corresponds to, reality, and [then] plays back into reality."[2]

Part of the reason for the indirect relationship between policy and persuasion has to do with the lingering distinction between "debate" and "result": between those few who arrogate to themselves the deliberative function and the many who retain the determinative function. This is a distinction that persists in pluralist democracies, and yet the line between "debate" and "result" had blurred by the middle of the nineteenth century. Changes in rhetoric furnish some evidence of the lower orders' assimilation into the deliberative order. In this long process of transformation, the press acted as the primary instrument in sealing this bond of identification between the wielders of power and the participants. The late eighteenth century saw the collision of two different political cultures and two very different forms of persuasion. The laudatory style of persuasion belonged to the ruling elite, communicated in print and in ritualized oral performances. The hortatory form of rhetoric belonged originally to the oral tradition of mass meetings and spontaneous oral speeches. The press reconciled these two traditions, first in the United States and later in Britain, by incorporating oral tradition on the printed page. The result was a remarkable transformation in the political culture. Visual communications also changed the political culture. Cartoons and illustrations mined the same sources of oral performance—the Bible and Shakespeare—that hortatory rhetoric employed.

A participatory political culture, in which the voters take more than an acquiescent role in politics, requires a form of rhetoric that intersects with their moral sensibilities, informs them of their obligations, and elicits their interest. In oral, printed, and visual appeals, a language had to be discovered which provided voters

<hr>

[2] Meyers, *Jacksonian Persuasion,* p. 102; see also E. E. Schattschneider, *The Semisovereign People: A Realist's View of Democracy in America* (Hinsdale, Ill., 1975), p. 68.

the means for determining the suitability of a candidate or a course of action. Voters cannot judge measures in the same way they do men; voters required a new language for appraising policy in the same way they had earlier evaluated personality. To make a political system in this sense "participatory" often meant phrasing electioneering appeals in hyperbolic language and supporting them with irrational argument. Creating a new language for evaluating policy paradoxically required a new political mythology.

Political mythology creates a dramatic narrative and links it to the hopes and fears of the whole society by personification. It focuses and stirs the "common will." Mythology is useful for a participatory regime because it encourages collective evaluation. The political leader personifies collective hopes; he or she is cast in heroic form in democratic mythology and often deified in totalitarian regimes. Collective fears, on the other hand, can be focused by the creation of "monsters."[3]

If political mythology addresses and focuses collective hopes and fears, the task of prophecy falls in the dominion of extrapolated history. Reinhard Koselleck has observed that since the eighteenth century our whole "linguistic inventory" has been attuned to the necessity of change. In a semantic sense, conceptions of change exert "a particularly stabilizing effect."[4] Historical allusions work by extrapolation to provide assurance that one human experience is analogous to another; the future is thus made to seem predictable and perhaps even inevitable.[5] George Canning, for example, reassured his audience in 1820 that the future would be more like the distant past than like the turbulent time of the Peterloo Massacre. In response, William Cobbett used a "future perfect" form of "history" (i.e., future historians looking back upon the present) to prophesy the triumph of Reform.[6]

History and myth had different weights in American and British electioneering. In Britain, for the better part of the nineteenth

---

[3] Leonard, *Power of the Press*, p. 116.

[4] Reinhart Koselleck, "Linguistic Change," p. 659.

[5] On the importance of historical allusions, see Cmiel, *Democratic Eloquence*, pp. 94–122; Simpson, *Politics of American English*, pp. 81–90.

[6] *Morning Herald*, 29 March 1820; *Cobbett's Political Register*, 8 April 1820; see Chapter 3, nn. 27, 28 herein.

century, the great task before the regime was that of managing change. For this reason, British electioneering relied more on historical than on mythic themes. Resonant historical themes had themselves often acquired mythological associations, however. In the longer span of European memory, myth and history were harder to separate. There were heroic deeds, valiant battles, unspeakable crimes, high honor, and foul shame. All these historical themes helped to define an English (and later a British) national identity.[7]

In the United States, however, mythological themes were more prevalent than historical themes. Americans required powerful symbols drawn from mythology because their national identity took form in the Enlightenment. Subsequent generations of Americans found themselves in the difficult position of sustaining an austere "civil religion" founded by patriarchs who disdained prophecy.[8] Their "sacred text," the Constitution, offered no explicit moral precepts. The Americans found it necessary to generate a national mythology, separate from Christianity and from the "civil religion." They borrowed their mythic inspiration first from classical texts, then from didactic fables, and later from parables of both secular and scriptural origin.[9] In our own age of persuasion by snippet, one can only marvel at the rich store of allusions comprehensible to American newspaper readers.

The weakness of the American "civil religion" ironically made American culture in the twentieth century more universal, more attractive, and ultimately more ubiquitous. Out of a "Unitarian" civil religion and vivid political language, American culture gradually transcended its Anglo-Saxon folk origins. The American yellow press, and later radio and television, helped to create the first

---

[7] Emile Durkheim, *The Elementary Forms of the Religious Life*, trans. by J. W. Swain (London, 1915) p. 427; Steven Lukes, "Political Ritual and Social Integration," in his *Essays in Social Theory* (New York, 1977), pp. 54–55, 68–69, 72.

[8] William H. Nelson, "The Revolutionary Character of the American Revolution," *American Historical Review* 70 (1965): 998–1014; Clark, *Language of Liberty*, p. 61.

[9] Robert Bellah has observed that the United States has built up "without any bitter struggle with the church powerful symbols of national solidarity." Robert N. Bellah, "Civil Religion in America," in *Religion in America*, ed. William G. McLoughlin and Robert N. Bellah (Boston, 1968), pp. 5–6, 9.

mass culture. This new culture defined itself more by consumption than by national memory.

Mass culture drew upon the popular interest in public spectacle (sports, crime, and scandal) and upon sanitized or invented versions of folk traditions (Robin Hood, Davy Crockett). It created a new form of persuasion primarily for advertising rather than for politics. In one sense the fusion of folk culture and public spectacle resembled the earlier collision of print culture and oral culture that produced hortatory rhetoric. In both cases the blending of these cultures helped absorb a hitherto unassimilated share of the population into the participating audience. Hortatory rhetoric assimilated the unenfranchised into active political participation. Mass culture assimilated Americans of every national origin—to a greater or lesser degree—into new identities as consumers. This new identity would prove attractive to Britons and the rest of the world as the new century wore on. However attractive mass culture proved to consumers, it seemed profoundly subversive to totalitarians and traditionalists. Attractive or subversive, or both, it did not prove to be political, at least in any sense that involved participatory mobilization.

The great bursts of political mobilization had occurred at times of rhetorical innovation. Most rhetorical innovation in the nineteenth century and in the twentieth century took advantage of an enlarged electorate, new technology, new market orientations, and transforming leaders. Extensions of voting rights, advances in printing and transportation, and the telegraph enabled hortatory rhetoric to reach a wider audience. Extension of the franchise was an obvious precondition for rhetorical innovation, but rhetoric was not transformed simply by virtue of a larger audience. Technology likewise provided a necessary but not a sufficient condition for innovation. *The Times* could sit on its monopoly of steam press technology while American penny press barons used it to generate a new kind of journalism. Bennett might not employ the new technology for political ends but another more political entrepreneur like Horace Greeley might see its utility for mobilizing a partisan audience. Chromolithography languished in serious journalism until the *New York Herald* and *Harper's Weekly* used it. New market orientation was a third important prerequisite for generating rhetorical innovation. Rhetorical changes occurred in the earliest newspapers of the eighteenth century, in the communications revolution of the Jeffersonian era, and the "penny press" of the 1830s. Elimination of restrictions on the press offered new market opportunities for expanding circulation of the *Daily Telegraph* and other British newspapers that catered to the middle and lower middle class. The cartoons of the weekly magazines caught the attention of the expanding middle class and the yellow newspapers stirred the interest of the reader as consumer. Finally, rhetorical innovation required the genius of the transforming leader. A mark of the transforming leader is a speaker or writer who can create a new pattern of resonant appeal from familiar themes at his disposal. Thomas Paine, Abraham Lincoln, and William E. Gladstone succeeded in bringing about a true rhetorical transformation. They were Skinner's revolutionaries marching "backwards into battle," who endowed old themes with a new meaning and devoted them to a new purpose. Paine, Lincoln, and Gladstone had the moral vision to frame issues and set them in a context that would be clear to their audience. Once launched, their rhetoric challenged and altered conventional politics. In a similar fashion, Thomas Nast transformed visual persuasion by seizing upon a set of recurrent pictorial themes and linking them to a didactic context. The rhetorical innovators exploited old themes, new technology, and market orientation to create new rhetorical opportunities for themselves and those that followed.

New rhetorical opportunities in the hands of these innovators illuminated the political landscape for their audience and their followers (both allies and opponents). Their rhetorical followers, however, often created more heat than light. Rhetorical innovation without moral inspiration exploited the extremes of the new form to maximize its novelty value. When inspiration was lacking the search for novelty often took its place, since it was easier to exploit a new form of rhetoric than to find something new to say. Rhetorical innovations needed time to establish limits; those limits are often established only after rhetorical forms have lost their novelty and at least some of their utility. The first stage of rhetorical transformation is the use of familiar themes set in a new context, usually by a rhetorical innovator; the second stage is exploitation of the form for its novelty value, often resulting in harsh exchanges; the third stage is a decline in the form's persuasive force. Eventually a new rhetorical innovation appears and the sequence more or less repeats itself. In the nineteenth century Lincoln and Gladstone introduced new rhetorical forms, taking advantage of instantaneous communication and the expanding audience of the press. Their successors, both allies and enemies, exploited the new rhetorical forms but, lacking inspiration, their language grew harsh and increasingly less persuasive. Illumination awaited another transforming leader.

Rhetorical innovation in the Anglo-American world of the nineteenth century seems to have flourished first in the United States before moving across the Atlantic. As Curzon recognized, Lincoln, not Gladstone, was the most gifted orator of the later nineteenth century. Part of the reason for the singular power of the American rhetorical idiom was its ability to exploit mythic imagery, as Lincoln ably demonstrated. British rhetoric, however, from the beginning of the century onward, was more articulate and more fluent than its American counterpart, as Gladstone's speeches attest. If the object of political discourse was to arouse and interest an audience, Americans seem to have been the better rhetoricians. If, on the other hand, the object of political discourse was to sustain high levels of participation, the British seem to have been more successful. From the Third Reform Act in 1884 to 1918, British participation increased, while from 1896 to 1928, American participation declined from levels set in the Gilded Age, the Jacksonian period, and the age of Jefferson.

Sustaining participation was but one problem affecting the participatory political culture. The question remains why the American and the British political culture did not produce an immediate change when voting rights were extended. The United States extended voting rights to adult white males on a nearly universal basis in every state before the Civil War. Britain extended voting rights more gradually, reaching universal suffrage only in 1918. Perhaps the answer lies in the difficulty, even with the best intentions, of creating a truly popular deliberative discourse compelling and comprehensible to all participants. The great misfortune of participatory government was that political appeals seldom posed a direct deliberative question to the people, unadorned by figurative sleight of hand. Politicians often reverted to Matthew Arnold's "clap-trap".[10] On those occasions when the parties experimented with pure deliberation, as in the American educational campaigns, they did not inspire the voters. Responsibility for this misfortune rests with the writers and speakers, not the readers or listeners.

In his observations of English and American society, J. A. Hobson noted that the "plain lessons" of the struggle for liberty "are branded by just, though formless, traditions upon the minds of millions who have never heard of Lord Acton or buried themselves in the archives of national history."[11] Over the course of the nineteenth century, Anglo-American rhetoric derived much of its inspiration and most of its persuasive power from the "just" but hardly "formless" traditions of folk imagery and vernacular speech.

E. E. Schattschneider said, "The most disastrous shortcomings of the system have been those of the intellectuals whose concepts of democracy have been amazingly rigid and uninventive."[12] George Orwell complained in 1944 that "all political parties alike have failed to interest the public in vitally important questions." Orwell thought democratic government would require a different kind of language:

> Some day we may have a genuinely democratic government, a government which will want to tell people what is happening, and what must be done next, and what sacrifices are necessary and why. It will need the mechanisms for doing so, of which the first are the right words, the right tone of voice. The fact that when you suggest finding out what the common man is like, and approaching him accordingly, you are either accused of being an intellectual snob who wants to "talk down to" the masses, or else suspected of plotting to establish an English Gestapo, shows how sluggishly nineteenth century our notion of democracy has remained.[13]

[10] Arnold, *Culture and Anarchy,* p. 152.

[11] J. A. Hobson, *A Modern Outlook: Studies of English and American Tendencies* (Boston, 1910), p. 313.

[12] Schattschneider, *Semisovereign People,* p. 132.

[13] George Orwell, "Propaganda and Demotic Speech," in *Collected Essays,* pp. 140–41.

"Sluggishly nineteenth-century" democracy in the United States and Britain has as yet failed to pose deliberative questions effectively for a mass audience. Ultimately, this is a failure of literature. Literature, as Walt Whitman observed, "has never recognized the People, and, whatever may be said, does not to-day." It seemed to him as if there were some "natural repugnance between a literary and professional life and the rude rank spirit of the democracies."[14] But Whitman also observed that language itself is a democratic instrument.[15] "Language, be it remember'd, is not an abstract construction of the learn'd, or of dictionary-makers, but is something arising out of the work, needs, ties, joys, affections, tastes, of long generations of humanity, and has its bases broad and low, close to the ground. Its final decisions are made by the masses, people nearest the concrete, having most to do with actual land and sea. It impermeates all, the Past as well as the present, and is the grandest triumph of the human intellect."

[14] Whitman, *Specimen Days*, p. 277.
[15] Walt Whitman, "Slang in America," was originally published in *North American Review* 141 (November 1885): 432, and reprinted in *Specimen Days*, p. 366.

# BIBLIOGRAPHY

PRIMARY SOURCES

Unpublished

Adams Family Papers. Massachusetts Historical Society
Blair Family Papers. Library of Congress
Broadside Collection. Library of Congress
Broadside Collection. New-York Historical Society
William Cobbett Papers. G. D. H. Cole Collection. Oxford University
Alexander Hamilton Papers. Library of Congress
Andrew Jackson Papers. Library of Congress
Jefferson Papers. Library of Congress
Pickering Papers. Massachusetts Historical Society
Charles Sumner Papers. Harvard University
The Times Archives. Printing House Square. London
Van Buren Papers. Library of Congress

American Newspapers and Periodicals

*Alexandria Gazette*
*Aurora and General Advertiser*
*Baltimore American*
*Baltimore Sun*
*Boston Gazette*
*Boston Gazette, Commercial and Political*
*Boston Post*
*Charleston Mercury*
*Chicago Daily News*
*Chicago Daily Tribune*
*The Connecticut Journal*
Atlanta, *The Constitution*
New York *Courier*
Portsmouth, New Hampshire, *Federal Address*
Baltimore *Federal Republican*
Philadelphia *Gazette of the United States*
Washington *Globe*
Springfield *Illinois State Journal*
Boston *Independent Chronicle*
*Indianapolis Daily Sentinel*

New York, *The Log Cabin*
*Louisville Courier-Journal*
*Massachusetts Spy: Or The Worcester Gazette*
New York *Mercantile Advertiser*
Washington *National Intelligencer*
Boston *New England Palladium*
Concord *New Hampshire Patriot*
*New Orleans Daily Picayune*
*New Orleans Times Democrat*
*New-York Commercial Advertiser*
*New York Evening Journal*
*New York Herald*
*New York Sun*
*New York Times*
*New-York Tribune*
*New York World*
*North Carolina Journal*
*Philadelphia Inquirer*
*Porcupine's Gazette*
*The Port Folio*
*Richmond Enquirer*
*San Francisco Examiner*
Philadelphia, *The Union*
Portsmouth, New Hampshire, *United States Oracle of the Day*


British Newspaper and Periodicals

London *Anti-Jacobin and Weekly Examiner*
London *Anti-Jacobin Review and Monthly Magazine*
London *Bee-Hive*
*Birmingham Argus*
*Bristol Gazette*
*Cambridge Independent Press*
*Cobbett's Political Register*
London *Daily Chronicle*
London *Daily Express*
London *Daily Mail*
London *Daily News*
London *Daily Telegraph*
*Edinburgh Courant*
London *Evening News*
London, *The Globe*
*Leeds Mercury*
*Liverpool Daily Post*
*Manchester Guardian*
London *Morning Chronicle and London Advertiser*
London *Morning Herald*

London *Morning Post and Fashionable World*
London *Morning Star*
*Pall Mall Gazette*
London *Poor Man's Guardian*
Edinburgh *Scotsman*
London, *The Spectator*
London *Standard*
London *Sun*
*The Times,* London
London *True Briton*
*Westminster Gazette*
*Yorkshire Post*

## Government Documents

*British*

United Kingdom. *Hansard Parliamentary Debates.*

*American*

U.S. Congress. *Congressional Globe.* 46 vols. Washington, D.C., 1834–73.
U.S. Department of Commerce, Bureau of the Census. *Historical Statistics of the United States, Colonial Times to the Present.* 2 vols. 1975; White Plains, N.Y.: Kraus International Publications, 1989.

## Books and Articles

Adams, John. *Works of John Adams.* 10 vols. Edited by Charles F. Adams. Boston: Little, Brown, 1850–6.
Adams, John Quincy. *Lectures on Rhetoric and Oratory.* 1810; New York: Russell and Russell, 1962.
Addison, Joseph. *Cato, A Tragedy.* 7th ed. London: Jacob Tonson, 1713.
*American Newspaper Annual, 1881.* Philadelphia: N. W. Ayer, 1881.
*American Newspaper Annual, 1891.* Philadelphia: N. W. Ayer, 1891.
*American Newspaper Directory, 1891.* New York: George P. Rowell, 1891.
Andrews, Alexander. *The History of British Journalism: From the Foundation of the Newspaper Press in England to the Repeal of the Stamp Act in 1855.* London: Richard Bentley, 1859.
Aristotle. *De Rhetorica.* In *The Basic Works of Aristotle.* Edited by Richard McKeon. New York: Random House, 1941.
Aristotle. *Topica.* Translated by E. S. Forster. London: Heinemann, 1971.
Arnold, Matthew. *Culture and Anarchy: An Essay in Political and Social Criticism.* Edited by R. H. Super. Vol. 5 of *The Complete Prose Works of Matthew Arnold.* 11 vols. 1867; Ann Arbor: University of Michigan Press, 1965.
Aspinall, Arthur, ed.. *Three Early Nineteenth Century Diaries.* London: Williams and Norgate, 1952.

Asquith, H. H. *Fifty Years in Parliament*. London: Cassell, 1926.

Bagehot, Walter. *The English Constitution*. London: Thomas Nelson, 1872.

Bangs, Edward. *What Cannot a Wise Choice of Rulers, and a Proper Confidence in Them . . . Perform! Oration Delivered at Worcester, on the Fourth of July, 1791*. Worcester, Mass.: American Antiquarian Society, Early American Imprints Series.

Bentham, Jeremy. *Bentham's Handbook of Political Fallacies*. Edited by Harold A. Larrabee. 1824; Baltimore, Md.: Johns Hopkins University Press, 1952.

Benton, Thomas Hart. *Thirty Years' View*. New York: D. Appleton, 1854.

Blair, Hugh. *Lectures on Rhetoric and Belles Lettres*. 2 vols. London: W. Stahan, 1783.

Brownlow, W. G., and A. Pryne. *Ought American Slavery to Be Perpetuated?* Philadelphia: J. B. Lippincott, 1858.

Bryan, William Jennings. *The Commoner Condensed*. 7 vols. Chicago: Henneberry, 1907.

Bryan, William Jennings. *The Credo of the Commoner*. Edited by Franklin Modisett. Los Angeles: Occidental College, 1968.

Bryan, William Jennings. *The First Battle: A Story of the Campaign of 1896*. Chicago: W. B. Conkey, 1896.

Bryan, William Jennings. *Speeches of William Jennings Bryan*. 2 vols. New York: Funk and Wagnalls, 1911.

Bryan, William Jennings, and Mary Baird Bryan. *The Memoirs of William Jennings Bryan*. Philadelphia: John C. Winston, 1925.

Bryce, James. *The American Commonwealth*. 2 vols. Chicago: Charles H. Sergel, 1891.

Buffon, Georges Louis Leclerc, Comte de. *Discours sur le style*. Paris: L'imprimerie royale, 1753.

Burke, Edmund. *The Works of the Right Honourable Edmund Burke*. Edited by Frank H. Wills. 6 vols. Oxford: Oxford University Press, 1907–34.

Cairnes, J. E. *The Slave Power: Its Character, Career, and Probable Designs*. London: Macmillan, 1863.

Campbell, George. *The Philosophy of Rhetoric*. 1776; Philadelphia: Mitchell, Ames and White, 1818.

Carpenter, F[rancis] B[icknell]. *Six Months at the White House with Abraham Lincoln: The Story of a Picture*. New York: Hurd and Houghton, 1866.

Chamberlain, Joseph. *Imperial Union and Tariff Reform: Speeches Delivered from May 14 to November 4, 1903*. London: G. Richards, 1903.

[Cicero]. *Rhetorica ad Herennium*. Translated by Harry Caplan. Cambridge, Mass.: Loeb Classical Library, 1954.

Clay, Henry. *Life and Speeches of Henry Clay*. 2 vols. New York: James B. Swain, 1843.

Cleveland, Grover. *Letters and Addresses of Grover Cleveland*. Edited by Albert Ellery Bergh. New York: Unit Book Publishing, 1909.

Cobbett, William. *Peter Porcupine in America: Pamphlets on Republicanism and Revolution*. Edited by David A. Wilson. Ithaca, N.Y.: Cornell University Press, 1994.

Conyngham, D[avid] P. *Sherman's March through the South.* New York: Sheldon, 1865.

Crockett, David [ascribed to Richard Penn Smith]. *The Autobiography of David Crockett.* New York: Scribner, 1923.

Croker, John Wilson. *The Correspondence and Diaries of the Late Right Honourable John Wilson Croker.* Edited by Louis J. Jennings. London: Murray, 1884.

Cromwell, Oliver. *Oliver Cromwell's Letters and Speeches.* Edited by Thomas Carlyle. New York: Harpers, 1855.

Curzon, George Nathaniel Curzon, Marquis of. *Modern Parliamentary Eloquence.* The Rede Lecture, Delivered by the Right Honourable Lord Curzon of Kedleston, Chancellor of Oxford University, at Cambridge University, 1913. Cambridge: Cambridge University Press, 1913.

Dewey, John. *The Ethics of Democracy.* In *The Early Works of John Dewey, 1882–1898.* Vol. 1, *1882–1888.* Carbondale, Ill.: Southern Illinois University Press, 1969.

Dickens, Charles. *American Notes for General Circulation.* 1842; Gloucester, Mass.: Peter Smith, 1968.

Dickens, Charles. *The Life and Adventures of Martin Chuzzlewit.* Edited by Margaret Cardwell. 1844; Oxford: Clarendon Press, 1982.

Durkheim, Emile. *The Elementary Forms of the Religious Life.* Translated by J[oseph] W[ard] Swain. London: Allen and Unwin, 1915.

Fehrenbacher, Don E. *Lincoln in Text and Context: Collected Essays.* Stanford, Calif.: Stanford University Press, 1987.

Franklin, Benjamin. *Benjamin Franklin: Representative Selections.* Edited by Chester E. Jorgensen and Frank Luther Mott. Rev. ed. New York: Hill and Wang, 1962.

George, Henry, Jr. *The Life of Henry George.* Garden City, N.Y.: Doubleday, Page, 1911.

Gladstone, William Ewart. *The Gladstone Diaries.* Edited by M. R. G. Foot and H. C. G. Matthew. 10 vols. Oxford: Clarendon Press, 1968–.

Gladstone, W. E. *Gleanings of Past Years, 1843–1878.* 2 vols. London: J. Murray, 1879.

Gladstone, William E. "Kin beyond Sea." *North American Review* 127 (September–October, 1878): 179–212.

Gladstone, William E. *Midlothian Speeches, 1879.* Leicester: Leicester University Press, 1971.

Gladstone, W. E. "On Eloquence." *Eton Miscellany* 2 (1827): 110.

Gladstone, William Ewart. *The Political Correspondence of Mr. Gladstone and Lord Granville.* Edited by Agatha Ramm. 2 vols. London: Offices of the Royal Historical Society, 1952.

Gladstone, W. E. *The Prime Minister's Papers.* Edited by John Brooke and Mary Sorensen. London: Her Majesty's Stationery Office, 1971.

Gladstone, William Ewart. *The Speeches and Public Addresses of the Right Hon. W. E. Gladstone.* Edited by A[rthur] W[ollaston] Hutton and H[ermann] J[oseph] Cohen. 10 vols. London: Methuen, 1892–94.

Grant, James. *The Newspaper Press: Its Origin, Progress, and Present Position.* 3 vols. London: Tinsley, 1871.

Greeley, Horace. "Recollections of a Busy Life." New York: J. B. Ford, 1868.

Greville, Charles C. F. *The Greville Memoirs, 1814–1860.* Edited by Lytton Strachey and Roger Fulford. 7 vols. (London: Macmillan, 1938).

Greville, Charles C. F. *A Journal of the Reigns of King George IV and King William IV.* Edited by Henry Reeve. 2 vols. London: Longman, 1874.

Greville, Charles C. F. *A Journal of the Reign of Queen Victoria, from 1837 to 1852.* Edited by Henry Reeve. 2 vols. London: Longman, 1885.

Hamilton, Alexander. *The Works of Alexander Hamilton.* Edited by Henry Cabot Lodge. New York: Putnam, 1885–86.

Hamilton, William Gerard. *Parliamentary Logic.* 1808; Cambridge: Heffer, 1927.

Harcourt, William Vernon. *"Resignation of the Gladstone Government": Speech of the Right Hon. Sir William Vernon Harcourt at the Meeting of the London and Counties Union at St. James's Hall, June 16, 1885.* London: National Press Agency, 1885.

Harrington, James. *The "Oceana" of James Harrington and His Other Works; . . . with An Exact Account of His Life, by John Toland.* Edited by John Toland. London: published by commission, 1700.

Hawthorne, Nathaniel. *The Complete Writings of Nathaniel Hawthorne.* 22 vols. Boston: Houghton, Mifflin, 1888.

Hazlitt, William. "The Periodical Press." *Edinburgh Review* 38 (May 1823): 349–78.

Herndon, William H. *Herndon's Life of Lincoln.* 1888; Cleveland, Ohio: World Publishing, 1942.

Hobson, J[ohn] A[tkinson]. "The Influence of Henry George in England." *Fortnightly Review* 62 (1897): 835–44.

Hobson, J[ohn] A[tkinson]. *A Modern Outlook: Studies of English and American Tendencies.* Boston: Dana Estes, 1910.

Hobson, J[ohn] A[tkinson]. *The War in South Africa: Its Causes and Effects.* London: J. Nisbet, 1900.

Hone, Philip. *The Diary of Philip Hone, 1828–1851.* Edited by Allan Nevins. New York: Dodd, Mead, 1927.

Hudson, Frederic. *Journalism in the United States from 1690 to 1872.* New York: Harper, 1873.

Hume, David. *Theory of Politics: Containing a Treatise of Human Nature, Book III, Parts I and II, and Thirteen of the Essays, Moral, Political, and Literary.* Edited by Frederick Watkins. 1740; Edinburgh: Nelson, 1951.

Hyde, Thomas W. *Following the Greek Cross; or, Memories of the Sixth Army Corps.* Boston: Houghton, Mifflin, 1894.

James, Henry. *The Letters of Henry James.* Edited by Percy Lubbock. 2 vols. New York: Scribner, 1920.

Julian, George W. *Political Recollections, 1840 to 1872.* Chicago: Jansen, McClurg, 1884.

King, William L. *The Newspaper Press of Charleston, South Carolina.* Charleston: Edward Perry, 1872.

Laski, Harold J. *The American Democracy: A Commentary and an Interpretation.* New York: Viking, 1948.

Lewis, George Cornewall. *Remarks on the Use and Abuse of Some Political Terms.* Oxford: Clarendon, 1898.

Lincoln, Abraham. *Complete Works.* Edited by John G. Nicolay and John Hay. 12 vols. 1894; New York: Tandy, 1905.

Lincoln, Abraham. *Selected Writings and Speeches of Abraham Lincoln.* Edited by T. Harry Williams. Chicago: Packard, 1943.

Locke, David Ross [Petroleum V. Nasby, pseud.]. *Divers Views, Opinions, and Prophecies.* Cincinnati, Ohio: R. W. Carroll, 1867.

Locke, David Ross [Petroleum V. Nasby, pseud.]. *"Swingin Round the Cirkle."* Boston: Lee and Shepard, 1867.

Lovejoy, Elijah. *The Barbarism of Slavery.* Speech Delivered in the House of Representatives, April 5, 1860 (Washington, D.C.: Buell and Blanchard, 1860).

Madison, James. "James Madison's Autobiography". *William and Mary Quarterly.* Edited by Douglass Adair. 3d ser., 2 (1945) 191–209.

Madison, James. *The Writings of James Madison.* Edited by Gaillard Hunt. 9 vols. New York: Putnam, 1900–1910.

Mill, John Stuart. *The Spirit of the Age.* In *Essays on Politics and Culture by John Stuart Mill,* edited by Gertrude Himmelfarb, pp. 3–50. Garden City, N.Y.: Doubleday, 1963.

Munford, Robert. "Robert Munford's *The Candidates."* *William and Mary Quarterly.* Edited by Jay B. Hubbell and Douglass Adair. 3d ser., 5 (1948): 217–57.

Orwell, George. *The Collected Essays, Journalism, and Letters of George Orwell: As I Please, 1943–1945.* Edited by Sonia Orwell and Ian Angus. New York: Harcourt, Brace, 1968.

Pease, Alfred E. *Elections and Recollections.* London: John Murray, 1932.

Peel, Lawrence. *A Sketch of the Life and Character of Sir Robert Peel.* London: Longman, 1860.

Peel, Robert. *Letter from Sir Robert Peel to the Electors for the Borough of Tamworth.* London: James Bain, 1847.

Plato. *The Gorgias.* Translated by Donald J. Zeyl. Indianapolis, Ind.: Hackett Publishing, 1986.

Poore, Benjamin Perley. *Perley's Reminiscences of Sixty Years in the National Metropolis.* Philadelphia: Hubbard Brothers, 1886.

Pray, Isaac Clark. *Memoirs of James Gordon Bennett.* New York: Stringer and Townsend, 1855.

Royce, Josiah. *The Philosophy of Loyalty.* New York: Macmillan, 1919.

Royce, Josiah. *Josiah Royce: Selected Writings,* Edited by John E. Smith and William Kluback. New York: Paulist Press, 1988.

Sampson, Henry. *A History of Advertising from the Earliest Times.* London: Chatto and Windus, 1874.

Smith, Adam. *Lectures on Rhetoric and Belles Lettres.* Edited by J. C. Bryce. 1763; Oxford: Clarendon Press, 1982.

Strong, Josiah. *Our Country: Its Possible Future and Its Present Crisis.* 2d ed. New York: Baker & Taylor, 1891.

Sumner, Charles. *The Crime against Kansas: Speech of Hon. Charles Sumner, of Massachusetts, in the Senate of the United States, May 19, 1856.* New York: Greeley and McElrath, 1856).

Tocqueville, Alexis de. *Democracy in America.* Edited by J. P. Mayer and Max Lerner. 1835; New York: Harper, 1966.

Tooke, John Horne. *EΠEA ΠTEPOENTA. Or, the Diversions of Purley.* 2 vols. 2d ed. London: printed for the author, 1798–1805.

Tooke, John Horne, *Two Pair of Portraits, Presented to All the Unbiassed Electors of Great Britain.* London: J. Johnson, 1788.

Twain, Mark [Samuel Longhorne Clemens], and Charles Dudley Warner. *The Gilded Age: A Tale of Today.* New York: Harper, 1915.

Tyler, Royall. *The Contrast, A Comedy in Five Acts.* Philadelphia: Thomas Wignell, 1790.

Van Buren, Martin. *Inquiry into the Origin and Course of Political Parties in the United States.* New York: Hurd and Houghton, 1867.

Watson Aaron. *A Newspaper Man's Memories.* London: Hutchinson, 1925.

Wayland, Francis. *The Elements of Moral Science.* 1835; London: W. Tegg, 1858.

Webb, Beatrice. *Beatrice Webb's American Diary, 1898.* Edited by David A. Shannon. Madison: University of Wisconsin Press, 1963.

Webster, Daniel. *The Papers of Daniel Webster.* Edited by Charles M. Wiltse and Alan R. Berolzheimer. Hanover, N.H.: University Press of New England, 1988.

Wells, H. G. *Experiment in Autobiography: Discoveries and Conclusions of a Very Ordinary Brain (Since 1866).* New York: Macmillan, 1934.

Wells, H. G. *The Future in America: A Search for Reality.* London: George Bell, 1906.

Whitman, Walt. "Slang in America." *North American Review* 141 (November 1985): 431–35.

Whitman, Walt. *Specimen Days, Democratic Vistas, and Other Prose.* Edited by Louise Pound. Garden City, N.Y.: Doubleday, 1935.

Wilkes, John. *The Controversial Letters of John Wilkes to the Rev. John Horne and Their Principal Adherents.* London: J. Williams, 1771.

Wingate, Charles F. "An Episode of Municipal Government." *North American Review* 120 (January 1875): 119–74.

Wirt, William. *The Life and Character of Patrick Henry.* Philadelphia: Desilver, Thomas, 1836.

SECONDARY SOURCES

Articles

Appleby, Joyce. "The New Republican Synthesis and the Changing Ideals of John Adams." *American Quarterly* 25 (1973): 578–95.

Appleby, Joyce. "What Is Still American in the Political Philosophy of Thomas Jefferson?" *William and Mary Quarterly*, 3d ser., 49 (1982): 287–309.

Banning, Lance. "Jeffersonian Ideology Revisited: Liberal and Classical Ideas in the New American Republic." *William and Mary Quarterly*, 3d ser., 43 (1986): 3–19.

Blewett, Neal. "The Franchise in the United Kingdom, 1885–1918." *Past and Present* 32 (1965): 31–56.

Boime, Albert. "Thomas Nast and French Art." *American Art Journal* 4 (Spring 1972): 43–65.

Bourke, Paul F. "The Status of Politics, 1909–1919: *The New Republic*, Randolph Bourne, and Van Wyck Brooks." *Journal of American Studies* 8 (August 1974): 171–202.

Briggs, Asa. "Thomas Attwood and the Economic Background of the Birmingham Political Union." *Cambridge Historical Journal* 9 (1948): 190–216.

Brown, Richard D. "Modernization and the Modern Personality in Early America, 1680–1865: A Sketch of a Synthesis." *Journal of Interdisciplinary History* 2 (1972): 201–28.

Brown, Richard H. "The Missouri Crisis, Slavery, and the Politics of Jacksonianism." *South Atlantic Quarterly* 45 (1966): 55–72.

Burke, Kenneth. "Rhetoric—Old and New." *Journal of General Education* 5 (1951): 202–9.

Burn, W. L. "Electoral Corruption in the Nineteenth Century." *Parliamentary Affairs* 4 (1951): 437–52.

Burnham, Walter Dean. "The Changing Shape of the American Political Universe." *American Political Science Review* 59 (1965): 7–28.

Cannon, J. " 'Poll Books': Short Guides to Records." *History* 67 (1963): 166–69.

Clarke, P. F. "Electoral Sociology of Modern Britain." *History* 57 (1972): 31–55.

Cox, Richard W. "Art Young: Cartoonist from the Middle Border." *Wisconsin Magazine of History* 61 (1977): 32–58.

Crouthamel, James L. "James Gordon Bennett, the *New York Herald*, and the Development of Newspaper Sensationalism." *New York History* 54 (1973): 294–316.

Davis, Richard W. "Deference and Aristocracy in the Time of the Great Reform Act." *American Historical Review* 81 (1976): 532–39.

Drake, Michael. "The Mid-Victorian Voter." *Journal of Interdisciplinary History* 1 (1971): 473–90.

Dunbabin, J. P. D. "Parliamentary Elections in Great Britain, 1868–1900: A Psephological Note." *English Historical Review* 81 (1966): 82–99.

Durey, Michael. "Thomas Paine's Apostles: Radical Emigrés and the Triumph of Jeffersonian Republicanism." *William and Mary Quarterly,* 3d ser., 49 (1987): 661–68.

Erickson, Paul D. "Daniel Webster's Myth of the Pilgrims." *New England Quarterly* 57 (1984): 44–64.

Formisano, Ronald P. "Deferential-Participant Politics: The Early Republic's Political Culture, 1789–1824." *American Political Science Review* 68 (1974): 473–87.

Formisano, Ronald P. "Political Character, Antipartyism, and the Second Party System." *American Quarterly* 21 (1969): 683–709.

Gilje, Paul A. "The Baltimore Riots of 1812 and the Breakdown of Anglo-American Mob Tradition." *Journal of Social History* 13 (1980): 547–64.

Ginter, Donald. "Financing of the Whig Party Organization." *American Historical Review* 71 (1966): 421–40.

Gombrich, E. H. "The Cartoonist's Armory." *South Atlantic Quarterly* 62 (Spring 1963): 188–227.

Haberkorn, Ruth E. "Owen Lovejoy in Princeton, Illinois." *Illinois State Historical Society Journal* 36 (1943): 291–99.

Habermas, Jurgen. "On Systematically Distorted Communication." *Inquiry* 13 (Autumn 1970): 205–18.

Hill, B. W. "Fox and Burke: The Whig Party and the Question of Principle." *English Historical Review* 89 (1974): 1–24.

Himmelfarb, Gertrude. "The Politics of Democracy." *Journal of British Studies* 6 (1966): 97–138.

Kemp, Betty. "Reflections on the Repeal of the Corn Laws." *Victorian Studies* 10 (1966): 189–204.

Kitson Clark, G. S. R. "The Electorate and the Repeal of the Corn Laws." *Transactions of the Royal Historical Society,* 5th ser., 1 (1951): 109–26.

Koselleck, Reinhard. "Linguistic Change and the History of Events." *Journal of Modern History* 61 (1989): 649–66.

Leff, Michael C., and G. P. Mohrmann. "Lincoln at Cooper Union: A Rhetorical Analysis of the Text." *Quarterly Journal of Speech* 40 (1974): 346–58.

Linkugel, Wil. "Lincoln, Kansas, and Cooper Union." *Speech Monographs* 37 (1970): 172–79.

Matthew, H. C. G., R. I. McKibbin, and J. A. Kay. "The Franchise Factor in the Rise of the Labour Party." *English Historical Review* 91 (1976): 723–52.

McCormick, Richard P. "New Perspectives on Jacksonian Politics." *American Historical Review* 65 (1960): 258–301.

McCormick, Richard P. "Suffrage Classes and Party Alignments: A Study in Voter Behavior." *Mississippi Valley Historical Review* 65 (1959–60): 397–410.

McGee, Michael Calvin. "The 'Ideograph': A Link between Rhetoric and Ideology." *Quarterly Journal of Speech* 66 (1980): 1–16.

Mohrmann, G. P., and Michael C. Leff. "Lincoln at Cooper Union: A Rationale for Neo-Classical Criticism." *Quarterly Journal of Speech* 40 (1974): 459–67.

Moore, D. C. "Concession or Cure: The Sociological Premises of the First Reform Act." *Historical Journal* 9 (1966): 39–59.

Moore, D. C. "The Matter of the Missing Contests: Towards a Theory of Nineteenth Century English Politics." *Albion* 6 (1974): 93–119.

Moore, D. C. "The Other Face of Reform." *Victorian Studies* 5 (1961): 7–34.

Moore, D. C. "Political Morality in Mid-Nineteenth Century England: Concepts, Norms, Violations." *Victorian Studies* 13 (1969): 5–36.

Nelson, William H. "The Revolutionary Character of the American Revolution." *American Historical Review* 70 (1965): 998–1014.

Nossiter, T. J. "Voting Behaviour, 1832–1872." *Political Studies* 18 (1968): 380–89.

Paine, Albert B. "The Origin of American Cartoon Symbols." *Harper's Weekly* 52 (19 September 1908): 11–12.

Phillips, John. "Popular Politics in Unreformed England." *Journal of Modern History* 3 (1968): 599–625.

Pocock, J. G. A. "An Appeal from the New to the Old Whigs? A Note on Joyce Appleby's 'Ideology and the History of Political Thought.' " *Intellectual History Newsletter* 3 (Spring 1981): 47–51.

Pocock, J. G. A. "The Classical Theory of Deference." *American Historical Review* 81 (1976): 516–23.

Pole, J. R. "Constitutional Reform and Election Statistics in Maryland, 1790–1812." *Maryland Historical Magazine* 4 (1955): 275–92.

Pole, J. R. "Election Statistics in North Carolina to 1861." *Journal of Southern History* 24 (1958): 225–28.

Pole, J. R. "Election Statistics in Pennsylvania, 1790–1840." *Pennsylvania Magazine of History and Biography* 82 (1958): 217.

Pole, J. R. "Representation and Authority in Virginia from the Revolution to Reform." *Journal of Southern History* 24 (1958): 16–50.

Pole, J. R. "Suffrage and Representation in Maryland from 1776 to 1810: A Statistical Note and Some Reflections." *Journal of Southern History* 24 (1958): 218–25.

Pole, J. R. "Suffrage and Representation in Massachusetts: A Statistical Note." *William and Mary Quarterly*, 3d ser., 14 (1957): 412–28.

Pole, J. R. "Suffrage and Representation in New Jersey, 1774 to 1844." *New Jersey Historical Society Proceedings* 71 (1953): 38.

Read, Allen Walker. "Could Andrew Jackson Spell?" *American Speech* 38 (October 1963): 188–95.

Read, Allen Walker. "The First Stage in the History of *O. K.*," *American Speech* 38 (February 1963): 5–27.

Read, Allen Walker. "The Folklore of *O. K.*," *American Speech* 39 (February 1964): 5–25.

Read, Allen Walker. "Later Stages in the History of *O. K.*," *American Speech* 39 (May 1964): 83–101.

Read, Allen Walker. "The Second Stage in the History of *O. K.,*" *American Speech* 38 (May 1963): 83–102.

Read, Allen Walker. "Successive Revisions in the History of *O. K.,*" *American Speech* 39 (December 1964): 243–67.

Rees, R. D. "Electioneering Ideals Current in South Wales, 1790–1832." *Welsh Historical Review* 2 (1965): 229–45.

Reid, Ronald F. "The Boylston Professorship of Rhetoric and Oratory, 1806–1904: Changing Concepts of Rhetoric and Pedagogy." *Quarterly Journal of Speech* 45 (1959): 239–57.

Russell, Henry M. W. "The Memoirs of Ulysses S. Grant: The Rhetoric of Judgment." *Virginia Quarterly Review* 66 (Spring 1990): 189–209.

Shalhope, Robert E. "Toward a Republican Synthesis: The Emergence of an Understanding of Republicanism in American Historiography." *William and Mary Quarterly,* 3d ser., 29 (1972): 49–80.

Smith, Robert W. "Political Organization and Canvassing: Yorkshire Elections before the Reform Bill." *American Historical Review* 74 (1969): 1538–60.

Speck, W. A. "A Computer Analysis of Pollbooks: A Further Report." *Bulletin of the Institute of Historical Research* 48 (1975): 64–90.

Speck, W. A. "A Computer Analysis of Pollbooks: An Initial Report." *Bulletin of the Institute of Historical Research* 43 (1970): 105–12.

Spring, David. "Walter Bagehot and Deference." *American Historical Review* 81 (1976): 524–31.

Stout, Harry S. "Religion, Communications, and the Ideological Origins of the American Revolution." *William and Mary Quarterly,* 3d ser., 34 (1977): 519–41.

Struever, Nancy. "The Study of Language and the Study of History." *Journal of Interdisciplinary History* 4 (Winter 1974): 401–15.

Thomas, P. D. G. "The Beginnings of Parliamentary Reporting in Newspapers, 1768–1774." *English Historical Review* 74 (1959): 623–36.

Wadsworth, A. P. "Newspaper Circulations, 1800–1954." *Manchester Statistical Society Papers* (1954–57): 1–40.

Wallace, Michael. "Changing Concepts of Party in the United States: New York, 1815–1828." *American Historical Review* 74 (1968): 453–91.

Wood, Gordon S. "Conspiracy and the Paranoid Style: Causality and Deceit in the Eighteenth Century." *William and Mary Quarterly,* 3d ser., 39 (1982): 401–41.

Zarefsky, Donald. "Conspiracy Arguments in the Lincoln-Douglas Debates." *Journal of the American Forensic Association* 21 (1984): 63–75.

Books

Aarslef, Hans. *From Locke to Saussure: Essays on the Study of Language and Intellectual History.* London: Athlone, 1982.

Adams, Henry. *History of the United States of America.* New York: Century, 1889–1911.

Albanese, Catharine L. *Sons of the Fathers: The Civil Religion of the American Revolution.* Philadelphia: Temple University Press, 1976.

Aly, Bower. *The Rhetoric of Alexander Hamilton.* New York: Columbia University Press, 1941.

Ames, William E. *A History of the "National Intelligencer."* Chapel Hill: University of North Carolina Press, 1972.

Andrews, J. Cutler. *The North Reports the Civil War.* Pittsburgh, Pa.: University of Pittsburgh Press, 1955.

Andrews, J. Cutler. *The South Reports the Civil War.* Princeton: Princeton University Press, 1970.

Appleby, Joyce. *Capitalism and a New Social Order: The Republican Vision of the 1790s.* New York: New York University Press, 1984.

Appleby, Joyce. *Liberalism and Republicanism in the Historical Imagination.* Cambridge: Harvard University Press, 1992.

Ashworth, John. *"Agrarians" and "Aristocrats": Party Political Ideology in the United States, 1837–1846.* London: Royal Historical Society, 1983.

Aspinall, Arthur. *Politics and the Press, c. 1780–1850.* London: Home and Van Thal, 1949.

Atkinson, Max. *Our Masters' Voices: The Language and Body Language of Politics.* London: Methuen, 1984.

Auer, J. Jeffrey. *Antislavery and Disunion, 1858–1861: Studies in the Rhetoric of Compromise and Conflict.* New York: Harper, 1963.

Austin, J. L. *How to Do Things with Words.* Cambridge: Harvard University Press, 1962.

Ayerst, David. *"Guardian": Biography of a Newspaper.* London: Collins, 1971.

Bailyn, Bernard. *The Ideological Origins of the American Revolution.* Cambridge: Belknap Press, 1967.

Bailyn, Bernard. *The Origins of American Politics.* New York: Knopf, 1967.

Bailyn, Bernard. *Pamphlets of the American Revolution, 1750–1776.* Cambridge: Harvard University Press, 1965.

Bailyn, Bernard, and John Hench. *The Press and the American Revolution.* Worcester, Mass.: American Antiquarian Society, 1980.

Bainton, Roland H. *Christian Attitudes toward War and Peace: A Historical Survey and Critical Re-Evaluation.* New York: Abingdon, 1960.

Baker, Jean H. *Affairs of Party: The Political Culture of Northern Democrats in the Mid-Nineteenth Century.* Ithaca, N.Y.: Cornell University Press, 1983.

Bakhtin, Mikhail. *Rabelais and His World.* Translated by Helene Iswolsky. Cambridge: MIT Press, 1968.

Baldasty, Gerald J. *The Commercialization of News in the Nineteenth Century.* Madison: University of Wisconsin Press, 1992.

Ball, Terence. *Transforming Political Discourse: Political Theory and Critical Conceptual History.* New York: Basil Blackwell, 1988.

Banner, James M. *To the Hartford Convention: Federalists and the Origins of Party Politics in Massachusetts, 1789–1815.* New York: Harper, 1970.

Banning, Lance. *The Jeffersonian Persuasion: Evolution of a Party Ideology.* Ithaca, N.Y.: Cornell University Press, 1978.

Barker, Michael. *Gladstone and Radicalism: The Reconstruction of the Liberal Policy in Britain.* London: Harvester, 1975.

Barton, William E. *Lincoln at Gettysburg: What He Intended to Say; What He Said; What He Was Reported to Have Said; What He Wished He Had Said.* New York: Peter Smith, 1950.

Baumgardner, Georgia B., ed. *American Broadsides: Sixty Facsimiles Dated 1689 to 1800.* Barre: Massachusetts Imprint Society, 1971.

Bebbington, D. W. *The Nonconformist Conscience: Chapel and Politics, 1870–1914.* London: Allen and Unwin, 1982.

Bell, Rudolph M. *Party and Faction in American Politics: The House of Representatives, 1789–1801.* Westport, Conn.: Greenwood Press, 1973.

Benewick, Robert, R. N. Berki, and Parekh Bhikhu. *Knowledge and Belief in Politics: The Problem of Ideology.* London: Allen and Unwin, 1973.

Benson, Lee. *The Concept of Jacksonian Democracy: New York as a Test Case.* Princeton: Princeton University Press, 1961.

Benson, Thomas W., ed. *American Rhetoric: Context and Criticism.* Carbondale: Southern Illinois University Press, 1989.

Bercovitch, Sacvan. *The American Jeremiad.* Madison: University of Wisconsin Press, 1978.

Berger, Meyer. *The Story of the "New York Times," 1851–1951.* New York: Simon and Schuster, 1951.

Besson, George. *Daumier.* Paris: Éditions Cercle d'Art, 1959.

Black, Eugene C. *The Association: British Extraparliamentary Political Organization, 1769–1793.* Cambridge: Harvard University Press, 1963.

Black, Jeremy. *The English Press in the Eighteenth Century.* London: Croom Helm, 1987.

Blake, Robert. *Disraeli.* London: St. Martin's, 1966.

Bloch, Maurice. *Political Language and Oratory in Traditional Society.* London: Academic Press, 1975.

Bloch, Ruth H. *Visionary Republic: Millennial Themes in American Thought, 1756–1800.* Cambridge: Cambridge University Press, 1985.

Blondel, Jean. *Introduction to Comparative Government.* London: Weidenfeld and Nicolson, 1970.

Blonsky, Michael, ed. *On Signs: A Semiotics Reader.* Oxford: Basil Blackwell, 1985.

Bloor, David. *Knowledge and Social Imagery.* London: Routledge and Kegan Paul, 1976.

Boles, John B., ed. *America, the Middle Period: Essays in Honor of Bernard Mayo.* Charlottesville: University Press of Virginia, 1973.

Bolt, Christine, and Seymour Drescher, eds. *Anti-Slavery, Religion, and Reform: Essays in Memory of Roger Anstey.* Folkestone, Eng.: W. Dawson, 1980.

Boorstin, Daniel J. *The Americans: The Colonial Experience.* New York: Random House, 1958.

Boorstin, Daniel J. *The Americans: The National Experience.* New York: Random House, 1965.

Bormann, Ernest G. *The Force of Fantasy: Restoring the American Dream.* Carbondale: Southern Illinois University Press, 1985.

Bostrom, Robert N. *Persuasion.* Englewood Cliffs, N.J.: Prentice-Hall, 1983.

Boulton, James T. *The Language of Politics in the Age of Wilkes and Burke.* London: Routledge and Kegan Paul, 1963.

Bourne, H[enry] R[ichard] Fox. *English Newspapers: Chapters in the History of Journalism.* 2 vols. London: Chatto and Windus, 1887.

Boyce, George, James Curran, and Pauline Wingate, eds. *Newspaper History: From the Seventeenth Century to the Present Day.* London: Constable, 1978.

Braden, Waldo W. *Abraham Lincoln, Public Speaker.* Baton Rouge: Louisiana State University Press, 1988.

Braden, Waldo W., ed. *Oratory in the New South.* Baton Rouge: Louisiana State University Press, 1979.

Braden, Waldo W., J. Jeffrey Auer, and Bert E. Bradley, eds. *Oratory in the Old South, 1828–1860.* Baton Rouge: Louisiana State University Press, 1970.

Brendon, Piers. *The Life and Death of the Press Barons.* London: Secker and Warburg, 1982.

Brent, Richard. *Liberal Anglican Politics, Whiggery, Religion, and Reform, 1830–1841.* Oxford: Clarendon Press, 1987.

Brewer, John. *Party Ideology and Popular Politics at the Accession of George III.* Cambridge: Cambridge University Press, 1976.

Brigance, William Norwood, ed. *A History and Criticism of American Public Address.* 12 vols. New York: McGraw-Hill, 1943–55.

Briggs, Asa. *The Age of Improvement.* London: Longman, 1959.

Briggs, Asa. *Chartist Studies.* London: Macmillan, 1959.

Briggs, Asa. *Victorian People: Some Reassessments of People, Institutions, Ideas, and Events, 1851–1867.* London: Odhams, 1954.

Briggs, Asa, and John Saville, eds. *Essays in Labour History.* London: Macmillan, 1967.

Brigham, Clarence S. *History and Bibliography of American Newspapers, 1690–1920.* 2 vols. Worcester, Mass.: American Antiquarian Society, 1947.

Brock, Michael. *The Great Reform Act.* London: Hutchinson University Library, 1973.

Brock, W. R. *Lord Liverpool and Liberal Toryism, 1820 to 1827.* London: Cass, 1967.

Brown, Francis. *Raymond of the "Times."* New York: Norton, 1951.

Brown, K. D. *The First Labour Party, 1906–1914.* London: Croom Helm, 1985.

Brown, Lucy. *Victorian News and Newspapers.* Oxford: Clarendon Press, 1985.

Brown, Richard D. *Knowledge Is Power: The Diffusion of Information in Early America.* New York: Oxford University Press, 1989.

Bryant, Donald C., ed. *The Rhetorical Idiom: Essays in Rhetoric, Oratory, Language, and Drama.* Ithaca, N.Y.: Cornell University Press, 1958.

Buel, Richard. *Securing the Revolution: Ideology in American Politics, 1789–1815.* Ithaca, N.Y.: Cornell University Press, 1972.

Bulmer-Thomas, Ivor. *The Growth of the British Party System.* 2 vols. London: J. Baker 1965.

Burke, Kenneth. *A Grammar of Motives.* 1945; Berkeley: University of California Press, 1969.

Burke, Kenneth. *A Rhetoric of Motives.* 1950; Berkeley: University of California Press, 1969.

Burke, Kenneth. *Permanence and Change: An Anatomy of Purpose.* 1936; Berkeley: University of California Press, 1984.

Burke, Kenneth. *The Philosophy of Literary Form: Studies in Symbolic Action.* Baton Rouge: Louisiana State University Press, 1967.

Burke, Peter. *The Historical Anthropology of Early Modern Italy: Essays on Perception and Communication.* Cambridge: Cambridge University Press, 1987.

Burn, W. L. *The Age of Equipoise.* London: Allen and Unwin, 1964.

Burnham, Walter Dean. *Critical Elections and the Mainsprings of American Politics.* New York: Norton, 1970.

Bushman, Richard L., Neil Harris, David Rothman, Barbara Miller Solomon, and Stephan Thernstrom, eds. *Uprooted Americans: Essays to Honor Oscar Handlin.* Boston: Little, Brown, 1979.

Butler, David E., and Donald Stokes. *Political Change in Britain.* 2d. ed. London: Macmillan, 1974.

Butler, J. R. M. *The Passing of the Great Reform Bill.* London: Longman, 1914.

Butterfield, Herbert. *George III and the Historians.* London: Collins, 1957.

Cannon, John Ashton. *Parliamentary Reform, 1640–1832.* Cambridge: Cambridge University Press, 1973.

Cash, W. J. *The Mind of the South.* New York: Knopf, 1941.

Cassirer, Ernst. *Language and Myth.* Translated by Suzanne K. Langer. New York: Dover, 1946.

Cassirer, Ernst. *Symbol, Myth, and Culture: Essays and Lectures of Ernst Cassirer, 1935–1945.* Edited by Donald Philip Verene. New Haven: Yale University Press, 1979.

Chambers, William Nisbet. *Political Parties in a New Nation: The American Experience, 1776–1809.* New York: Oxford University Press, 1963.

Chambers, William Nisbet, ed. *The First Party System.* New York: John Wiley, 1972.

Chambers, William Nisbet, and Walter Dean Burnham, eds. *The American Party System: Stages of Party Development* 2d. ed. New York: Oxford University Press, 1975.

Champfleury. *Histoire de la caricature moderne.* Edited by E. Dentu. Paris: Librairie de la société de gens des lettres, 1885.

Charles, Joseph. *The Origins of the American Party System.* New York: Harper, 1961.

Christie, I. R. *Myth and Reality in Late Eighteenth Century Politics.* Berkeley: University of California Press, 1970.

Christie, I. R. *Wilkes, Wyvil, and Reform.* London: Macmillan, 1962.

Christie, O. F. *The Transition to Democracy, 1867 to 1914: A Political and Social History of England from the Second Reform Act to the War.* London: Routledge, 1934.

Clair, Colin. *A History of Printing in Britain.* London: Cassell, 1965.

Clark, J. C. D. *English Society, 1688–1832: Ideology, Social Structure, and Political Practice during the Ancien Regime.* Cambridge: Cambridge University Press, 1985.

Clark, J. C. D. *The Language of Liberty, 1660–1832: Political Discourse and Social Dynamics in the Anglo-American World.* Cambridge: Cambridge University Press, 1994.

Cmiel, Kenneth. *Democratic Eloquence: The Fight over Popular Speech in Nineteenth-Century America.* New York: William Morrow, 1990.

Cohen, Murray. *Sensible Words: Linguistic Practice in England, 1640–1785.* Baltimore, Md.: Johns Hopkins University Press, 1977.

Cohn, Norman. *The Pursuit of the Millennium.* Fairlawn, N.J.: Essential Books, 1957.

Colbourn, Trevor, ed. *Fame and the Founding Fathers,* New York: Norton, 1974.

Cole, G. D. H. *The Life of William Cobbett.* 3d ed. London: Home and Van Thal, 1947.

Collet, Collet Dobson. *History of the Taxes on Knowledge: Their Origin and Repeal.* London: Unwin, 1899.

Conacher, J. B. *The Aberdeen Coalition: A Study in Mid-Nineteenth Century Politics.* Cambridge: Cambridge University Press, 1968.

Conacher, J. B. *The Peelites and the Party System, 1846–1852.* Newton Abbot, Eng.: David and Charles, 1972.

Cone, Carl B. *The English Jacobins: Reformers in Late Eighteenth Century England.* New York: Scribner, 1968.

Conrad, Peter. *Imagining America.* New York: Oxford University Press, 1980.

Corbett, Edward P. J. *Classical Rhetoric for the Modern Student.* 2d ed. New York: Oxford University Press, 1971.

Craig, F. W. S. *British Parliamentary Results, 1885–1918.* London: Macmillan, 1974.

Craig, F. W. S. *British Parliamentary Results, 1832–1885.* London: Macmillan, 1977.

Cranfield, G. A. *The Press and Society: From Caxton to Northcliffe.* London: Longman, 1978.

Crenshaw, Ollinger. *The Slave States in the Presidential Election of 1860.* Gloucester, Mass.: Peter Smith, 1969.

Crocker, Lionel, ed. *An Analysis of Lincoln and Douglas as Public Speakers and Debaters.* Springfield, Ill.: Charles C. Thomas, 1968.

Crook, David Paul. *American Democracy in English Politics, 1815–1850.* Oxford: Clarendon Press, 1965.

Culler, Jonathan. *Saussure.* London: Harvester, 1976.

Cunningham, Noble E. *The Jeffersonian Republicans: The Formation of Party Organization, 1789–1801.* Chapel Hill: University of North Carolina Press, 1957.

Cunningham, Noble E. *The Jeffersonian Republicans in Power: Party Operations, 1801–1809.* Chapel Hill: University of North Carolina Press, 1963.

Curtis, L. Perry. *Apes and Angels: The Irishman in Victorian Caricature*. Washington, D.C.: Smithsonian Institution Publications, 1971.

Dangerfield, George. *The Era of Good Feelings*. London: Methuen, 1953.

Dangerfield, George. *The Strange Death of Liberal England*. London: MacGibbon and Kee, 1966.

Dauer, Manning J. *The Adams Federalists*. Baltimore, Md.: Johns Hopkins University Press, 1953.

David, Paul T. *Party Strength in the United States, 1872–1890*. Charlottesville: University of Virginia, 1972.

Davidson, Donald. *Inquiries into Truth and Interpretation*. Oxford: Clarendon Press, 1984.

Davis, Natalie Zemon. *Society and Culture in Early Modern France*. Stanford, Calif.: Stanford University Press, 1975.

Davis, Richard W. *Political Change and Continuity*. Newton Abbot, Eng.: David and Charles, 1972.

Dawidoff, Robert. *The Education of John Randolph*. New York: Norton, 1979.

Demos, John P. *Entertaining Satan: Witchcraft and the Culture of Early New England*. New York: Oxford University Press, 1982.

Derrida, Jacques. *Dissemination*. Translated by Barbara Johnson. Chicago: University of Chicago Press, 1981.

Derrida, Jacques. *Writing and Difference*. Translated by Alan Bass. Chicago: University of Chicago Press, 1978.

DeVos, George, and Lola Romanucci-Ross. *Ethnic Identity: Cultural Continuities and Change*. Palo Alto, Calif.: Mayfield, 1975.

Dickey, Dallas C. *Seargent S. Prentiss: Whig Orator of the Old South*. Baton Rouge: Louisiana State University Press, 1945.

Diggins, John Patrick. *The Lost Soul of American Politics: Virtue, Self-Interest, and the Foundations of Liberalism*. New York: Basic Books, 1984.

Dillon, Merton L. *Elijah P. Lovejoy: Abolitionist Editor*. Urbana: University of Illinois Press, 1961.

Dinkin, Robert J. *Voting in Provincial America: A Study of Elections in the Thirteen Colonies, 1689–1776*. Westport, Conn.: Greenwood Press, 1977.

Dinkin, Robert J. *Voting in Revolutionary America: A Study of Elections in the Original Thirteen States, 1776–1789*. Westport, Conn.: Greenwood Press, 1982.

Donald, David. *Charles Sumner and the Coming of the Civil War*. New York: Knopf, 1960.

Drescher, Seymour. *Capitalism and Antislavery: British Mobilization in Comparative Perspective*. London: Macmillan, 1986.

Du Parcq, Herbert, Baron. *Life of David Lloyd George*. 2 vols. London: Caxton Publishing, 1912–13.

Duverger, Maurice. *Political Parties: Their Organisation and Activities in the Modern State*. London: Methuen, 1954.

Eaton, Clement. *Freedom of Thought in the Old South*. Durham, N.C.: Duke University Press, 1940.

Edelman, Murray J. *Political Language: Words That Succeed and Policies That Fail*. New York: Academic Press, 1977.

Edelman, Murray J. *Politics as Symbolic Action: Mass Arousal and Quiescence.* London: Academic Press, 1971.

Edelman, Murray J. *Symbolic Uses of Politics.* Urbana: University of Illinois Press, 1967.

Edwards, John. *Language, Society, and Identity.* Oxford: Basil Blackwell, 1985.

Elkins, Stanley, and Eric McKitrick. *The Age of Federalism: The Early American Republic, 1788–1800.* New York: Oxford University Press, 1993.

Ellis, Richard E. *The Jeffersonian Crisis: Courts and Politics in the Young Republic.* New York: Oxford University Press, 1971.

Erickson, Paul D. *The Poetry of Events: Daniel Webster's Rhetoric of the Constitution and the Union.* New York: New York University Press, 1986.

Ewen, Stuart, and Elizabeth Ewen. *Channels of Desire: Mass Images and the Shaping of American Consciousness.* New York: McGraw-Hill, 1979.

Eyck, Erich. *Pitt versus Fox: Father and Son, 1735–1806.* Translated by Eric Northcott. London: Bell, 1950.

Feaver, William. *Masters of Caricature: From Hogarth and Gillray to Scarfe and Levine.* Edited by Ann Gould. London: Weidenfeld and Nicolson, 1981.

Felling, Keith Grahame. *The Second Tory Party, 1714–1832.* London: Macmillan, 1951.

Fermer, Douglas. *James Gordon Bennett and the "New York Herald": A Study of Editorial Opinion in the Civil War Era, 1854–1867.* New York: St. Martin's Press, 1986.

Feuchtwanger, E. J. *Disraeli, Democracy, and the Tory Party: Conservative Leadership and Organization after the Second Reform Bill.* Oxford: Clarendon Press, 1968.

Fischer, David Hackett. *Albion's Seed: Four British Folkways in America.* New York: Oxford University Press, 1989.

Fischer, David Hackett. *The Revolution of American Conservatism: The Federalist Party in the Era of Jeffersonian Democracy.* New York: Harper, 1965.

Fite, Emerson David. *The Presidential Campaign of 1860.* New York: Macmillan, 1911.

Foner, Eric. *Free Soil, Free Labor, Free Men: The Ideology of the Republican Party before the Civil War.* New York: Oxford University Press, 1970.

Foner, Eric. *Tom Paine and Revolutionary America.* New York: Oxford University Press, 1976.

Fontana, Biancamaria. *Rethinking the Politics of Commercial Society: The "Edinburgh Review," 1802–1832.* Cambridge: Cambridge University Press, 1985.

Forgie, George B. *Patricide in the House Divided: A Psychological Interpretation of Lincoln and His Age.* New York: Norton, 1979.

Formisano, Ronald P. *The Birth of Mass Political Parties: Michigan, 1827–1861.* Princeton: Princeton University Press, 1971.

Formisano, Ronald P. *The Transformation of Political Culture: Massachusetts Parties, 1790–1840.* New York: Oxford University Press, 1983.

Foster, R[obert] F[itzroy]. *Lord Randolph Churchill: A Political Life.* Oxford: Clarendon Press, 1981.

Fredrickson, George. *The Inner Civil War: Northern Intellectuals and the Crisis of the Union*, New York: Harper, 1965.

Frye, Northrop. *The Critical Path: An Essay on the Social Context of Literary Criticism*. Bloomington: Indiana University Press, 1971.

Frye, Northrop. *The Stubborn Structure: Essays on Criticism and Society*. Ithaca, N.Y.: Cornell University Press, 1970.

Fuchs, Eduard. *Der Maler Daumier*. Munich: A. Langen, 1930.

Furtwangler, Albert. *American Silhouettes: Rhetorical Identities of the Founders*. New Haven: Yale University Press, 1987.

Gash, Norman. *Aristocracy and Politics: Britain, 1815–1865*. London: Arnold, 1979.

Gash, Norman. *Politics in the Age of Peel: A Study in the Technique of Parliamentary Representation, 1830–1850*. London: Longman, 1953.

Gash, Norman. *Reaction and Reconstruction in English Politics, 1832–1852*. Oxford: Clarendon Press, 1965.

Gash, Norman. *Sir Robert Peel: The Life of Sir Robert Peel after 1830*. London: Longman, 1972.

Gay, Peter. *The Cultivation of Hatred*. Vol. 3 of *The Bourgeois Experience, Victoria to Freud*. New York: Norton, 1993.

Geertz, Clifford. *The Interpretation of Cultures: Selected Essays by Clifford Geertz*. New York: Basic Books, 1973.

Geertz, Clifford. *Works and Lives: The Anthropologist as Author*. Stanford, Calif: Stanford University Press, 1988.

George, M. Dorothy. *English Political Caricature, 1793–1832: A Study of Opinion and Propaganda*. Oxford: Clarendon Press, 1959.

George, M. D. *English Political Caricature to 1792*. Oxford: Clarendon Press, 1959.

George, M. Dorothy. *Hogarth to Cruikshank: Social Change in Graphic Satire*. New York: Walker, 1967.

Gérard, Alice. *La révolution française: Mythes et interprétations, 1789–1970*. Paris: Flammarion, 1970.

Gienapp, William E. *The Origins of the Republican Party, 1852–1856*. New York: Oxford University Press, 1987.

Goen, C. C. *Broken Churches, Broken Nation: The Denominational Schism and the Coming of the American Civil War*. Macon, Ga.: Mercer University Press, 1985.

Gollin, A. M. *The "Observer" and J. L. Garvin: A Study in a Great Editorship*. London: Oxford University Press, 1960.

Gramsci, Antonio. *Selections from the Prison Notebooks*. Edited and translated by Quinton Hoare and Geoffrey Nowell Smith. London: Lawrence and Wishart, 1971.

Green, David. *Shaping Political Consciousness: The Language of Politics in America from McKinley to Reagan*. Ithaca, N.Y.: Cornell University Press, 1987.

Greene, Jack P. *Pursuits of Happiness: The Social Development of Early Modern British Colonies and the Formation of American Culture*. Chapel Hill: University of North Carolina Press, 1988.

Greene, Jack P. *The Reinterpretation of the American Revolution, 1763–1789*. New York: Harper, 1968.

Gretton, Thomas. *Murders and Moralities: English Catchpenny Prints, 1800–1860*. London: British Museum Publications, 1980.

Gunderson, Robert Gray. *The Log-Cabin Campaign*. Lexington: University of Kentucky Press, 1957.

Gustafson, Thomas. *Representative Words: Politics, Literature, and American Language, 1776–1865*. New York: Cambridge University Press, 1992.

Habermas, Jurgen. *Communication and the Evolution of Society*. Translated by Thomas McCarthy. Boston: Beacon Press, 1979.

Halévy, Elie. *England in 1815*. 2d ed. Translated by E. I. Watkin and D. A. Barker. London: Ernest Benn, 1961.

Haley, William, ed. *C. P. Scott, 1846–1932: The Making of the "Manchester Guardian."* London: Muller, 1946.

Hall, David, John M. Murrin, and Thad W. Tate, eds. *Saints and Revolutionaries: Essays on Early American History*. New York: Norton, 1984.

Hamilton, Sinclair. *Early American Book Illustrators and Wood Engravers, 1670–1870*. Princeton: Princeton University Press, 1958–1968.

Hammond, J. L., and Barbara Hammond. *The Age of the Chartists, 1832–1854: A Study of Discontent*. London: Longman, 1930.

Hanham, H. J. *Elections and Party Management: Politics in the Time of Disraeli and Gladstone*. London: Longman, 1959.

Harrison, Stanley. *Poor Man's Guardians: A Record of the Struggle for a Democratic Newspaper Press, 1763–1973*. London: Lawrence and Wishart, 1974.

Hartz, Louis. *The Liberal Tradition in America: An Interpretation of American Political Thought since the Revolution*. New York: Harcourt, Brace, 1955.

Higham, John. *Writing American History: Essays on Modern Scholarship*. Bloomington: Indiana University Press, 1970.

Hill, Brian W. *British Parliamentary Parties, 1742–1832: From the Fall of Walpole to the First Reform Act*. London: Allen and Unwin, 1985.

Hilton, Boyd. *The Age of Atonement: The Influence of Evangelicalism on Social and Economic Thought, 1795–1865*. Oxford: Clarendon Press, 1988.

Hirschman, Albert O. *The Rhetoric of Reaction: Perversity, Futility, Jeopardy*. Cambridge, Mass.: Belknap Press, 1991.

*History of "The Times."* 4 vols. London: Times Publishing Company, 1952.

Hobsbawn, Eric, and Terence Ranger. *The Invention of Tradition*. Cambridge: Cambridge University Press, 1983.

Hoff, Syd[ney]. *Editorial and Political Cartooning*. New York: Stravan Press, 1976.

Hofstadter, Richard. *The Age of Reform: From Bryan to F.D.R.* New York: Knopf, 1956.

Hofstadter, Richard. *The Idea of a Party System: The Rise of Legitimate Opposition in the United States, 1780–1840*. Berkeley: University of California Press, 1969.

Hofstadter, Richard. *The Paranoid Style in American Politics and Other Essays*. New York: Knopf, 1965.

Hollis, Patricia. *The Pauper Press: A Study in Working Class Radicalism of the 1830s.* Oxford: Oxford University Press, 1970.

Holt, Michael F. *The Political Crisis of the 1850s.* New York: John Wiley, 1978.

Holzer, Harold, Gabor S. Boritt, and Mark E. Neely, Jr. *The Lincoln Image: Abraham Lincoln and the Popular Print.* New York: Scribner, 1984.

Honour, Hugh. *The Image of the Black in Western Art.* 4 vols. Cambridge: Harvard University Press, 1976–1989.

Horner, Harlan H. *Lincoln and Greeley.* Urbana: University of Illinois Press, 1953.

Howe, Daniel Walker. *The Political Culture of the American Whigs.* Chicago: University of Chicago Press, 1979.

Howell, Wilbur Samuel. *Eighteenth-Century British Logic and Rhetoric.* Princeton: Princeton University Press, 1971.

Hoyt, Edwin P., Jr. *Jumbos and Jackasses: A Popular History of the Political Wars.* Garden City, N.Y.: Doubleday, 1960.

Hunt, Lynn, ed. *The New Cultural History: Essays.* Berkeley: University of California Press, 1989.

Isaac, Rhys. *The Transformation of Virginia, 1740–1790.* Chapel Hill: University of North Carolina Press, 1982.

Iseley, Jeter A. *Horace Greeley and the Republican Party, 1853–1861.* Princeton: Princeton University Press, 1947.

Jaffa, Harry V. *Crisis of the House Divided: An Interpretation of the Issues in the Lincoln-Douglas Debates.* Garden City, N.Y.: Doubleday, 1959.

Jakobson, Roman. *Verbal Art, Verbal Sign, Verbal Time.* Edited by Krystyna Pomorska, Stephen Rudy, and Brent Vine. Oxford: Basil Blackwell, 1985.

Jamieson, Kathleen Hall. *Eloquence in an Electronic Age: The Transformation of Political Speechmaking.* New York: Oxford University Press, 1988.

Jamieson, Kathleen Hall, and David S. Birdsell. *Presidential Debates: The Challenge of Creating an Informed Electorate.* New York: Oxford University Press, 1988.

Jamieson, Kathleen Hall, and Karlyn Kohrs Campbell. *Deeds Done in Words: Presidential Rhetoric and the Genres of Governance.* Chicago: University of Chicago Press, 1990.

Jefferson, Ann, and David Robey. *Modern Literary Theory: A Comparative Introduction.* London: Batsford, 1982.

Jenkins, Alan. *The Social Theory of Claude Levi-Strauss.* New York: St. Martin's, 1979.

Jensen, Richard. *The Winning of the Midwest: Social and Political Conflict.* Chicago: University of Chicago Press, 1971.

Johannsen, Robert W. *Lincoln, the South, and Slavery: The Political Dimension.* Baton Rouge: Louisiana State University Press, 1991.

Jones, Andrew. *The Politics of Reform, 1884.* Cambridge: Cambridge University Press, 1972.

Jones, Michael Wynn. *The Cartoon History of Britain.* London: Tom Stacey, 1971.

Jupp, Peter. *British and Irish Elections, 1784–1831.* Newton Abbot, Eng.: David and Charles, 1973.

Kammen, Michael. *Mystic Chords of Memory: The Transformation of Tradition in American Culture.* New York: Knopf, 1991.

Kammen, Michael. *A Season of Youth: The American Revolution and the Historical Imagination.* New York: Knopf, 1978.

Keller, Morton. *Affairs of State.* Cambridge: Harvard University Press, 1977.

Keller, Morton. *The Art and Politics of Thomas Nast.* New York: Oxford University Press, 1968.

Kelley, Robert. *The Cultural Pattern in American Politics: The First Century.* New York: Knopf, 1979.

Kelley, Robert. *The Transatlantic Persuasion: The Liberal Democratic Mind in the Age of Gladstone.* New York: Knopf, 1969.

Kerber, Linda K. *Federalists in Dissent: Imagery and Ideology in Jeffersonian America.* Ithaca, N.Y.: Cornell University Press, 1970.

Ketcham, Ralph. *Presidents above Party: The First American Presidency, 1789–1829.* Chapel Hill: University of North Carolina Press, 1984.

Kinsley, Philip. *The "Chicago Tribune": Its First Hundred Years.* Chicago: Chicago Tribune, 1945.

Kitson Clark, George. *Peel and the Conservative Party: A Study in Party Politics, 1832–1841.* London: Cass, 1964.

Kleppner, Paul. *The Cross of Culture: A Social Analysis of Midwestern Politics, 1850–1900.* New York: Free Press, 1970.

Kleppner, Paul, ed. *The Evolution of American Electoral Systems.* London: Greenwood, 1981.

Kloppenberg, James T. *Uncertain Victory: Social Democracy and Progressivism in European and American Thought, 1870–1920.* New York: Oxford University Press, 1986.

Kluger, Richard. *The Paper: The Life and Death of the "New York Herald Tribune."* New York: Knopf, 1986.

Knott, John. *Popular Opposition to the 1834 Poor Law.* London: Croom Helm, 1986.

Koss, Stephen. *The Rise and Fall of the Political Press in Britain.* 2 vols. London: Hamish Hamilton, 1981.

Krippendorff, Klaus. *Content Analysis: An Introduction to Its Methodology.* London: Sage, 1980.

Kuhn, Thomas S. *The Structure of Scientific Revolutions.* Chicago: University of Chicago Press, 1965.

LaCapra, Dominick. *History and Criticism.* Ithaca, N.Y.: Cornell University Press, 1985.

Lakoff, George, and Mark Johnson. *Metaphors We Live By.* Chicago: University of Chicago Press, 1980.

Land, Stephen K. *From Signs to Prepositions: The Concept of Form in Eighteenth Century Semantic Theory.* London: Longman Linguistic Library, 1974.

Lapalombara, Joseph, and Myron Weiner, eds. *Political Parties and Political Development.* Princeton: Princeton University Press, 1966.

Larkin Oliver W. *Daumier: Man of His Time.* New York: McGraw, 1966.

Lassaigne, Jacques. *Daumier.* Translated by Eveline Byam Shaw. New York: French and European Publications/Hyperion Press, 1938.

Lasswell, Harold, Nathan Leites, and Associates. *Language of Politics: Studies in Quantitative Semantics.* Cambridge: MIT Press, 1965.

Lears, T. J. Jackson. *No Place of Grace: Antimodernism and the Transformation of American Culture, 1880–1920.* New York: Pantheon, 1981.

Leavis, F. R. *The Great Tradition: George Eliot, Henry James, Joseph Conrad.* London: Chatto and Windus, 1948.

Lee, Alan J. *The Origins of the Popular Press in England, 1855–1914.* London: Croom Helm, 1976.

Lee, Alfred McClung. *The Daily Newspaper in America: The Evolution of a Social Instrument.* New York: Macmillan, 1937.

Leonard, Thomas C. *The Power of the Press: The Birth of American Political Reporting.* New York: Oxford University Press, 1986.

LePore, Ernest. *Truth and Interpretation: Perspectives on the Philosophy of Donald Davidson.* New York: Basil Blackwell, 1986.

Leverenz, David. *Manhood and the American Renaissance.* Ithaca, N.Y.: Cornell University Press, 1990.

Levy, Leonard W. *The Emergence of a Free Press.* New York: Oxford University Press, 1985.

Levy, Leonard W. *Jefferson and Civil Liberties: The Darker Side.* Cambridge: Harvard University Press, 1963.

Levy, Leonard W. *Liberty of the Press from Zenger to Jefferson.* Indianapolis, Ind.: Bobbs-Merrill, 1966.

Lincoln, Bruce. *Discourse and the Construction of Society: Comparative Studies of Myth, Ritual, and Classification.* New York: Oxford University Press, 1989.

Linderman, Gerald F. *The Mirror of War: American Society and the Spanish-American War.* Ann Arbor: University of Michigan Press, 1974.

Lippmann, Walter. *Public Opinion.* New York: Macmillan, 1932.

Lipset, Seymour Martin. *The First New Nation: The United States in Historical and Comparative Perspective.* New York: Basic Books, 1963.

Lipset, Seymour Martin, and Stein Rokkan, eds. *Party Systems and Voter Alignments.* New York: Free Press, 1967.

Lloyd, T. O. *The General Election of 1880.* London: Oxford University Press, 1968.

Longmore, Paul K. *The Invention of George Washington.* Berkeley: University of California Press, 1988.

Lowance, Mason I., and Georgia B. Baumgardner, eds. *Massachusetts Broadsides of the American Revolution.* Amherst: University of Massachusetts Press, 1976.

Lukes, Steven. *Essays in Social Theory.* New York: Columbia University Press, 1977.

Lynch, Denis Tilden. *"Boss" Tweed: The Story of a Grim Generation.* New York: Boni and Liveright, 1927.

Lynd, Helen Merrill. *England in the Eighteen-Eighties: Towards a Social Basis for Freedom.* London: Oxford University Press, 1945.

McCord, Norman. *The Anti–Corn Law League, 1838–1846.* London: Allen and Unwin, 1958.

McCormick, Richard P. *The Presidential Game: The Origins of American Presidential Politics.* New York: Oxford University Press, 1982.

McCormick, Richard P. *The Second American Party System: Party Formation in the Jacksonian Era.* New York: Norton, 1966.

McCoy, Drew R. *The Elusive Republic: Political Economy in Jeffersonian America.* Chapel Hill: University of North Carolina Press, 1980.

McCoy, Drew R. *The Last of the Fathers: James Madison and the Republican Legacy.* New York: Cambridge University Press, 1989.

McDonald, Forrest. *Novus Ordo Seclorum: The Intellectual Origins of the Constitution.* Lawrence: University Press of Kansas, 1985.

McDonald, Forrest. *The Presidency of Thomas Jefferson.* Lawrence: University Press of Kansas, 1976.

McGerr, Michael E. *The Decline of Popular Politics: The American North, 1865–1928.* New York: Oxford University Press, 1986.

McJimsey, George T. *Genteel Partisan: Manton Marble, 1834–1917.* Ames: Iowa State University Press, 1971.

McKenzie, Robert, and Allan Silver. *Angels in Marble: Working Class Conservatives in Urban England.* Chicago: University of Chicago Press, 1968.

McLoughlin, William G., and Robert N. Bellah, eds. *Religion in America.* Boston: Houghton, Mifflin, 1968.

McPherson, James M. *Abraham Lincoln and the Second American Revolution.* New York: Oxford University Press, 1990.

Mandler, Peter. *Aristocratic Government in the Age of Reform, 1830–1852.* Oxford: Clarendon Press, 1990.

Mannheim, Karl. *Ideology and Utopia: An Introduction to the Sociology of Knowledge.* Translated by Louis Wirth and Edward Shils. New York: Harcourt, Brace, 1936.

Mansfield, Harvey. *Statesmanship and Party Government: A Study of Burke and Bolingbroke.* Chicago: University of Chicago Press, 1965.

Matthew, H. C. G. *Gladstone, 1809–1974.* Oxford: Clarendon Press, 1986.

Matthew, H. C. G. *The Liberal Imperialists: The Ideas and Politics of a Post-Gladstone Elite.* Oxford: Oxford University Press, 1973.

Maxwell, Herbert. *The Life and Times of the Right Honourable William Henry Smith, M.P.* 2 vols. Edinburgh: William Blackwood, 1893.

Meadow, Robert G. *Politics as Communication.* Norwood, N.J.: Ablex Publishing, 1980.

Meyers, Marvin. *The Jacksonian Persuasion: Politics and Belief.* Stanford, Calif.: Stanford University Press, 1957.

Michael Ian. *English Grammatical Categories and the Tradition to 1800.* Cambridge: Cambridge University Press, 1970.

Miller, John C. *Crisis in Freedom: The Alien and Sedition Acts.* Boston: Little, Brown, 1951.

Mitchell, Austin. *The Whigs in Opposition, 1815–1830.* Oxford: Clarendon Press, 1967.

Mitgang, Herbert, ed. *Abraham Lincoln: A Press Portrait*. Chicago: Quadrangle, 1971.

Moneypenny, William Flavelle, and George Earle Buckle. *The Life of Benjamin Disraeli*. 2 vols. Rev. ed. London: John Murray, 1929.

Moore, D. C. *The Politics of Deference: A Study of the Mid-Nineteenth Century Political System*. New York: Harper, 1976.

Moore, James R. *The Post-Darwinian Controversies: A Study of the Protestant Struggle to Come to Terms with Darwin in Great Britain and America, 1870–1900*. Cambridge: Cambridge University Press, 1979.

Moorhead, James H. *American Apocalypse: Yankee Protestants and the Civil War, 1860–1869*. New Haven: Yale University Press, 1978.

Moran, James. *Printing Presses: History and Development from the Fifteenth Century to Modern Times*. London: Faber, 1973.

Morison, Samuel Eliot. *Three Centuries of Harvard, 1636–1936*. Cambridge: Harvard University Press, 1936.

Morison, Stanley. *The English Newspaper, 1622–1932*. Cambridge: Cambridge University Press, 1932.

Morley, John. *The Life of William Ewart Gladstone*. 3 vols. London: Macmillan, 1903.

Mulkay, Michael. *The Word and the World: Explorations in the Early Form of Sociological Analysis*. London: George Allen, 1985.

Murrell, William. *A History of American Graphic Humor (1865–1938)*. New York: Macmillan, 1938.

Namier, L. B. *The Structure of Politics at the Accession of George III*. 2d ed. London: Macmillan, 1957.

Namier, L. B., and John Brooke. *The House of Commons, 1754–1790*. 3 vols. London: Her Majesty's Stationery Office, 1964.

Nash, Gary B. *The Urban Crucible: Social Change, Political Consciousness, and the Origins of the American Revolution*. Cambridge: Harvard University Press, 1979.

Neale, R. S. *Class and Ideology in the Nineteenth Century*. London: Routledge and Kegan Paul, 1972.

Nevett, T. R. *Advertising in Britain: A History*. London: Heinemann, 1982.

Nevins, Allan. *The "Evening Post": A Century of Journalism*. New York: Boni and Liveright, 1922.

Nevins, Allan, ed. *Lincoln and the Gettysburg Address: Commemorative Papers*. Urbana: University of Illinois Press, 1964.

Nicholas, H. G., ed. *To the Hustings: Election Scenes from English Fiction*. London: Cassell, 1966.

Nichols, Roy F. *The Invention of the American Political Parties: A Study of Political Improvisation*. New York: Macmillan, 1967.

Nordlinger, E. A. *The Working Class Tories: Authority, Deference, and Stable Democracy*. London: MacGibbon and Kee, 1967.

Nossiter, T. J. *Influence, Opinion, and Political Idioms in Reformed England: Case Studies from the North-east, 1832–74*. Hassocks, Sussex: Harvester, 1975.

O'Gorman, Frank. *The Rise of Party in England: The Rockingham Whigs, 1760–82.* London: Allen and Unwin, 1975.

O'Leary, Cornelius. *Elimination of Corrupt Practices in British Elections.* Oxford: Clarendon Press, 1962.

Olney, R. J. *Lincolnshire Politics, 1832–1885.* London: Oxford University Press, 1973.

Ong, Walter J. *Orality and Literacy: The Technologizing of the Word.* London: Methuen, 1982.

Ostrogorski, M. *Democracy and the Organisation of Political Parties.* 2 vols. Translated by Frederick Clarke. London: Macmillan, 1902.

Owen, Frank. *Tempestuous Journey: Lloyd George, His Life and Times.* London: Hutchinson, 1954.

Ozouf, Mona. *Festivals and the French Revolution.* Translated by Alan Sheridan. Cambridge: Harvard University Press, 1988.

Paechter, Heinz, Bertha Hellman, Hedwig Paechter, and Karl O. Paetel. *Nazi-Deutsch: A Glossary of Contemporary German Usage.* New York: Frederick Ungar, 1944.

Paine, Albert Bigelow. *Th. Nast: His Period and His Pictures.* New York: Macmillan, 1904.

Pares, Richard, and A. J. P. Taylor, eds. *Essays Presented to Sir Lewis Namier.* London: Macmillan, 1956.

Parry, J. P. *Democracy and Religion: Gladstone and the Liberal Party, 1867–1875.* Cambridge: Cambridge University Press, 1986.

Parton, James. *The Life of Horace Greeley.* New York: Mason Brothers, 1855.

Pelling, Henry. *America and the British Left, From Bright to Bevan.* London: Adam and Charles Black, 1956.

Pelling, Henry. *Popular Politics and Society in Late Victorian Britain.* London: Macmillan, 1968.

Pelling, Henry. *Social Geography of British Elections, 1885–1910.* London: Macmillan, 1967.

Pemberton, W. Baring. *Lord Palmerston.* London: Batchworth, 1954.

Perelman, Ch[aim], and L. Olbrechts-Tyteca. *The New Rhetoric: A Treatise on Argumentation.* Translated by John Wilkinson and Purcell Weaver. South Bend, Ind.: University of Notre Dame Press, 1969.

Peterson, Merrill D. *The Great Triumvirate: Webster, Clay, and Calhoun.* New York: Oxford University Press, 1987.

Peterson, Merrill D. *The Jefferson Image in the American Mind.* New York: Oxford University Press, 1985.

Philbin, J. H. *Parliamentary Representation, 1832.* New Haven: Yale University Press, 1965.

Phillips, John A. *Electoral Behavior in Unreformed England: Plumpers, Splitters, and Straights.* Princeton: Princeton University Press, 1982.

Phillips, K. C. *Language and Class in Victorian England.* Oxford: Basil Blackwell, 1984.

Pitkin, Hannah F. *The Concept of Representation.* Berkeley: University of California Press, 1967.

Plumb, J. H. *England in the Eighteenth Century.* Baltimore, Md.: Johns Hopkins University Press, 1966.

Pocock, J. G. A. *The Machiavellian Moment: Florentine Political Thought and the Atlantic Republican Tradition.* Princeton: Princeton University Press, 1975.

Pocock, J. G. A. *Politics, Language, and Time: Essays on Political Thought and History.* New York: Athenaeum, 1971.

Pocock, J. G. A. *Virtue, Commerce, and History: Essays on Political Thought and History, Chiefly in the Eighteenth Century.* Cambridge: Cambridge University Press, 1985.

Pocock, J. G. A., ed. *Three British Revolutions, 1641, 1688, 1776.* Princeton: Princeton University Press, 1980.

Pole, J. R. *Paths to the American Past.* New York: Oxford University Press, 1979.

Pole, J. R. *Political Representation in England and the Origins of the American Republic.* London: St. Martin's, 1966.

Popkin, Jeremy D. *Revolutionary News: The Press in France, 1789–1799.* Durham, N.C.: Duke University Press, 1990.

Pred, Allan R. *Urban Growth and the Circulation of Information: The United States System of Cities, 1790–1840.* Cambridge: Harvard University Press, 1973.

Prest, John. *Politics in the Age of Cobden.* London: Macmillan, 1979.

Ramsay, A. A. W. *Sir Robert Peel.* London: Constable, 1928.

Rea, Robert R. *The English Press in Politics, 1760–1774.* Lincoln: University of Nebraska Press, 1963.

Read, Donald. *Press and People, 1750–1850: Opinion in Three English Cities.* London: Arnold, 1961.

Remini, Robert V. *The Election of Andrew Jackson.* Philadelphia: Lippincott, 1963.

Remini, Robert V. *Martin Van Buren and the Making of the Democratic Party.* New York: Columbia University Press, 1959.

Rice, Kenneth A. *Geertz and Culture.* Ann Arbor: University of Michigan Press, 1980.

Richards, I. A. *The Philosophy of Rhetoric.* 2d ed. New York: Oxford University Press, 1964.

Ricoeur, Paul. *The Conflict of Interpretations: Essays in Hermeneutics.* Edited by Don Ihde. Evanston, Ill.: Northwestern University Press, 1974.

Ritchie, Donald A. *Press Gallery: Congress and the Washington Correspondents.* Cambridge: Harvard University Press, 1991.

Robbins, Caroline. *The Eighteenth-Century Commonwealthman: Studies in the Transmission, Development, and Circumstance of Liberal Thought from the Restoration of Charles II to the War with the Thirteen Colonies.* Cambridge: Harvard University Press, 1959.

Robinson, William A. *Jeffersonian Democracy in New England.* New Haven: Yale University Press, 1916.

Robson, R[obert], ed. *Ideas and Institutions of Victorian England: Essays in Honour of George Kitson Clark.* London: Bell, 1967.

Roche, John P. *Origins of American Political Thought: Selected Readings.* New York: Harper, 1967.

Roche, John P. *Shadow and Substance: Essays on the Theory and Substance of Politics.* New York: Macmillan, 1964.

Rodgers, Daniel T. *Contested Truths: Keywords in American Politics since Independence.* New York: Basic Books, 1987.

Rorty, Richard. *Contingency, Irony, and Solidarity.* Cambridge: Cambridge University Press, 1989.

Rorty, Richard, J. B. Schneewind, and Quentin Skinner, eds. *Philosophy in History: Essays on the Historiography of Philosophy.* Cambridge: Cambridge University Press, 1984.

Rosengren, Karl Erik. *Advances in Content Analysis.* London: Sage, 1981.

Royster, Charles. *A Revolutionary People at War: The Continental Army and American Character, 1775–1783.* Chapel Hill: University of North Carolina Press, 1979.

Rubin, Richard L. *Press, Party, and the Presidency.* New York: Norton, 1981.

Rudé, George. *The Crowd in History: A Study of Popular Disturbances in France and England, 1730–1848.* London: Wiley, 1964.

Rugoff, Milton, ed. *America's Gilded Age: Intimate Portraits from an Era of Extravagance and Change, 1850–1890.* New York: Henry Holt, 1989.

Ryan, A. P. *Lord Northcliffe.* London: Collins, 1953.

Saville, John, ed. *Democracy and the Labour Movement.* London: Lawrence and Wishart, 1954.

Saussure, Ferdinand de. *Course in General Linguistics.* Translated by Roy Harris. London: Duckworth, 1983.

Schattschneider, E. E. *The Semisovereign People: A Realist's View of Democracy in America.* Hinsdale, Ill.: Dryden Press, 1975.

Schiller, Dan. *Objectivity and the News: The Public and the Rise of Commercial Journalism.* Philadelphia: University of Pennsylvania Press, 1981.

Schlesinger, Arthur M., Jr. *The Age of Jackson.* Boston: Little, Brown, 1945.

Schoyen A. R. *The Chartist Challenge: A Portrait of George Julian Harney.* London: Heinemann, 1958.

Schudson, Michael. *Discovering the News: A Social History of American Newspapers.* New York: Basic Books, 1978.

Schwartz, Barry. *George Washington: The Making of an American Symbol.* New York: Free Press, 1987.

Searle, Geoffrey Russell. *The Quest for National Efficiency: A Study in British Politics and Political Thought, 1899–1914.* Berkeley: University of California Press, 1971.

Searle, John R. *Speech Acts: An Essay in the Philosophy of Language.* London: Cambridge University Press, 1977.

Seymour, Charles. *Electoral Reform in England and Wales: The Development and Operation of the Parliamentary Franchise, 1832–1885.* New Haven: Yale University Press, 1915.

Seymour-Ure, Colin. *The Political Impact of Mass Media.* London: Constable, 1974.

Shannon, R. T. *Gladstone.* Vol. 1. London: Hamish Hamilton, 1982.

Shannon, R. T. *Gladstone and the Bulgarian Agitation, 1876.* London: Nelson, 1963.

Sharp, James Roger. *American Politics in the Early Republic: The New Nation in Crisis.* New Haven: Yale University Press, 1993.

Shaw, Peter. *American Patriots and the Rituals of Revolution.* Cambridge: Harvard University Press, 1981.

Shaw, Peter. *The Character of John Adams.* Chapel Hill: University of North Carolina Press, 1976.

Shikes, Ralph E. *The Indignant Eye: The Artist as Social Critic in Prints and Drawings from the Fifteenth Century to Picasso.* Boston: Beacon Press, 1969.

Silbey, Joel H. *The Partisan Imperative: The Dynamics of American Politics before the Civil War.* New York: Oxford University Press, 1985.

Silbey, Joel H. *The Transformation of American Politics, 1840–1860.* Englewood Cliffs, N.J.: Prentice-Hall, 1967.

Silverman, Kaja. *The Subject of Semiotics.* Oxford: Oxford University Press, 1983.

Simpson, David. *The Politics of American English, 1776–1850.* New York: Oxford University Press, 1986.

Sisson, Daniel. *The American Revolution of 1800.* New York: Harper, 1974.

Skinner, Quentin, " 'Social Meaning' and the Explanation of Social Action." In *Meaning and Context: Quentin Skinner and His Critics,* edited by James Tully. Princeton: Princeton University Press, 1989.

Smith, Culver H. *The Press, Politics, and Patronage: The American Government's Use of Newspapers, 1789–1875.* Athens: University of Georgia Press, 1977.

Smith, F. B. *The Making of the Second Reform Bill.* Cambridge: Cambridge University Press, 1966.

Smith, James Morton. *Freedom's Fetters: The Alien and Sedition Laws and American Civil Liberties.* Ithaca, N.Y.: Cornell University Press, 1956.

Smith, Jeffrey A. *Printers and Press Freedom: The Ideology of Early American Journalism.* New York: Oxford University Press, 1988.

Smith, Olivia. *The Politics of Language, 1791–1819.* Oxford: Clarendon Press, 1984.

Smith, R. A. *Eighteenth Century English Politics: Patrons and Place-Hunters.* New York: Holt, Rinehart and Winston, 1972.

Smith, R. J. *The Gothic Bequest: Medieval Institutions in British Thought, 1688–1863.* Cambridge: Cambridge University Press, 1987.

Southgate, Donald G. *The Passing of the Whigs, 1832–1886.* London: Macmillan, 1962.

Speck, W. A. *Tory and Whig: The Struggle in the Constituencies, 1701–1715.* London: Macmillan, 1970.

Spender, J. A. *The Public Life.* 2 vols. London: Cassell, 1925.

Stedman Jones, Gareth. *Languages of Class: Studies in English Working Class History, 1832–1982.* Cambridge: Cambridge University Press, 1983.

Steffen, Charles G. *The Mechanics of Baltimore: Workers and Politics in the Age of Revolution, 1763–1812.* Urbana: University of Illinois Press, 1984.

Stephenson, William. *The Play Theory of Mass Communication.* Chicago: University of Chicago Press, 1967.

Stewart, Donald H. *The Opposition Press of the Federalist Period.* Albany: State University of New York Press, 1969.

Stourzh, Gerald. *Alexander Hamilton and the Idea of Republican Government.* Stanford, Calif.: Stanford University Press, 1970.

Summers, Mark W. *The Plundering Generation: Corruption and the Crisis of the Union, 1849–1861.* New York: Oxford University Press, 1987.

Swanberg, W. A. *Citizen Hearst: A Biography of William Randolph Hearst.* London: Longman, 1962.

Sydnor, Charles S. *American Revolutionaries in the Making: Political Practices in Washington's Virginia.* 1952; 2d ed. New York: Free Press, 1965.

Tannen, Deborah. *Talking Voices: Repetition, Dialogue, and Imagery in Conversational Discourse.* Cambridge: Cambridge University Press, 1989.

Tanner, Henry. *The Martyrdom of Lovejoy: An Account of the Life, Trials, and Perils of Rev. Elijah P. Lovejoy.* Chicago: Fergus Printing Co., 1881.

Taylor, A. J. P. *Beaverbrook.* London: Hamish Hamilton, 1972.

Taylor, George Rogers. *The Transportation Revolution.* New York: Rinehart, 1951.

Thomas, W. E. S. *The Philosophic Radicals: Nine Studies in Theory and Practice, 1817–1841.* Oxford: Clarendon Press, 1979.

Thompson, E. P. *The Making of the English Working Class.* London: Victor Gollancz, 1963.

Thompson, F. M. L. *English Landed Society in the Nineteenth Century.* London: Routledge and Kegan Paul, 1963.

Thompson, P. D. G. *The House of Commons in the Eighteenth Century.* London: Longman, 1922.

Thomson, Mark A. *A Constitutional History of England, 1642 to 1801.* London: Methuen, 1938.

Trevelyan, George Macaulay. *The Life of John Bright.* London: Constable, 1913.

Tulis, Jeffrey K. *The Rhetorical Presidency.* Princeton: Princeton University Press, 1987.

Tully, James, ed. *Meaning and Context: Quentin Skinner and His Critics.* Princeton: Princeton University Press, 1989.

Turner, Victor. *Dramas, Fields, and Metaphors: Symbolic Action in Human Society.* Ithaca, N.Y.: Cornell University Press, 1974.

Turner, Victor. *The Forest of Symbols: Aspects of Ndembu Ritual.* Ithaca, N.Y.: Cornell University Press, 1967.

Turner, Victor W. *The Ritual Process: Structure and Anti-Structure.* Chicago: Aldine, 1969.

Tuveson, Ernest Lee. *Redeemer Nation: The Idea of America's Millennial Role.* Chicago: University of Chicago Press, 1968.

Van Deusen, Glyndon G. *Horace Greeley: Nineteenth Century Crusader.* Philadelphia: University of Pennsylvania Press, 1953.

Vestergaard, Torben, and Kim Schroder. *The Language of Advertising.* Oxford: Basil Blackwell, 1985.

Veth, Cornelis. *Comic Art in England.* Introduction by James Greig. London: Edward Goldston, 1930.

Vincent, Howard P. *Daumier and His World*. Evanston, Ill.: Northwestern University Press, 1968.

Vincent, John R. *The Formation of the British Liberal Party, 1857–1868*. Harmondsworth, Middlesex: Penguin, 1966.

Vincent, J. R. *Poll Books: How Victorians Voted*. Cambridge: Cambridge University Press, 1967.

Wald, Kenneth. *Crosses on the Ballot: Patterns of British Voting Alignment since 1885*. Princeton: Princeton University Press, 1983.

Waller, Philip J., ed. *Politics and Social Change in Modern Britain: Essays Presented to A. F. Thompson*. New York: St. Martin's, 1987.

Walvin, James, ed. *Slavery and British Society, 1776–1846*. London: Macmillan, 1982.

Walzer, Michael. *The Revolution of the Saints*. New York: Athenaeum, 1970.

Ward, John William. *Andrew Jackson: Symbol for an Age*. New York: Oxford University Press, 1955.

Wardlaugh, Ronald. *An Introduction to Sociolinguistics*. Oxford: Basil Blackwell, 1986.

Watts, Steven. *The Republic Reborn: War and the Making of Liberal America, 1790–1820*. Baltimore, Md.: Johns Hopkins University Press, 1978.

Wertenbaker, Thomas J. *Princeton, 1746–1896*. Princeton: Princeton University Press, 1946.

White, Hayden. *Tropics of Discourse: Essays in Cultural Criticism*. Baltimore, Md.: Johns Hopkins University Press, 1978.

White, Hayden, and Margaret Brose, eds. *Representing Kenneth Burke*. Baltimore, Md.: Johns Hopkins University Press, 1982.

Wiebe, Robert. *The Opening of American Society: From the Adoption of the Constitution to the Eve of Disunion*. New York: Knopf, 1984.

Wiebe, Robert. *The Search for Order, 1877–1920*. New York: Hill and Wang, 1967.

Wiebe, Robert. *The Segmented Society: An Introduction to the Meaning of America*. New York: Oxford University Press, 1975.

Wiener, Joel H. *The War of the Unstamped: The Movement to Repeal the British Newspaper Tax, 1830–1836*. Ithaca, N.Y.: Cornell University Press, 1969.

Wilentz, Sean. *Chants Democratic: New York City and the Rise of the American Working Class, 1788–1850*. New York: Oxford University Press, 1984.

Williams, E. M. *The Eighteenth Century Constitution*. Cambridge: Cambridge University Press, 1965.

Williams, Francis. *Press, Parliament, and People*. London: Heinemann, 1946.

Williams, Harold A. *The "Baltimore Sun," 1837–1987*. Baltimore, Md.: Johns Hopkins University Press, 1987.

Williams, Raymond. *Keywords: A Vocabulary of Culture and Society*. Rev. ed. Oxford: Oxford University Press, 1985.

Williamson, Chilton. *American Suffrage from Property to Democracy, 1760–1860*. Princeton: Princeton University Press, 1960.

Wills, Garry. *Cincinnatus: George Washington and the Enlightenment*. Garden City, N.Y.: Doubleday, 1984.

Wills, Garry. *Explaining America*. Garden City, N.Y.: Doubleday, 1981.

Wills, Garry. *Inventing America: Jefferson's Declaration of Independence.* Garden City, N.Y.: Doubleday, 1978.

Wills, Garry. *Lincoln at Gettysburg: The Words That Remade America.* New York: Simon and Schuster, 1992.

Wilson, David A. *Paine and Cobbett: The Transatlantic Connection.* Kingston, Ont.: McGill-Queen's University Press, 1988.

Winslow, Ola Elizabeth. *American Broadside Verse: From Imprints of the Seventeenth and Eighteenth Centuries.* New Haven: Yale University Press, 1930.

Wirt, William. *Sketches of the Life and Character of Patrick Henry.* Philadelphia: DeSilver, Thomas, 1836.

Wood, Gordon S. *The Creation of the American Republic, 1776–1787.* Chapel Hill: University of North Carolina Press, 1969.

Wood, Gordon S. *Leadership in the American Revolution.* Washington, D.C.: Library of Congress, 1974.

Wood, Gordon S. *The Radicalism of the American Revolution.* New York: Knopf, 1992.

Wood, James M. *The Story of Advertising.* New York: Ronald Press, 1958.

Woodward, E. L. *The Age of Reform, 1815–1870.* Oxford: Oxford University Press, 1946.

Wrigley, E. A., ed. *Nineteenth Century Society.* Cambridge: Cambridge University Press, 1972.

Young, Alfred F., ed. *The American Revolution: Explorations in the History of American Radicalism.* De Kalb: Northern Illinois University Press, 1976.

Young, James Sterling. *The Washington Community, 1800–1823.* New York: Columbia University Press, 1966.

Zarefsky, David. *Lincoln, Douglas, and Slavery: In the Crucible of Public Debate.* Chicago: University of Chicago Press, 1990.

Zenderland, Leila, ed. *Recycling the Past.* Philadelphia: University of Pennsylvania Press, 1978.

Zvesper, John. *Political Philosophy and Rhetoric: A Study of the Origins of American Party Politics.* Cambridge: Cambridge University Press, 1977.

Unpublished Sources

Aamodt, Terry Dopp. "Righteous Armies, Holy Cause, Apocalyptic Imagery, and the Civil War." Ph.D. diss., Boston University, 1986.

Avery, Donald R. "The Newspaper on the Eve of the War of 1812: Changes in Content Patterns, 1808–1812." Ph.D. diss., Southern Illinois University, 1982.

Berridge, Virginia. "Popular Journalism and Working Class Attitudes." Ph.D. diss., University of London, 1976.

Coltham, Stephen. "George Potter and the *Bee-Hive* Newspaper." Ph.D. diss., Oxford University, 1956.

Edmondson, Ricca. "Rhetoric and Sociological Explanation." Ph.D. diss., Oxford University, 1979.

Lucas, Stephen Edwin. "Rhetoric and the Coming of the Revolution in Philadelphia, 1765–1776: A Case Study in the Rhetoric of Protest and Revolution." Ph.D. diss., Pennsylvania State University, 1973.

Matthew, H. G. C. "Rhetoric and Public Opinion in Late-Victorian Britain." Paper delivered at the Conference on Europe in the Struggle for Political and Social Democracy, 1870–1890, held in Bologna, Italy, April 1983.

Wisan, Joseph E. "The Cuban Crisis as Reflected in the New York Press (1895–1898)." Ph.D. diss., Columbia University, 1934.

# INDEX

Aberdeen Coalition, 112
"Abolitionism" (epithet), 91, 127
Adams, John, 31
Adams, John Quincy, 36, 42, 52
Addison, Joseph 149
admonitory rhetoric: and Bryan, 161;
    and "combat" 124, 128; and
    conspiracy 153; in educational
    campaigns, 160; and hortatory
    rhetoric, 16, 163; and voters'
    conduct, 120
advertising, 14, 17, 23, 35, 54–55, 71,
    97, 130, 188
African Americans: and emancipation,
    122; and Jefferson, 42; and
    suffrage, 1, 127; visual stereotypes of,
    189, 209
*Alexandria Gazette*, 50
Alien and Sedition Acts. *See* repressive
    legislation
American Civil War, 73, 151, 216; and
    British imagery, 136, 167–68;
    disillusionment after, 16, 129, 163;
    illustrations during, 188; Gilded
    Age imagery, 95, 160; political
    rhetoric during, 116–17; and
    primacy of events, 117
American Revolution, 1, 2–3, 5, 9–10,
    12, 20, 28, 37, 39, 43, 49, 73–74,
    76–77, 87, 92, 94–95, 120–21,
    186–87
Anglicans, 14, 100, 102, 114
Anglo-American discourse, 4, 10–13,
    216–17; and repression, 28–29,
    31–35; rhetorical polarization in,
    31–32; in 1790s, 20–28
Anti-Corn Law agitation, 96, 106, 110,
    113, 132, 183
*Anti-Jacobin Review*, 33, 183
anti-Semitism, 111, 162
antithetical contrasts, 37, 70, 111;
    coercion/conciliation, 203–4;
    continent of wrong/realm of right,
    174; free trade/protection, 202;

man/mammon, 161; monarchy/
    republicanism, 102; safety/chaos,
    169; unity/disruption, 172; weak,
    divided/strong, united, 173. *See also*
    rhetorical schemes: antithesis
argument, forms of; *ad metum*, 74; *ad
    odium*, 208; *ad personam*, 30; *reductio
    ad absurdum*, 85
aristocracy, 76, 77, 103, 104, 124
Aristotle, 3, 7, 21, 211
Arnold, Matthew, 16–18, 150,
    175–76, 218
Asian Americans, 189
Aspinall, Arthur, 55
Asquith, Herbert H., 179
Atlanta *Constitution*, 156, 158

Bache, Benjamin Franklin, 13
Ballot Act of 1872, 168
*Baltimore Sun*, 151, 154
Bank of the United States, 73, 79, 104
"Bank War," 74, 76–80
Banneker, Benjamin, 42
battle metaphors, American: in Civil
    War, 117–18, 127–28; Gilded Age,
    148–49, 151; William Jennings
    Bryan, 161
battle metaphors, British: late
    nineteenth-century, 166–68, 170,
    172; in myth and history, 214; naval,
    139; in reform struggle, 103
Beecher, Henry Ward, 152, 157–58
Bennett, James Gordon, 69, 118–19,
    126, 215
Bentham, Jeremy, 56
Benton, Thomas Hart, 83
Bible, references to, 77, 88, 89; New
    Testament, (Luke) 41; (Mark) 89;
    (Matthew) 34, 89; (Revelation) 77;
    Old Testament, 165; (Daniel) 158,
    192, 198–99; (Exodus) 102, 122;
    (Genesis) 161, 169; (Judges) 121;
    (Kings) 162, 174; (Leviticus) 125;
    (Proverbs) 101–2